JERSEY BOY TAKES FLIGHT

JERSEY BOY TAKES FLIGHT

*One Man's Story
of Life, Loss, and Love
During the Vietnam Era*

by
FRANK FOX

Jersey Boy Takes Flight © by Frank Fox, 2024.
All rights reserved. No part of this book shall be reproduced,
stored in a retrieval system, or transmitted by any means, electronic,
mechanical, photocopying, recording, or otherwise,
without written permission from the publisher.

The materials contained herein represent the opinions of the author.

Hardcover ISBN: 979-8-2183-6641-4
Paperback ISBN: 979-8-8229-5316-1
eBook ISBN: 979-8-8229-5455-7

Project Director: Jean Heckhaus Neubauer
Cover and Jacket Design: Drew Robinson
Editor and Book Design: Lisa Allen
Reviewer: Michael J. Henry
Publisher: Palmetto Publishing

IN LOVING MEMORY—WE WILL NEVER FORGET
Matthew Patrick Fox
03/13/72 – 11/28/76

Acknowledgments

Grandfather John Keena, who "jumped" ship in New York in the early part of the 20th century, thus becoming our "illegal" immigrant who became a U.S. citizen, raised a large family, and forever changed life's trajectory for all who followed him!

MaryEllyn Turowski (nee Keena), who was the last surviving sibling of the "original" **Keenas** and who in 2010 provided me with a fascinating oral history of her family from an "insider's" perspective.

The "original" Keena family in America. (Left to right) MaryEllyn, Betty, Norah, John, Eileen, Alice, and father John Keena, Sr.

Acknowledgments

Francis M. (Sr.) and Eileen R. Fox (nee Keena), my parents, who were always there for my brother Jim and me and who, without our "knowing," and maybe without our fully appreciating, laid a good foundation for life...from whence we came!

Sons Thomas J. Fox and Andrew F. Fox, who continually urged me to "keep writing...just get it down," and who while growing up and experiencing life together, made our family a family, which included a big boxer dog named **Alli**!

Georgia and Jake Fox, my grandchildren, who are the reason I embarked upon putting this "term paper" together. It is my hope that it will provide a small glimpse into their family's life before they were born.

Michelle Fox (nee Cole), my daughter-in-law, who lent her assistance in creating the necessary "cloud" file that forever protected the manuscript while in development...it was a mystery to me.

Becky Santorios, who worked hard at "breaking" the computer code between systems, allowing my editing team and me to view the document in real time, thus eliminating conflicts and speeding up the work in progress.

Acknowledgments

And lastly, my wife **Kathy Fox,** the **best** of the **best**!!! My best friend and life partner...we've shared both the good times and the hard times, and you were the **Rock**! In looking back over the almost four years of my "project," you must have grown weary listening to the telling and retelling of my "story." Thank you for being a good listener and a discerning and friendly critic. **I Love You!**

Special Thanks To…

Jean Heckhaus Neubauer, my "executive producer," who, while making homemade pizza with me on my "electric griddle" and listening to some of my life's stories, told me to "get serious" and start thinking in terms of putting them in a book. She became the prime mover for me and helped "structure" the entire project, and I loved working with her!

Lisa Allen, my "editor-in-chief" with an eagle's eye, the patience of a saint, and a consummate professional's touch. She helped get this work into a manageable format and turned an "endless stream" of run-on sentences into something very readable, and I also loved working with her!

Drew Robinson, my "jacket" design engineer, who, after only talking with us for maybe 15 minutes, suggested the "final" book title (something we had been struggling with) and had me wondering "why didn't I think of that"…creative minds!

Special Thanks To...

Michael Henry, my critical reader, who reviewed my efforts at a crucial juncture. His spot-on corrective suggestions put the story line in sync and kept me from "spoiling" a major theme too early in the script. Well-thought-out comments and critique, when applied, allowed for a much smoother transition through the story!

Contents

Prologue 1

Chapter 1 – From Whence I Came! 11

Chapter 2 – The After High School Graduation Wilderness 43

Chapter 3 – A Working Chance, or "When the Moon Hits Your Eye Like a Big Pizza Pie" 49

Chapter 4 – What's a Bitulithic? 55

Chapter 5 – Should I or Shouldn't I? 67

Chapter 6 – Wow, I Really Did Get Drafted 93

Chapter 7 – So, It Was Settled—You're in
the Army Now 97

Chapter 8 – Army Basic Combat Training 113

Chapter 9 – Ft. Benning—"I Am the Infantry,
Queen of Battle, Follow Me" 133

Chapter 10 – First Assignment—Real Army 161

Chapter 11 – Off to Flight School 175

Chapter 12 – Moving On—
Savannah Here We Come! 219

Chapter 13 – Beyond Flight School
and Preparing for the Unknown 239

Chapter 14 – Off to Vietnam .245

Chapter 15 – Vietnam, November 1, 1968:
The Start of a Long Year! 253

Chapter 16 – "Freedom Bird" and
Homeward Bound 407

Chapter 17 – Vietnam—The War and
Its Aftermath, Still Hard to Figure 413

Chapter 18 – Life After Vietnam—
And Then Some! 427

Chapter 19 – 16 Months an Instructor Pilot 439

Chapter 20 – What a Day! 447

Epilogue 453

Prologue

I was a WWII "baby boomer" born in Jersey City, New Jersey, at the Margaret Hague Hospital on March 22, 1947. It was the hospital where everyone I ever knew from my part of New Jersey seemed to have been born. It was to a point that I remember a specific casual encounter with a girl at the Jersey Shore in the 1960s and she asked me where I had been born. When I said Jersey City, she, without hesitation, said, "Oh yes, the Margaret Hague Hospital." So for me, that made it "official"—and if you hadn't been born at the "Maggie Hague," as I later heard it referred to, then you must have been from Mars, or maybe even from across the river in New York. And if that was the case, you hadn't "properly" entered the world, or more specifically, New Jersey. So, growing up, I always felt good knowing I had that going for me—a proper entry!

My mom and dad, Eileen Rose Fox nee Keena and Francis Matthew Fox, both from Newark, New Jersey, were pretty much from working lower middle class families who I'm sure "struggled" through the Depression years; my dad more so than many others. My mother was child number

Prologue

two of six, five girls and one boy, born to an Irish family on May 8, 1920. Her father was born in County Longford, Ireland, in 1883, the 13th of 16 children, and only he and his older sister, the first-born, Nantny, immigrated to the United States.

The family story was related to me and my wife while visiting my Aunt Mary Ellyn, my mom's sister and the youngest in her family, in San Diego around 2010. What spawned the "family story" was that while listening to the news on a local TV station there was a piece about "immigrants" being picked up after entering the United States illegally. My aunt said something to the effect, "Wow those poor people. All they want is to be able to get into the United States to find good paying work and to raise a family." She looked at me and said, "Just like your grandfather did," to which I said, "You mean your father?" She said, "Yes, Poppa!"

She went on to describe how my grandfather was an ocean-going, able-bodied seaman working aboard transport steamers. At some point, circa 1905–1908, after voyaging from Europe to New York City, he contacted his much older sister Nantny in Boston. She told him to "jump ship" and come north to join her. He did, and thus he became our family's "illegal" alien for the times. This occurred in the early 20th century when legal/illegal entry into the United States was somewhat blurred and

Prologue

likely hard to track by the authorities. The long and short of it for him was that after reaching his sister in Boston, he was "officially sponsored" by her employer, who later offered him employment as a boilerman, likely as a result of having had experience tending to steam engines and boilers aboard ship.

By the grace of God and with the help of his sister, grandpa got a "break" that a lot of people wish they could've gotten. The act of sponsorship during that time in U.S. history essentially gave him what's known today as "green card" status. Along the way, he met and married Catharine Fox, an Irish girl raised in the Ironbound section of Newark, whose family hailed from County Cork, Ireland. He gained his U.S. citizenship, and he and Catharine raised a family of six children. Grandpa's "ship jumping" caper has, to date, led to as many as 30 offspring inheriting Grandpa's "big break." And it goes without saying that many more will follow without knowing the hows or whys...a lucky bunch are we to have inherited U.S. citizenship—thanks to Grandpa Keena!

By all accounts, he was a hard worker who, during the Depression, was an ironworker doing construction in New York and likely took part in building some of the "skyscrapers" of the period—maybe even the Empire State Building! Although it was the Depression, and he was a "very blue collar worker," he did OK. My mom always

My grandparents, Catharine and John Keena (left), with friends Theresa and Jimmie Mullins, all dressed up for a St. Patrick's Day parade, Newark, New Jersey, late 1940s.

remembered having "meat" on the table for Papa, head of the household, which was a big deal during the Depression. He was ultimately able to purchase his own home and rented an upper floor apartment that provided some additional income.

I think it can also be said that he had a good heart. As the story goes, and I knew and remember these people well, during the 1950s he took in a single mother of two girls and provided them with the third-floor apartment on Summer Avenue in Newark for little or no rent. I have great memories of me and my brother Jim playing "marathon" Monopoly games that would last long into the night with Margie, the youngest girl in that family. It seemed every time we visited during the late 1950s into the early 1960s, we all got to stay up after midnight—great fun! This family of three truly became members of the Keena "family," participating in most holidays, birthday gatherings, anniversaries, and even a wedding or two!

Prologue

My father was one of three children, all boys, of Irish descent, and as we understand it, he was born in April 1919 into a working middle class family that would likely be considered dysfunctional. His mother passed away early in his life, and it is said that his "out of work" father abandoned the three children, who were then raised by their maternal grandparents. Life was tough and three boys were a handful in the mid to late 1920s. With the onset of the Depression, it seems that his family was "on hard times" and they couldn't afford to have three more mouths to feed. My father and his two brothers were remanded to St. Peter's Catholic Orphanage in Newark. Since my father was the oldest of the three, he essentially was the "protector" of his brothers, even though he was only 10–12 years old. As it turned out, his youngest brother fell from a dormitory window and died of a fractured skull. It was never talked about, but I'm sure it weighed heavy on my father through the years.

His family history is sketchy at best, and I only ever heard him talk of an Uncle Bill. I believe my father worked on Uncle Bill's truck making "freight" runs from New Jersey to Boston and points in between during the mid 1930s. He never finished formal high school, but he and his remaining brother, Ed, made it through the tough times. They both served in the military during WWII, and after being honorably discharged, they joined the Newark Police Department.

Prologue

My mom and dad as newly engaged to be married, Newark, New Jersey, 1940.

Moving through the Depression as teenagers, my mom and dad met at a church-sponsored play in the mid 1930s, and they married on November 2, 1941. They entered into matrimony only a month and a few days before the outbreak of WWII. Subsequently, my Dad was drafted into the Army Air Corps, and as the story goes, he took basic military training in and around the boardwalk of Atlantic City, New Jersey. He was billeted, along with thousands of others, in one of Atlantic City's famous seashore hotels, which had been commandeered by the government and essentially turned into a rather opulent looking "barracks building."

Prologue

He spent his entire time in service as an Army Air Corps-trained radio operator, first on B-17s and later on B-29 bombers. He never deployed overseas, and it was all "luck of the draw" or, if you prefer, fate. For him, it was the result of a torn meniscus, which occurred shortly before his B-29 unit was to depart for the Pacific. Knee surgery in those days was very invasive, with a long time in recovery and rehabilitation. WWII came to a close about the time he was cleared to return for duty, so he ended up not deploying and was honorably discharged in early 1946.

During his almost four years in the Air Corps, after basic and technical training, he was stationed in Chanute Field, Illinois; Paiute, Texas; Colorado Springs, Colorado; and Mountain Home, Idaho. All the men in my mother's family served in the military during WWII. The one exception was her father who was over 50 years old at the start of the war. My father's brother also served as a U.S. Marine, and he spent part of his "enlistment" in the South Pacific.

After military service, my dad worked for Congoleum Nair, an industrial floor covering company in Kearny, New Jersey, and then started a painting business with a partner, which I believe focused on big jobs such as factory and warehouse interiors. It didn't pan out, and I suspect it was overwhelming in scope with start-up and investment costs

Prologue

My mom and dad as newlyweds, Colorado Springs, Colorado, 1942.

putting the enterprise totally out of reach. In 1948, he became a police officer with the Newark Police Department, serving honorably for 36 years as a foot ("beat") patrolman, highway motorcycle officer, and finally detective.

My mom, on the flip side of the coin, was a camp follower of sorts. She traveled with my dad to at least two of his Air Corps assignments, and she lived and worked for a period of time in both Colorado Springs and Mountain Home. She became a "certified" telephone operator and, as a result, always had steady work, and it seemed as though she enjoyed working in this field at that time. She became pregnant in Colorado Springs but had a "serious" miscarriage when my dad was on a stateside training deployment. She always credited her landlord, the Hubertys on Bijou Street, for essentially saving her

Prologue

life. For her, the miscarriage was traumatic, as I'm sure it is for all women, and she never spoke of it to my brother or me.

Throughout her life, she spoke fondly of the Hubertys, and for many years they exchanged Christmas cards and other correspondence. In 1975, when I was stationed at Ft. Carson, Colorado, my parents visited for the Christmas holidays and we drove up and down Bijou Street, her wartime home site, looking for a familiar landmark, to no avail. Everything had changed so dramatically in the 30 years since WWII that we could not find the house they had lived in.

Chapter 1
From Whence I Came!

Chapter 1

My first memories of home and life in general were at 27 Sherman Avenue, East Newark, New Jersey, across the street from the East Newark Fire Station #1, in an apartment above a corner delicatessen operated by Mollie and Harry Goldberg. I spent a fair amount of time running errands for my mom or Grandpa Keena whenever they needed something from the corner deli, which literally had everything. I was in awe of the big pickle barrel, along with freshly killed chickens hanging from hooks and the bins of penny candy that were right adjacent to the cash register—Mary Janes, two for a penny!

Whenever my grandfather visited, he would give me a quarter and have me pick him up two packs of Old Gold cigarettes (that's right—two packs for a quarter). Mollie would always ask if I was old enough to buy cigarettes, to which I would respond by saying, "Yes I am, I'm 5." Funny the things you remember!

I lived there from 1950 until 1955. I welcomed my brother James P. Fox into the world in 1952 and started school at the East Newark Elementary School, skipping a grade from kindergarten to first grade. At the time, my mother thought she had a "budding" genius on her hands. She didn't, and as it turned out, skipping a grade hurt me later on because of the age difference. When you get to high school, you can be as much as 18 months younger than some of your classmates. Not good. Word to the

Me, 1951/1952, East Newark, New Jersey. The firehouse in the background (on the left) is the starting point for my great train adventure. Goldberg's Deli is on the corner to the right.

wise—don't let your children "skip a grade." It might make you feel special, but it likely won't help your child. It didn't help me. So just let them evolve, they'll be fine!

I was raised in the Catholic faith and my first Holy Communion was at St. Anthony's, a little Catholic church down the street. I probably didn't really know what was going on with the Communion, but the pictures are angelic—and the whole episode likely got me started on the "straight and narrow."

Chapter 1

My first BIG adventure ocurred just as I turned seven years old. It involved climbing into an empty train box car with three other "daredevils" after, I'm sure, having been "double dog dared." We rode the train from behind the firehouse in East Newark to West Side Park in Kearny, a distance of probably four to six miles. Thank God the train slowed to a stop at this point, allowing my little "band of brothers" a chance to jump off. If it hadn't, it's a wonder where we would have ended up. And yes, we were scared and all babbling something about our "mommies"!

In 1955, my family moved to the country, Old Bridge, New Jersey, into a completely new community surrounded by pine forests adjacent to a lake. I did all the things boys did at that time. There was always something to participate in such as Little League Baseball, Boy Scouts, summer/winter camping, fishing, stamp collecting—yeah, stamp collecting—and even a little hunting with a rifle under the supervision of a friend's dad. We also started recognizing that girls were fundamentally different from boys and sometimes they were nice to look at and fun to be with. They brought a different perspective along with them, and to our amazement, at that same age level, a few of them could hit a baseball as far as we boys could!

A big spring and summer adventure was sliding down the spillway at the dam into the North Fork of the South River. I know, I know, DANGEROUS, but fun like you wouldn't believe. On one particular afternoon after just having slid down the spillway into the river, I looked up to the fenced-in observation area at the top of the spillway and, to my horror, I saw my dad. He gave me a slight wave of acknowledgement, then turned and walked away. I dreaded going home that afternoon, expecting to be banished to my room until I reached the age of 21, but my dad never said a word. When I arrived at the dinner table that evening, he just gave me a "father/son" look of "saw you today…not sure that's real smart…but it sure looked like fun…be careful." The topic never again came up, and I suspect my mother never knew—and was I ever relieved!

We followed this up by something even worse in the winter, and that was ice skating the entire length of Duhernal Lake as a group of 12–15 kids, 10–12 years old. We didn't have a clue as to how thick the ice was or should be to hold our weight, and while I remember being "concerned" about the ice, it didn't stop us. And of course, we never informed anyone, meaning parents, of our whereabouts. They all thought we were skating on the three-foot-deep pond at the end of our street. If they had ever found out, our skating adventures would have been "verboten" or in plain English, FORBIDDEN FOREVER! God, no doubt, was looking out for us on many occasions, and we were thankful that he was because it was really great fun!

Chapter 1

At the start of one of those skating adventures, Old Bridge, New Jersey, 1958.

The couple of years we did that the ice was like glass, and we could fly across the lake in what seemed like minutes. We would skate to a town called Spotswood, about 15 miles from our community by car but likely "only" eight or nine miles by "ice." It was a kick, and I'll bet we were doing 25–30 mph across the ice. I don't think we've had ice like that in this part of the world in years, so if you haven't experienced something like that it's probably hard to imagine. And if our mothers had ever found out—there'd have been hell to pay!

From 1958 through 1960, I was a Boy Scout in Troop 3 of Old Bridge. I've got great memories of Scouting events such as participating in our town's Memorial Day parade and camping with the Scout troop during the summers of 1959 and 1960. During those two summer camps, I worked hard on completing merit badge requirements, such as swimming, lifesaving, rifle marksmanship, rowing, canoeing, etc., with the long-term goal of becoming an Eagle Scout. It was a goal too far; however, I did complete the requirements for being a Life Scout (one rank below Eagle Scout) during the summer of 1960.

In January 1959, my dad and I participated in a father/son "winter" camping trip to Camp Sakawawin near Sparta, New Jersey. This was the summer camping area run by the Boy Scouts of America, but in the winter it was very wintery (read cold), virtually dormant, desolate, and remote, which provided for a very different type of camping

Boy Scout winter camp (I'm on the left) near Sparta, New Jersey, 1959.

Chapter 1

My dad, Frank Sr., at Boy Scout winter camp, 1959.

experience from summertime. Not every Boy Scout group was overly interested in challenging the elements during a north Jersey winter of the time. But our Troop 3 braved the wild for at least two years that I know of. We would be housed as two groups of about 25 boys and dads in log-type cabins that were void of amenities, with no heat, except for a large fireplace one could literally walk into, no electric lights, and no running water.

Daytime temperatures hovered in the 20s, and it snowed heavily, making "normal" activities like collecting firewood a rigorous event. We would take our water from the creek running off the mountain into the lake—very cold. And I distinctly remember a few fathers, mine being one of them, and a bunch of us boys brushing our teeth right out of the creek. That water would make your teeth ache—a hardy group we were!

Another distinct memory I have of winter camping was scraping off and smoothing out a portion of the lake so we could play night ice hockey. It's hard to believe but car headlights provided the lighting, and I actually recall two cars venturing onto the ice to light up the entire "arena." I'm not sure what constitutes a "safe condition" for driving out on the ice, but the men were very confident. They cited a little known to the rest of the world "mathematical formula" of depth of ice, to strength of ice, to weight of cars. There was probably a fair amount of "Kentucky windage" involved, but hey, it worked! Another example of our WWII vet fathers figuring it out and doing it! Again, hard to believe, but it really happened that way.

Has "global warming" caused real winter to become somewhat moderate in this part of the country or is it just cyclical? Whatever the case, as I sit here in Mendham, New Jersey, during Christmas of 2022, not far from Camp Sakawawin and some great remembrances of my youth, I'm watching a heavy snowfall. Overnight temperatures will be dipping into the single digits with the wind chill factor at -10 to -15 degrees. The weeklong forecast resembles something right out of those long-ago days of the 1950s. So, how do these types of weather events happen during a "period" of global warming? I'm sure someone could

Chapter 1

provide a scientific answer, but there are times when it won't jive with actual "ground truth"!

Well, 1955 quickly turned into 1960, and we moved back to the city because all Newark police officers, of which my dad was one, were directed to move back into the city limits if they wanted to keep their jobs. That was a no-brainer, so we moved back to Newark in the summer of 1960 after I graduated from grammar school.

Speaking of grammar school, I attended Our Lady of Hungary Catholic School in Perth Amboy, New Jersey. I, along with a pile of other kids, was bussed the 25 miles from Old Bridge to the Catholic school. This essentially happened because the public school system was overwhelmed by the "housing and baby boom" that had taken place in that part of New Jersey to accommodate post-

My school picture, 9 years old, from Our Lady of Hungary Catholic School in Perth Amboy, New Jersey.

WWII families and the "baby boomer" generation. Because there were so many new students, the school system went to what was called "split sessions," and school administrators erected trailer-type buildings around the main school building. My parents thought that environment was "undesirable," so they opted for private school even though it meant long-distance bussing and surely cut down on me developing friendships and participating in after-school activities. But, I had no complaints, and I understood why my parents did what they did.

I attended Our Lady of Hungary for five years. The school was so named after the eastern European nation of Hungary and the Blessed Virgin Mary. In 1956, Russian Communists invaded Hungary and brutally put down a countrywide anti-Communist revolt. As a result, and because of mass refugee migrations to Western Europe and the United States, our school accepted about 25 displaced war children whose families fled their country to avoid the Communist onslaught. Sounds familiar doesn't it, like in Ukraine circa 2022 to the present? Nothing has changed for the Russians in 67 years.

It was an interesting time, as these children were placed in our various classes even though they were three to four years older than we were. For them, it was English immersion as none of them spoke the language. After a few months, and as they became more proficient with English,

Chapter 1

we learned more about their ordeal against the Russians, and it was something that stayed with me for the rest of my life. They were no friends of the Russian Bear or of the Communist philosophy. It made all of us wide-eyed, American grammar schoolers happy and proud to have been "born in the USA"! Needless to say, they were very happy to be in the United States. As I recall, they stayed with our classes for about six months, through the summer break, and then they were placed into classes appropriate for their age, with some moving up to high schools in and around the Perth Amboy area.

The summer of 1960 was hard for my brother and me as we had just moved into the Weequahic section of Newark, and we didn't know a soul. I didn't know the city bus system, and even if I had, I didn't know where to go or what to do. There were no city pools in the area, and our family was not planning on going to the Jersey Shore that summer. So, there I was, confined to 230 Leslie Street, and as far as I was concerned, high school couldn't start soon enough.

But not so fast, big fella! When my parents were in the process of moving, they thought I would be attending the Weequahic Public High School, which was about three long city blocks from where we moved. It was a nice looking facility with a good reputation, so I was looking forward to attending classes there. However, while my family was in the process of moving from the country back to the city, the school authorities voted in favor of going to a junior high school system. So, instead of attending Weequahic Public High School as a ninth grader, I was designated to attend Clinton Place Junior High. My parents thought that wasn't going to work, so a week before classes were set to begin my dad took me to see the principal of St. James High School for an interview.

Three days later, right after Labor Day weekend in September 1960, I began attending St. James High. I didn't know a soul there and wasn't at all familiar with the location. For me it was just somewhere in the city and across town from where we lived! After a few weeks of classes, I found out that St. James was an accredited "commercial" high school, which meant it offered no college prep courses. In lieu of college prep course work, it offered typing, stenography, business math and accounting, and general science and basic biology. It also offered the "core" courses of English language and literature, world and U.S. history, religious studies (you know, Catholic school), and Spanish.

At the time, it didn't matter to me and I think it went right past my parents, as I'm not sure they were thinking much beyond high school. As things turned out, however, the typing, stenography, and business math courses were very useful during my lifetime. Hey, the keyboard for typing…think laptops/computers…who da thunk? And stenography enabled me to take verbatim notes while working in the private sector and during my early years in the military.

My experience at St. James was better than OK. I had some very good teachers, both lay people and clergy, and I was favorably influenced by three good teachers, including a former U.S. Marine and a newly ordained "baby" priest.

Mr. Richard Gill, our history teacher, brought history to life for his students—and didn't always stay on the syllabus, which was good. Instead, he addressed the issues we were interested in within a historical period or relative to what was going on in the present. We had lively discussions about our form of democracy and the nuances of a republic, states' rights and the federal system, the Civil War, slavery, the difference between Democrats and Republicans, a third political party, certain Supreme Court decisions such as *Brown vs. the Board of Education,* and Eisenhower's decision to send in the 101st Airborne Division to support integrating the Little Rock, Arkansas, high school. Of particular interest was John F. Kennedy's dramatic winning of the 1960 presidential election and his carrying New Jersey with less than 1% of the vote. And then there were always the Yankees, and then the Mets. All of it was history!

Sister Margaret, our English language and literature teacher, made Shakespeare interesting and relevant. She was famous for her ability to turn an appropriate phrase from the most obscure pieces of "classical" literature. She had a twinkle in her eye and the "computer" between her shoulders was always working. She loved her job but wasn't always happy with the boys in the class; however, she worked with us tirelessly until the bitter end…she was a hoot in a good way!

Mr. Bill Murphy, an alum who graduated in the early 1940s, joined the Army at the height of WWII. He was a hulking, broad-shouldered, 6'5", no-nonsense kind of guy who played basketball for St. James while a student. After the war, he taught physical fitness and personal health at his alma mater. He was also our basketball and baseball coach.

He participated in the D-Day invasion of Normandy in June 1944, and he was "shot in the forehead" after landing ashore. The bullet entered the front of his helmet, grazed his skull, and traveled "around" the INSIDE of his helmet, exiting out the back side. Us smart ass, brainless schoolboys affectionately nicknamed him "bullet head." Little did we know, or appreciate, the horrors he must have endured. Miraculously, the wound did not cause any permanent damage or disfigurement, and he only sustained a smallish star-shaped scar just below the hairline. Inevitably, he surely endured emotional trauma, but all in all, he was a very lucky young man seemingly no worse for wear.

Because of his actions in combat on D-Day and the days following, he received a battlefield commission to 2nd lieutenant as a young 20-something and fought with an infantry unit for the remainder of WWII. He was a very disciplined and methodical teacher, who at times seemed overly stern and demanding. Sticking to it and never giving in were core traits of his, which paid out dividends to me, and likely many of my classmates, years after graduating from high school.

In retrospect, I'm sure his goal was to make it a little tough on us so that we might know what tough "felt like." His approach likely was to ensure that we would be able to muster the internal fortitude needed to overcome bad times and adverse conditions if they should ever come our way. He was a good mentor who had no use for quitters and a knack for passing along some of life's constants, as in "who led you to believe it would be easy…and if it is…something might be wrong"! Life came at him (and thousands like him) real fast on June 6, 1944, and he became a survivor in a very tough environment!

And then there was Monsignor Thomas M. Reardon. He was the pastor of St. James Church, which made him the superintendent of the high school and the director of the St. James Hospital, which served all of the "Down Neck" area of Newark. It turns out that as a 31-year-old Marine Corps chaplain during WWII, he landed with the 5th Marine Division on Guadalcanal, which turned out to be one of the more lengthy and nastiest battles of the

Pacific Campaign. He spent 85 straight days on the beach, declaring it "his parish," and he tended the wounded and comforted the dying, all while celebrating Mass for Marines needing spiritual uplifting! During his time on the "Canal," he lost 50 pounds and contracted malaria, which he suffered with for the remainder of his life.

How did malaria manifest itself in him? He would inexplicably be "away" from St. James for maybe weeks at a time, and the nuns, under their breath, would mention that he contracted malaria during WWII. As a result, he would be hospitalized periodically throughout his lifetime. To my amazement, I discovered his wartime exploits specifically cited in the book "Serving God and Country, U.S. Military Chaplains in World War II" (pages 75, 78, 79) by Lyle W. Dorsett. His actions were also noted by Richard Tregaskis in "Guadalcanal Diary," the definitive history of that battle.

He walked amongst us every day, and we never knew his "complete" story. He was soft spoken in a comforting way, and he had a firm but gentle manner highlighted by piercing, clear, light blue eyes accentuated by "bushy" eyebrows. Something that all of us students noticed was the sterling silver belt buckle he wore with his priestly garb that was always polished and featured the Marine Corps "anchor, ball, and chain" emblem. Once a Marine, always a Marine. Semper Fi, Monsignor Thomas M. Reardon!

Chapter 1

Overall, I made good friendships, "dated" a few classmates, whatever that meant, attended the senior prom, won a couple of ball games at the plate for St. James, and generally had good experiences in the classroom of only 48 students (the entire size of my class).

And oh, the "baby" priest—Father Al Arvay came to St. James in our junior year when we were 16 and 17 years olds. Father Arvay was newly ordained and probably 23 or 24, not much older than our senior classmates. He had a great personality, was athletic, and had a good way with the high school-aged kids. He became our athletic director, and he attended most of our basketball games and some of our baseball games. He knew each one of us by name and easily struck up conversations, which centered on how we were each doing in particular, likes and dislikes, and sports in general. He was a likable guy!

So, my class graduated, and for all intents and purposes, I pretty much forgot about Father Arvay. You know, it just happens that way. Well, sometime early in 1968, I received a letter from one of my high school friends, Richie Silva, who was in Vietnam and who literally ran into Father Arvay conducting Mass at some outpost in the middle of nowhere. Turns out, Father Arvay joined the U.S. Army Chaplain Corps and he served in Vietnam in 1967–1968.

Fast-forward to 1979…and I was assigned to an Army Mobile Training Team at Ft. Sill, Oklahoma. I attended

Sunday Mass with members of my team. While listening to the homily (the priest's Sunday message to the congregation), I thought the priest's voice sounded very familiar. After some thought, I harkened back to my friend Rich Silva's letter about his having met Father (Captain/Chaplain) Arvay in Vietnam and while that had been ten years prior, I thought maybe the "good father" had remained on active duty in the Chaplain Corp. Long story short, as Mass was winding down I informed my team members that I wanted to be the last one to exit the chapel so I could have words with the priest.

As I approached Father Arvay, I was convinced it was him. Reaching out to shake hands, I said, "Father, while you probably don't remember me, my name is Frank Fox, and I was a student at St. James when you were there in the early 1960s." Without skipping a beat, he looked me in the eye, put his arm around my shoulder, and said, "I do remember you, not very good at basketball, pretty good at baseball." I almost fell down howling—how 'bout that, he nailed it and he did remember! Over the next two weeks, we had dinner a few times and just talked about his time at St. James, his and my time in Vietnam, him being an Army chaplain and me being an Army helicopter pilot, and life in general. It was good meeting him again and getting to spend some time with him.

A few years later, when I was assigned to the Pentagon, I attempted to reestablish contact with him through the

Chapter 1

Military Chaplain section located within the building. I inquired about Father Arvay, and a records clerk quickly conducted a search and determined, to my disappointment, that he left the Chaplain Corps and likely the priesthood. I wasn't totally surprised, as during our dinners at Ft. Sill he seemed betwixt and between about his being in the priesthood as he seemed to harbor a desire to have a family. I lost track after that but have thought about him a fair amount of times since and I hope he found what he was looking for!

As high school freshmen in the fall of 1960, my friend Richie Silva and I responded to an ad for volunteers to "work" for the John F. Kennedy presidential campaign. And, as 13 year olds, we were both "hired." We ended up handing out Kennedy literature on opposite corners of Broad and Market streets in Newark for the last four weekends of the presidential campaign season. On October 12, Columbus Day, 1960, I got to see JFK up close, from about 50 feet away, when he passed in front of me while sitting up on the back of a convertible during a parade down Broad Street. The parade, organized by the New Jersey Democratic Party, proceeded through the heart of Newark after he addressed thousands at a rally in front of Newark City Hall. Kennedy really looked good. He was youngish and had a "glowie" kind of tanned complexion, which I'm sure he brought with him from Palm Beach, and he really looked the part—exuding confidence while looking very "presidential."

On that day, my dad was on the Newark Police Department presidential security detail at the lower level of City Hall when, as the story goes, Kennedy stopped near a Coca-Cola machine and was making small talk with some of the "city government workers." While doing so, he got some change from an aide and bought Cokes for himself, three Catholic nuns, and a few City Hall workers. So, there he was, sipping on a Coke for a brief moment in the midst of adoring fans—translated, a real man of the people!

It was a great photo op, and it did appear in the *Newark Evening News*. I'm sure it contributed to his winning the state of New Jersey by a mere 22,000 votes, or slightly less than 1% of the total vote. New Jersey had been a Republican state for years, but 1960 was the year the "worm" turned! I was a young Kennedy supporter, as was my entire high school class. You know, he was Irish and a Catholic—seemed as if we all knew him—the tawdry stuff came out later!

His assassination in 1963 was a "shocker," and it greatly impacted everyone I knew, as in grown men weeping and our nation seemingly coming to a standstill over the following three days leading up to his funeral. I experienced a sense of loss that is hard to describe, but it was real and it took a fair amount of time to get over it. And after it was

Chapter 1

all said and done, something had changed profoundly—news commentators would say "we had lost our innocence as a country." Not sure about that, but, as a teenager, the "feeling" was different.

The early 1960s, during my high school years, was a period when the United States and Russia were in a competition, of sorts, in the race to space. It turned out the Russians put the first satellite in space, something called Sputnik, and they also placed the first human in space orbit. The Russian cosmonaut was Yuri Gagarin, the first person in space and the first to orbit Earth!

The United States was shocked to the core and, in an effort to not be "outperformed," even though we had been outperformed, we quickly followed up with a satellite of our own, followed by a "sub-orbital" manned space flight piloted by Commander Alan Shepard of the U.S. Navy. His flight blasted him into space from Cape Canaveral, Florida, as planned, and he traveled in space several hundred miles "down range" into the central Atlantic Ocean. He successfully splashed down in the ocean and was airlifted to an awaiting Navy aircraft carrier by a spaceship recovery team. Shepard was America's first person to travel into space.

This remarkable achievement was followed by that of Lieutenant Colonel John Glenn of the U.S. Marine Corps. His flight from Cape Canaveral took him into orbital flight, and he circumnavigated Earth three times. He too splashed down in the Atlantic Ocean and was also retrieved by the Navy's spaceship recovery team.

These space missions happened in pretty quick succession, and our country was enthralled by their success. It also put us on par with the Russians, and it started to look like we might, in fact, achieve President Kennedy's challenge to send people to the moon by the end of the decade, which at that time, was only eight years away!

My father, like most, was caught up with spacemania, and so when New York City announced it would hold a ticker-tape parade for the Mercury 7 astronauts, of which Shepard and Glenn were members, my dad told my mom, brother, and me that we would all go to New York, attend the parade, and make a day of it! What was really incredible was that my brother Jim and I would be kept out of school as it was going to happen on a weekday/school day, and we thought that was pretty cool. What was really amazing to us brothers was that we had never missed a day of school for anything as frivolous as a "parade"—we were from a household that went to school even when you didn't feel well! Whatever, we were excited and on our way to a parade, and my mom and dad were all in—and so were us brothers.

So, on the appointed day, our family made its way to New York. We drove into the city early and somehow

Chapter 1

my dad actually found a parking space on a city street near the Empire State Building. It was a choice spot, as the parade route would bring it right down 34th Street and it would pass right in front of the Empire State Building's main entrance.

After parking the car, we went to a Horn and Hardart Automat (essentially a self-serve cafeteria). These eateries were located all over the city and, while not considered a fine dining venue, they were unique for the way in which you selected and received your food. As you walked into the automat, you would walk down a wall of see-through glass doors behind which was displayed breakfast, lunch, dinner, salads, desserts, and many more epicurean delights. All one had to do was choose what you wanted, deposit the appropriate amount of coins to open the door, and wah-lah! I'd never been to one of these places before and it made a lasting impression on me—and it was fun and tasty to boot!

We had time to burn before the parade began, so my dad thought it would be a treat to go up to the top floor of the Empire State Building for a little sightseeing. Up to the 102nd floor (1,000+ feet) and out we went onto the observation deck—amazing! We could see all the way back to our home in Newark (because we knew where to look), and with New York harbor laid out in front of us, we could clearly see the comings and goings of the Staten

Island Ferry, the George Washington Bridge about eight miles up the river, Governors Island (at the time a Coast Guard base), the famous Brooklyn Navy Yard (what was left of it), and the Statue of Liberty. We even witnessed the docking of the transatlantic ocean liner SS *France*, a ship my wife and I would later sail on in 1990, renamed the SS *Norway*!

At the appointed time, we came back down to street level and found a suitable viewing spot on West 34th Street along with thousands and thousands of others. The parade consisted of marching bands, state and city of New York officials, the New York Police Department horse-mounted patrol, and the New York Fire Department honor guard, along with many school children marching in the mile-long procession. NASA officials and the Mercury 7 astronauts all rode in individual limos in a slow-moving motorcade with their family members.

As the parade moved closer to our location, we could hear cheers and applause rolling up the parade route. There was a syncopation to it all with the combined "noise" reverberating off the "canyon walls" of the skyscrapers at ever-increasing decibels. After a point, the orchestrated chaos was accompanied by finely shredded ticker tape thrown from the upper stories of the skyscrapers lining the route. We were engulfed in the excitement of all the noise and the sight of all the ticker tape drifting over the parade

Chapter 1

as if it was a snow blizzard. And then boom, the entire event was directly in front of us, not more than 50 feet away. So, there they were, our astronauts and their families waving to the approving throngs of onlookers and, in general, happily taking it all in—the two recent space travelers, Alan Shepard and John Glenn, followed by Walter Schirra, Donald "Deke" Slayton, Scott Carpenter, Virgil "Gus" Grissom, and L. Gordon Cooper. And as quickly as it appeared, it was gone—the motorcade, the bands, the cheers, and the "paper blizzard," including the thousands of onlookers who just melted back into midtown Manhattan. I later read that upwards of 1.5 million onlookers were in attendance—a big, and I'll add, good natured, and orderly crowd!

The final event of the day, and another lasting impression in the making, was the attack of the garbage trucks on line from curb to curb, accompanied by a hundred or more city sanitation workers. The entire operation appeared to have been choreographed with a shoulder to shoulder "chorus line" of men swooshing big push brooms ever forward while keeping up with the slow-moving trucks. The men on line were supported by shovelers who would scoop the growing piles of paper waste into the "bellies" of the large, green, 10-wheeled beasts. It was impressive, and I still remember the cleanup squad to this day, in "living color," as I do the entire day's events.

In 20 minutes, the entire show had come to a close, and if you arrived on scene shortly afterward, you would never have guessed that just moments before, New York had hosted an epic event—one of its fabled ticker-tape parades!

So, let me travel forward through time a little. When our son, TJ, was a student at Virginia Tech, he roomed with a fellow named Brett Steward. And as it turns out, Brett married Lark, who was the granddaughter of America's first astronaut, Alan Shepard. Well, while TJ was working in Denver in the early 2000s, he was neighbors with Brett and Lark, and during one of our Christmas visits we met Lark's mom, Laura Shepard Churchley, Alan Shepard's daughter, and chit-chatted about all things in general during the course of the evening.

Long after that encounter, in 2019, the Naval Academy planned a ceremony to honor all graduates who went into the space program. By that time, Alan Shepard had passed away, but his daughter Laura was asked to represent the family and attend the festivities, which were held in Annapolis, Maryland, our hometown. When finding out Laura had been asked to attend the ceremony, TJ asked if I would host Laura and her daughter Lark aboard my boat, the "Fox Sea Lady," for a cocktail cruise. We were happy to host and had them meet us at the city dock area of Ego Alley in Annapolis. We had on-board cocktails one afternoon, followed by a lunch cruise to a local Chesapeake

Chapter 1

Bay crab shack the following day. We all had a great time bantering about her being a Navy brat (her dad Alan was a Navy guy), my wife being an Air Force brat, and me, worst of all, being a career Army guy.

At one point over cocktails, I told Laura, to her surprise, that she and I had met at a ticker-tape parade in New York City a long time ago and almost in a different universe. And, although hard to believe, I told her that we had briefly caught each other's eye that day amid the tumult of thunderous cheering, the block's long ripple of applause, and the dizzying effect of floating ticker tape. She thought about that for a New York second, gave me a long, hard, steely look, and said, "So that was you, huh—well, now that you bring it up, I do remember that moment!" We all had a big, lengthy belly laugh at that and reminisced about how long ago that was—58 years to be precise. A good memory!

In late 2021, Laura followed her father into space aboard a Blue Horizon "New Shepard" commercial spacecraft, thereby becoming the first father/daughter astronauts in the history of space flight—bravo Laura!

And just to close the loop on our "adventures" with Laura, my wife and I hosted her and her husband Fred for lunch at our winter hideout in Florida this past winter. While talking to her about her "astronaut" experience, I reminded her about our "meeting" at a certain ticker-tape parade honoring the Mercury 7 astronauts so long ago. In acknowledging that, she asked me if I was interested in "trivial" history, to which I replied yes I was. She looked at me and said well then I have a little surprise, something for you and I'll get it off to you when I return home.

Within six weeks, I received a small package that contained a "sampling" of ticker tape that had been dropped from the New York City skyscrapers stuffed into a "shoe shine pocket" marked "The Waldorf Astoria Hotel." Laura's note to me said "ticker tape" from the "parade" and yes, the Mercury 7 families stayed in New York's famed Waldorf Astoria Hotel—incredible trivia!

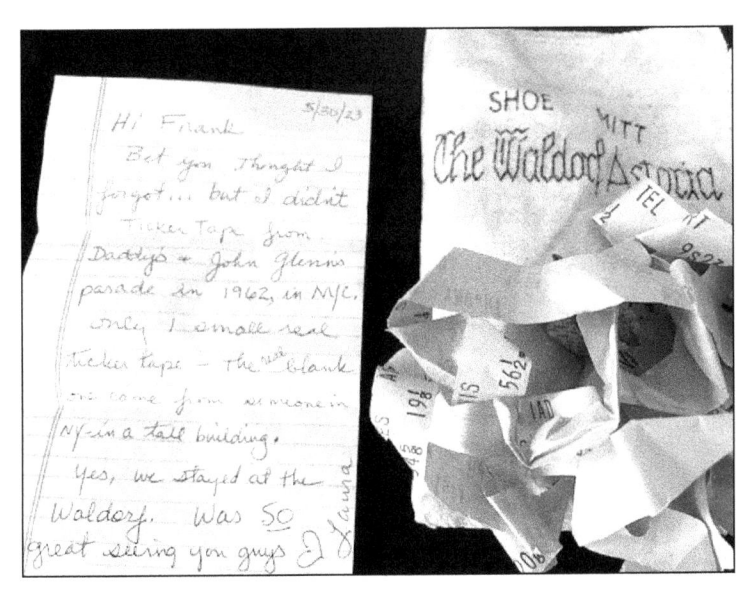

A handwritten note from Laura Shepard Churchley to me, accompanied by "ticker tape" from the grand parade honoring the Mercury 7 astronauts.

Chapter 1

Me, "not very good at basketball," St. James High School "Dukes," 1964.

St. James High School baseball team, "Murderers' Row," 1963. (Left to right) Joe Conklin, me, Tom Gerrity, and his brother Mike Gerrity.

Incredible as that was, how ironic is this? When our granddaughter started grammar school in a Chicago suburb, the school was named after Commander Alan Shepard, Laura's dad—a random happenstance type thing but mind boggling at the same time.

Back to my high school days...I played on both the basketball (not so good) and baseball (thinking better than average) teams from sophomore year on, and participating in these activities likely kept me out of trouble as the season for both teams covered fall, winter, and spring. There was lots of physical training and actual practice, so for the most part that meant I normally arrived home from school around 5:30 pm. It was a long day!

The total student population at St. James was just over 200, and we were a mixed group, looking a lot like Newark

My dad, Frank Sr., and me, the graduate, at St. James High School graduation, Newark, New Jersey, 1964.

Chapter 1

The Fox family, Silver Beach, New Jersey, 1964. (Left to right) Mom, my brother Jim, Dad, and me.

looked in general. The only real downside to attending St. James for me was that it was on the other side of the city and a long bus ride and walk of about 45 minutes each way. I spent too much time traveling to school and back. The bigger downside was that the school didn't confer an academic diploma, so I had to attend "night" high school for a couple of semesters in order to be considered for college. That's not a complaint, though, because in actuality it gave me a year or so to catch up on the year I "lost" when skipping a grade in grammar school.

I graduated from high school during the second week of June 1964 and immediately departed for the Jersey Shore to spend the summer working and enjoying the beach scene.

Chapter 2
The After High School Graduation Wilderness

Chapter 2

The war in Vietnam escalated significantly after two incidents occurred in the Gulf of Tonkin on August 2 and 4, 1964, a mere two months after I graduated from high school. At the time, it was alleged that a U.S. Navy destroyer, the USS *Maddox*, was engaged by three North Vietnamese torpedo boats in the Gulf of Tonkin off the coast of North Vietnam in international waters.

These incidents resulted in Congress passing the Gulf of Tonkin Resolution, which granted President Lyndon B. Johnson the authority to assist any Southeast Asian country considered "jeopardized by Communist aggression." Prior to passing the Tonkin Resolution, and since 1963, the United States had been providing "Special Ops" forces to train and shape the South Vietnamese military into a cohesive and, hopefully, "stand-alone" force.

From that time forward, we had as many as 13,000 advisors on the ground assisting the government of Vietnam. Did our having a "significant" presence in South Vietnam cause the North Vietnamese to ratchet up their activities in a form of "saber rattling," which at some point "crossed the line" that then opened the door to more involvement on the part of the United States?

With that as a little backdrop, life after high school in June 1964 became ever more full of reports from Vietnam citing increased U.S. involvement, meaning ground combat operations, with casualties rising accordingly. Correspondingly, Congress kept, slowly but surely, allowing for an increase in total end strength for the U.S. military, a harbinger of things to come as these actions supported deploying additional forces for the purpose of expanding the war effort.

As events unfolded, there became a time when the casualty tally was shown on the nightly news with accompanying news footage of some aspect of military operations. It got intense, and in the back of every late teenager or early 20-something's head was the thought that we all might get caught up in this event. It was always in the background for my age group, and a heck of a lot of us did get caught up in it.

I'm sitting here now writing this during the coronavirus outbreak, watching news show hosts going over the total number of virus cases, virus-related deaths, and numbers of people who have recovered. It's different for sure, but reminiscent of Vietnam reporting with the same intense effect—total soldiers killed in action (KIA) for the week followed by total since our involvement in Vietnam. KIAs would be followed by wounded along with those missing in action (MIA). At some point, service members' pictures would be displayed on screen, which made everything much more personal and real, putting a face with a name. It started to weigh on people over time!

Chapter 2

While most in my age group, including me, were concerned about having to serve in the military during a time of war, there were alternatives to outright military service. The things you could do to defer or maybe avoid the draft, and maybe military service altogether, were as follows:

1. Gain acceptance into a four-year college and carry a full credit load while maintaining a certain grade point average (GPA). The same applied if you attended an accredited night college; the credit load was less on a semester basis, but you had to attend the entire year, including summer semesters. Being able to maintain the credit load and the GPA would give you a student deferment from military service with no threat of being drafted during your time spent as a student. You would become eligible for the draft after completion of college. Note: Anyone who exercised this option in the 1965–1966 time frame likely figured the war in Vietnam would surely be over by 1969–1970. It wasn't, and so it seemed more college grads were in the enlisted ranks in the early 1970s.

2. Enlist in the National Guard or the Reserve Forces. This meant you were in the military service, and your commitment was generally for six years with monthly weekend training drills and a two-week summer training period. National Guard forces were rarely called to active duty and deployed overseas, save for very select Air National Guard units. Once you finished this obligation,

you were through with military service, but a six-year commitment was viewed by many as a very long time to put life on hold.

3. Seek deferment from military service for physical reasons, whatever they might be. This status was called being 4F, and it exempted one from military service. Famous among these maladies are "bone spurs," flat feet, deficient eyesight, and so on.

4. Being a sole surviving son. I believe it had to be applied for and, if granted, exempted one from military service. You had to be a sole surviving son for starters.

I received a full-time college student deferment by virtue of attending Seton Hall University in Newark for night classes during the fall 1965 and spring 1966 semesters. I was, however, drafted in summer 1966. What happened? I'll explain later, and it's all about fate being the hunter and the sun, the moon, and the stars aligning!

Chapter 3
A Working Chance, or "When the Moon Hits Your Eye Like a Big Pizza Pie"

Chapter 3

After graduating from St. James High School in 1964 and intent on spending the summer at the Jersey Shore, I found work as a dishwasher in an Italian restaurant and pizzeria in Ortley Beach (you know, it was New Jersey). I never saw so many dishes or such large/deep pots in my life before that point. The fast learner that I am, in only one week's time on the job, I graduated to pizza chef, or sous chef, if you prefer, ever expanding my job skill set! Actually, I was a full-time dishwasher and part-time pizza chef, and things were good.

The restaurant owner's name was Pat Scaglione, and he was a great guy who would always tell me at the beginning of my shift that there would be a little lasagna, some apple pie with ice cream, and a couple of cold beers for me after we finished for the night, which was normally around midnight. Pat must have thought I wasn't being fed enough at home, don't know, but I was. Whatever the case, it was remarkable how much better the beer tasted when you were under age!

Pat had lost his wife five years earlier and his daughter Patricia became the steadying force within the family, which included Patricia, her dad Pat, and her brother John. Patricia was 20 years old that summer, and she was the head waitress, concierge, overseer, handler of the money, and the keeper of her father. She was also beautiful and just as nice as could be!

A Working Chance, or "When the Moon Hits Your Eye Like a Big Pizza Pie"

At the end of a weekend, Pat always paid me a little extra, and sometimes a lot more than what had been agreed to when he hired me. He would say, "Frankie, we had a good weekend, sold a lot of pizzas, so here's a little something extra." His little something extra would be $50, which was twice and again what I should have received. Pat always paid in cash, you know, no record for tax purposes! I should have been paid $1.25 per hour for a total of 18 hours of work on a Friday, Saturday, and Sunday night. That would've totaled $22.50 for the weekend. Instead, I'd go home on Sunday night sometimes with $75—a nice amount of cash for 18 hours of work in 1964 when you were 17 and still living at home.

New Jersey being what it is, there were many family godfathers, particularly if your name ended in a vowel. Working for Pat I felt as if I was looking into one of those families. About every other week during that summer, a big black Cadillac would show up in front of the pizzeria. It would always park a ways down the block, and after the engine was turned off, it would sit awhile before the occupants stepped out.

I always figured they were checking out the area and seeing that it was all clear. You know, the godfather couldn't be too careful. After all, this was New Jersey, it was in the 1960s, and strange things still happened. All of this was probably my teenage brain running a little wild and maybe I had watched too many episodes of "The Untouchables," but hey!

After parking, and at an appropriate time, two younger men would get out of the car, followed by an older man (when you're 17, everyone over 22 looks a lot older). They would be dressed all in black and looking dapper. It turned out that the older man was a Mr. Lou Monte, and the story went that he was a singer/entertainer/Italian favorite who in fact had been the occasional opening act for New Jersey's own Frank Sinatra! I later found out that Lou Monte's real name was Luigi Scaglione. So, he was likely my boss Pat's brother or uncle, hence he might have been a real-life godfather who may have helped Pat after he lost his wife.

Lou was quite accomplished and revered in the Italian community, having sold millions of records, which included his biggest hit "Pepino the Italian Mouse" (I know, that's what I thought, but you can Google it, it's true). It had become a hit in, you guessed it, 1964. Lou used to love going up to the boardwalk in Seaside Heights, sitting out at the open air joints lining the boards, and eating mussels and clams while drinking a beer or two—lemonade was also a favorite!

I was invited to join them on two separate occasions and found them to be friendly, fun, and generous. I was the Irish kid in with the Italian family, as it were, who after the first five minutes was made to feel right at home.

I liked working in that pizzeria. It was hot as hell in the kitchen during July and August, the pots kept coming, and there were too many pizzas in the oven at the same time (Pat would say we're cooking now!), but my couple of colleagues were good and the boss was fair. Over the years I often thought of Pat Scaglione and the way he treated me, and I tried to apply his "touch" to various situations in my life.

Chapter 4
What's a Bitulithic?

Chapter 4

After the summer of 1964, I was hired by Standard Bitulithic Company, a smallish road paving company. I know, what's a bitulithic, you ask? Well, it's a mixture of bitumen and aggregate, which together makes what's commonly called asphalt paving. The first modern asphalt facility was built in Cambridge, Massachusetts, in 1901 by the Warren Brothers Company, the parent company of the company I worked for.

The Standard Bitulithic Company of Newark was located at the end of Brill Street on the Passaic River in the Ironbound section of Newark. My first job there was assistant payroll clerk and numbers checker. I worked directly for Mr. Chris Kergen, who at the time was 66 years old and drove to Newark from Brooklyn every day. As the crow flies, it was probably only 16–18 miles, but the traffic on the Holland Tunnel approaches could be brutal even in the 1964–1966 timeframe.

Chris appeared to be sort of a curmudgeon until you got to know him. He suffered from polio as a kid and had to use crutches to get around, but his brain was laser sharp and he could be damn funny in a smart, sophisticated way. Because of that, it was easy to miss his humor, which ended up sometimes being even funnier, in a "who's the dumbshit here" kinda way.

Not long after being hired, Chris was working the quarterly plant accounting report, and he gave me a series of manually developed spreadsheets accompanied by 20 or so long strands of calculator paper tapes. Together it just looked like a tangled nightmare.

Chris wanted me to check the numbers to ensure that they matched/balanced. Well, I worked those numbers for three hours and everything was off about $40,000. On the second or third go—remember, everything was manual—I found what appeared to be a series of transposition errors. Not wanting to linger over it all morning, I went to Chris and presented my findings, not feeling at all sure about what I was saying. Chris started to re-check and together we found what he called offset errors. He looked at me and said, "Son (everybody was son to him), thanks for sticking with this and bringing it to my attention." If this had made it into the final report, it would have taken days to sort out.

The lessons for me were attention to detail, stick-to-it-ive-ness (even after you become very frustrated), and something about not being afraid to show the boss the bad news because it doesn't get better over time. Fascinating stuff in this real world!

A little side thing that Chris used to orchestrate was something called the 13-run pool. It was a benign game of chance based on Major League Baseball. If you paid to be in the pool and a team scored 13 runs in any one game, and if that was your randomly selected team, you won the pool. The amount of payout would then go back to zero, with money being added for every game when 13 runs weren't scored. This was all based on when there were only 16 Major League teams, so I'm not sure it could apply today, as there are so many more teams involved.

Nowadays, you would probably need to get an actuarial type involved to do the calculations, and in order to actually get into the pool, you'd probably need a username, password, and pin…ugh! It was a neat little pool and ran the entire season to include the World Series. I won that pool more than a couple of times over the almost two years I worked there, and I clearly remember my first win of $58—not bad when you consider that I took home $105.05 for a two-week pay period!

On the other hand, being the payroll clerk was as real as it got. I was the one who received the data and cut the checks for the union day workers, who were paid daily at the end of a shift. The men wanted their "pay due," and it was mandated by law/union rules. If you screwed it up, you might not get the union day workers reporting to your job site in the future. That would not be good. So, it was a little hectic as it was well before computers and quick data transmission, so we did everything by phone (landline), walkie-talkie radio (range limited), or, believe it or not, passing a handwritten note from the job site foreman personally delivered to me. These notes would contain the worker's name, job position, pay rate, hours on the job, and whatever else was necessary at the time to satisfy union/government mandates. Checks would be cut and then delivered back out to the site right at quitting time.

I learned how to drive a pick-up truck with a stick shift one day when I volunteered to drive the paychecks out to the job site. The plant manager, Pete Soccoro, asked me if I knew how to drive a truck with a stick shift. I said, "Sure do," and he threw me the keys to one of the company pick-up trucks. In fact, I hadn't ever done either—drive a pick-up truck or work a stick shift on the column. My only experience with a stick was watching my dad work it while driving his 1952 Studebaker. So, with that much "experience" under my belt, I thought I could figure it out.

I did figure it out and, without hesitation, I jumped in the truck, started it up, and literally "bucked" that truck out of the company's construction yard. The "bucking" effect happened when you were unsure as to how to "gently" synchronize the movements of the floor-mounted clutch pedal with a column or floor-mounted stick shift, all while applying the gas pedal as appropriate. I saw Pete's face in the rear-view mirror and never forgot his perplexed look. I got better at the stick while heading out to the site on Route 22 near Union, New Jersey. Gear shift, clutch, and gas pedal synchronization is now a lost art, which faded away with the introduction and total integration of the automatic transmission—a good thing, bad thing!

Chapter 4

After five months on the job, I was promoted to accounts receivable/payable clerk in the main building. Being promoted was good; however, I missed the plant office and the men who were in and out of there. They were a little bit on the rough hewn side and either worked with heavy equipment in the yard or drove big dump trucks hauling asphalt out to the job sites. They were all characters, and most were WWII vets who had a "can-do" attitude about getting stuff done—an attribute, I suspect, they picked up in military service while winning a war!

There was a time when I briefly thought about becoming a heavy equipment operator. What sparked my interest was a discussion I had with the yard's steam shovel operator, a Mr. Henry Bennet. He learned his trade by "luck of the draw" in the 1930s as a "walk-on" at a road construction site. During the war, and because he had heavy equipment experience, he was placed with the Army's Combat Engineers and worked on road and airfield construction projects. Anyway, it turns out that because of union-negotiated pay rates, Henry was the highest paid person in the entire company, including the company president. Old Henry made $73K in 1965, which included overtime and a few minor job performance bonuses. That caught my eye when working year-end payroll stuff and getting the end-of-year W-2 forms out to the employees. That kind of money was a tidy sum for the times. I didn't

What's a Bitulithic?

pursue it as my life was taking a little different turn with the opportunity of attending college…who knows!

I believe my promotion really happened because the guy who had the job before me could never quite get to work on time. The straw that broke the camel's back for him was when he went on a one-week vacation and came back three weeks later. Another lesson learned: keep management informed and show up on time. Throughout life, it seems like the "showing up" on time part is about 40% of getting the job done!

Working with Standard Bitulithic was the first real job I had, and it turned out to be a really good experience. I didn't know it or really appreciate it at the time, but President George Landers, Vice President Vinny Flynn, and Treasurer Bob Sherry were great people to work for. They were good examples and wonderful mentors and teachers who were very tolerant of a new, young guy's mistakes. I always thought that if I were in a similar position, I hoped I could apply their examples to my life experiences.

Vinny did something for me that I would never forget. One day, in probably November 1965, he asked me to join him to run an errand and go to lunch. The errand was to a place called Yokz's Ski Shop in Elizabeth, New Jersey. He was picking up new skis for his oldest son. While there he asked me if I had ever skied, and I told him I hadn't but that

Chapter 4

I was interested in it. He took me over to the used equipment section and talked to me about boots, skis, bindings, and everything that went with it. While talking, one of the salespeople came over and indicated he could get me into a set of used skis, bindings, poles, and boots for $150. A great offer, but I didn't have that kind of money, particularly for something I had never done before. Hell, I was all about trying to put some "coin" away to buy that Pontiac Tempest or Sunbeam Alpine Convertible I kept eyeing up in the newspaper used car section.

Fast-forward to our company Christmas party a few weeks later. Mr. Landers handed out company Christmas gift "bonus" envelopes along with a turkey, a ham, and an assorted box of liquor to be "brought home to the parents," of course. I brought most of the liquor home. I can't remember all the details, but if you can believe it, I think I still have a bottle of Cutty Sark scotch from that gift package still in the original box. That bottle was in my dad's bar and has been in mine since his passing, which means that scotch has been "fermenting," more like sitting, in the bottle for at least 55 years. Ought to crack it open some day!

In addition to the gift from Mr. Landers, Vinny called me to his office and gave me a Christmas card with a note inviting me to join him and his son for a day of skiing in early January. Vinny's gift was $100, a lot of "bread" in

1964, which meant I had enough to buy the set of skis I had been shown at the ski shop.

I know that Vinny's gift was out of his own pocket, and it knocked me over. I went skiing with him and his son and had a great time. It started me on a 25-year sojourn to many "world famous" ski areas in the United States and Europe. I introduced my children to skiing, and my oldest son has introduced his children to the sport, along with buying a "ski" home in Utah. Might this all be attributable to Vinny's long-ago Christmas "bonus" to me? Who knows, but what a nice thing to have happen to you!

Wow, two good work experiences in a row, the pizza place and the paving company. I was a very lucky young guy! Things sort of lined up right. But it didn't just happen. I helped the situation along by taking the job with the hours no one else wanted, and I tried to put a "happy face" on it!

I always tried to put my "best foot forward"! I made it a point to show up a little before starting time (might be the most important part of a project—being on time), in the right mindset, and, if necessary, would stay beyond quitting time. (Yeah, yeah, I know you're a "brown-noser"—don't let those kinds of comments bother you. Whatever the circumstances are, working a "real" job or even doing volunteer work such as with the community homeowners' association, your colleagues will appreciate you being a team player.)

I would lend a hand if it was needed, even if it wasn't in my job description (think of it as broadening your horizons—remember the "bucking" pick-up truck?). I tried to present myself well (you know, make your bed, brush your teeth, comb your hair, clean shaven, with a pair of pressed chinos and an open at the neck dress shirt or polo, depending on the occasion, sometimes accompanied with a "whimsical" necktie). And I was respectful to those whom I worked for, who, I'm sure, had gone through all this many years before me. Most, if not all of this, stuck with me to varying degrees and without a doubt helped me navigate through life's everyday little and occasionally big events!

I worked in the main office at Standard with two others who were the same age as me. One was Carla Lee Quinn, whom I went to school with. While we attended high school together, we really didn't know each other well, but we became great friends over the two years we worked in the same office. She became engaged to our regular UPS driver, Gus—who da thunk—and oh by the way, a great guy who had just been honorably discharged from the Army. I was invited to their wedding in September 1967, but much to my chagrin, I was unable to attend. At that time, I was stationed at Ft. Benning, Georgia, as an infantry platoon leader in the 197th Infantry Brigade, and it wasn't so easy to get out and back from Columbus, Georgia, over a weekend in 1967. As the newly assigned 2nd lieutenant in an infantry company, I was at the bottom of the pecking order when it came to requesting and receiving leave or an extended weekend pass.

The other person in the office was Mike Washington, who became the payroll clerk in the plant office when I moved to the main office. Mike and I shared a lot of good times together, like Mets, Yankee, and Knicks games in New York; a couple of St. Paddy's Day parades; a ski weekend or two; and basketball games at Seton Hall, all of which included some fun bar hopping and carousing (not what you think—but we were trying). Mike and I would end up being drafted into the Army on the same day in August 1966; a real stunner on that Monday morning in July when we walked into the office at Standard Bitulithic and announced almost simultaneously that we had received the letter from Uncle Sam that started out with the salutation: Greetings!

Chapter 5

Should I or Shouldn't I?

Chapter 5

After moving to the main office at Standard Bitulithic, I settled in and started working with one of the company's head accountants in the accounts payable/receivable department. It was all numbers work with zero chance of getting out to a job site or of changing the routine, as things pretty much happened in the same manner week after week. Branch offices in New Jersey, New York, and Maryland would send in their data, and I would break it down and log it into the ledgers. Afterward, I would present it all to the accountant I was working with.

At the end of each week, we would balance the books across the company and close out weeks, months, and quarters. Ditto for the months, ditto for the quarters, and ditto again for the year! Sounds somewhat mundane, but that's the way it was done in the manual age. Dull as it sounds, you had to pay attention during the entire process or else a careless mistake, such as improper ledger entries, transposition, or just flat out entering the wrong numbers, would cause one big headache at the end of any given period.

When the books didn't balance, then an entry-by-entry assessment would ensue covering a couple thousand entries until the errors were resolved and the books balanced. It wasn't much fun at the individual level, knowing your error(s) may have caused five colleagues to spend three to four hours, or longer, drilling down into the ledgers after

Should I or Shouldn't I?

the normal workday. One of these sessions lasted a couple of days, after which it was determined that one of the branch offices had submitted a completely wrong set of numbers for the entire month. It was a careless error, as the numbers turned out to be real enough but they were for a period two months earlier. I walked away from that drill just being happy that it wasn't my careless error. Another lesson learned, however—continuous attention to detail! The work was boring but pleasant, and it came with a steady paycheck, working with good people, and for the most part a regular 9-to-5 day after day with weekends off. All things considered, not bad at all!

In the fall of 1964, I started attending night high school in order to make up for college credit courses I didn't get while I was attending regular high school. The school I graduated from conferred a commercial diploma, not the necessary academic diploma required for consideration for college entry. Although I didn't have any say at the time, I often wondered why I attended a commercial high school. It was all mixed in with having moved from the country in Old Bridge back to the city of Newark during the summer of 1960. Because it was very late in the summer, St. James High School was the only private school that would accept my application with only three days left until school opened. So, who knows! But here's one thing I do know—I learned a few skills in commercial high school that have served me well for most of my life. In fact, one is still working as I type this "memoir." I learned how to type, the proper way, a skill that carried over into the computer age. I also learned Gregg Shorthand, which allowed me to take verbatim notes my first few years in the workforce and for some years after entering the Army.

So, in addition to the "exotic" courses, we also had the usual dose, for the times, of history and civics, literature, language (Spanish), geography, and general science, along with a commercial school staple of business math, which didn't hurt either as it exposed me to the stuff of life, such as savings, checking account management, interest rates, investing, taxes, and insurance—all very useful skills!

In the world as it was at the time, having attended commercial high school meant I would have to take a couple of math courses and a science course or two in order to comply with college entry requirements. So, in order to do this, I attended Central High School's night program in Newark, which offered classes in the areas I was deficient in. Specifically, I needed two math courses and a biology course. Between fall of 1964 and summer of 1965, I completed those courses and satisfied the college entry requirements.

When I finished the high school evening classes, Vinny Flynn asked me into his office and offered me the chance to attend night college, with the company paying for tuition and books. It was a great opportunity, which I agreed to accept. The hook in the offer, however, was that I would have to study/major in accounting. I didn't see myself doing that forever, but thought it a good idea to see what it was like. Needless to say, when I told my parents about the offer of free college, they were ecstatic.

Going to college hadn't really been talked about a whole lot in my family for probably more than a couple of reasons, but one of them was surely the fact that there wasn't money in the budget to pay for college. My dad was a police officer in Newark who also worked a few part-time jobs along the way to stay ahead of the curve. But the plain and simple truth was that things were likely a little tight. I never felt like things were tight, but I did have an inkling that there wasn't a whole lot of excess spendable income just based on my parents' lifestyle, which was basic to say the least. I never felt like we were wanting for anything—life was good, food on the table, a color TV, loving family, and a little money in my pocket.

Speaking of money in one's pocket, my mom had me kick in $10 a week of my $55 per week after-tax salary to "help out." I'm not complaining, but just saying something about "back in the day" as these idiot rappers keep saying.

And speaking of "back in the day," my father, being a police officer, had a fair number of police officer friends, all good guys, all WWII vets, all can-do people, and all with

Chapter 5

young families, who we, my family, would meet at various police functions such as picnics, during parades in the city, or visits to the beach.

One of these "friends" made a lasting impression on me to the point that I really looked forward to seeing him throughout my teenage years. I don't know why but he was easy to like...could've been your father and was big into "boy" things. He had two daughters and I suspect he longed to have a boy to share boy "adventures" with. We hit it off and I would occasionally run into him when catching a bus home from school as he worked with the Newark Police Rescue Squad "housed" in a former firehouse just two blocks south of Broad and Market streets, the epicenter of Newark.

His name was Louie Goc, and he was easy to talk to about "stuff," most of which I recall being centered around fishing for flounder off the Jersey beaches, baseball (probably the Yankees), and airplanes...yes, airplanes! Turns out he was a B-17 "waist" gunner during WWII and flew the required 25 missions over Europe before being returned to the United States. He never really got into it except when talking about how cold it was in the "non-pressurized" B-17 flying at 28,000 feet, essentially with the windows open. I think the temps reached -35 degrees and the crewmen wore sheepskin fur lined full leather "flying" suits, which made them look like Michelin men!

Should I or Shouldn't I?

An adventure I shared with Louie was all about one of the things I loved to do at the Jersey Shore, and that was fishing for "fluke" as they were called (fluke was the local Jersey name given to summer flounder, a fish that at the time was found in abundance along the coast and in the inlets and rivers). The way "my" adventure started was a conversation at a "police" picnic in which I told Louie about my love for surf fishing for fluke. By the end of the picnic, Louie had talked to my dad and arranged for me to join him on a "party" boat fluke fishing trip the following week.

On the designated day, my dad dropped me off at the boat basin in Pt. Pleasant, New Jersey, where I met Louie for a very early breakfast, an o'dark thirty event before I knew what o'dark thirty was all about. Fishing is fun, but why do you have to start so early…cause that's when the fish get up! I was really looking forward to a full day of fishing off the coast with someone I knew could probably catch fish out of a rain barrel after a heavy thunderstorm! Speaking of thunderstorms, the weather forecast for the day called for strong winds and light rain with possible thunderstorms.

In spite of this, our group of about 35 or so intrepid fishermen headed out to the dock to board the Miss Tambo, a 41-foot center cockpit, old-looking, wooden "party" boat. All the fishermen were outside in the elements with only the boat's captain and first mate under cover. At 6:30 am sharp, we undid the dock lines and headed out toward the Manasquan Inlet into a boiling Atlantic Ocean. The weather forecast didn't disappoint; wind was up and the seascape was flecked with frothy white caps and a steady rain…naturally!

Once outside the inlet, we turned south and pounded our way through four-foot seas heading for the Seaside Heights fishing grounds about 15 miles away. The southbound trip took about an hour, and it was not a fun time as the wind kept blowing sea spray the length of the boat, ensuring all aboard were soaking wet before reaching our destination. Louie, the fisherman, had a set of rubber "slickers" that kept him dry. I did not—a lesson learned! Regardless, I was looking forward to putting a line in the water as soon as the captain gave the word.

Louie had put us in the ideal spot on the boat for drift fishing over the ocean floor—a stern corner. Why ideal you ask? Well, as the boat drifts, the lines on either side of the boat will go under the keel, depending on the drift, making it harder to bring in a catch. It also increases the chances of tangling lines on the other side of the boat. A stern corner position tends to eliminate the hazards mentioned and the natural action of the boat drift will keep the lines free and away from the hull. Our lines were in the water less than 10 minutes when I felt a hard tug followed by a steady bouncing motion at the rod tip. Exciting! I had the first hit of the day and with help from the first mate, who netted the fish, I landed a nice sized fluke after a 10-minute up-and-down tug of war.

By this time, half of the "fishermen" on board were seasick and in no mood for standing on a rocking boat jigging a line for fish that had probably paid attention to the weather report and headed for cover. I didn't feel that way, and after eating a "famous" New Jersey baloney sandwich that my mom had packed me, I got my line back in the water and bada bing, in only a few minutes of bouncing my line along the bottom, I had another nice fluke in the bag! I was a happy camper, and when the captain announced that he was calling an end to our adventure and heading back to port because of the weather, I dove into another baloney sandwich with, I think, a package of Twinkies.

Turns out that only three fish were caught that morning, and the fellow who caught "the other one" gave it to me so that "I could have a nice fish fry" when we got home. I ended up with all the fish, and I won the pool of $75, which paid for the day and then some! Louie got "skunked," meaning zero fish, but he was really happy for me and somewhat amazed at how seasickness didn't get to me and the fact that I ate everything in my lunch bag in a rolling sea!

Chapter 5

Over the next couple of summers, I fished with Louie a few more times, and although they weren't as "memorable," I always enjoyed the day and picked up some fishing "tips," which I've been able to pass along to my family. Incidentally, I've taken my gang fishing for fluke out of Pt. Pleasant aboard the Miss Norma K on several occasions over the years—good memories! And, oh by the way, my wife caught the biggest fish of the day on one of our family outings, winning the pool of about $150. It paid for the day and then some—I taught her everything I ever learned about fishing from Louie!

While fishing with Louie a few times, I found out that he was a real baseball fan—Yankees, of course, after all we all lived very near New York. The Yankees were the team until the Mets came in to being, giving the "Yanks" a little competition. Turns out, Louie wasn't just a fan, he was quite a baseball player before the "war." He was a pitcher, and one weekend during an early 1960s summer, Louie and his family came to spend the day at the beach with my family.

My brother and I always had baseball gloves laying around (Rawlings "Heart of the Hide"), and while getting ready to walk up to the beach, Louie asked us to bring the gloves and ball so we could play a little "catch." OK with us, as we played catch with my dad all the time—we knew how to play catch. About an hour into our day at the beach, Louie motioned for us to grab the gloves and up the dune we went to find a little space where we could throw the ball. Louie starts a three-way "catch" with us, and a short time later he starts pitching to my brother Jim, who had the catcher's mitt on. Well, Louie started out just pitching back and forth, and then he picked up the pace a little, no problem for Jim to handle, until he started throwing THE "knuckleball" and that's when the fun started!

The "knuckleball" is a pitch that is thrown at a minimal speed, unlike a "fastball" or even a "curveball." It is grasped by the pitcher in such a way that the ball is held by the knuckles of one's hand as opposed to holding the ball in the palm and extended fingers of the hand. In order to master the knuckleball, the pitcher needs to have BIG hands to essentially surround the baseball with the knuckles. When thrown, the baseball is released with minimal spin on it, which causes erratic and unpredictable airflow over the seams of the baseball while in flight to the batter. Typically, a knuckleball travels at about 60–65 mph, as compared to a fastball, which sometimes hits 100 mph.

Well, Louie had enormous "beefy" hands, and he did surround the baseball with his knuckles. His knuckleball was diabolical! It dipped up and down, slid sideways, right or left, and seemed to just sit in the air with no rotational spin at all. Bottom line for me and my brother Jim was that

Chapter 5

eight times out of 10, we couldn't catch the ball. It bounced in the sand or literally hit us on the arms or legs, and when you did catch it, it would hit with a resounding "thud" and actually hurt your hand even though the ball was traveling a lowly 60+ mph. Jim and I laughed the entire time. Louie's knuckleball was so good he could make you look silly. Don't know how any batter could hit it. From where we were sitting, Louie missed his calling—he should have been pitching for the Yanks…might have had something to do with WWII—he was playing in a different league!

And speaking of pitching for the Yanks—sometime during the summer of 1961, my dad came by four tickets to a Yankees vs. KC Athletics game at Yankee Stadium (the original house that "Ruth Built") for a Sunday

The Goc family. (Left to right) My mom Eileen, Louie Goc, "the Knuckleballer," and his family.

afternoon game. So it was my dad, Louie, my brother Jim, and me, all baseball guys, headed to the Bronx on a beautiful summer day.

In addition, this was the year that Roger Maris and Mickey Mantle were both chasing Babe Ruth's home run record of 60 in a season. At this point, before the All Star break, Maris had already hit 27 homers and the sportswriters were already "talking." Added to the "drama," Mantle had already hit 25 homers and he was "chasing" Maris. Mantle and Maris, they were fun to watch—the "M&M boys" as they were referred to by the New York sports press. They batted third and fourth in the lineup, and when they were up in the same inning there was great anticipation that one or the other of them would hit a homer or maybe even both of them would hit it out.

Entering Yankee Stadium was a "grand" event unto itself. When you walked up to the main entrance, which was directly behind home plate, you passed through a plaza-like area, which directly to your front and high above had YANKEE STADIUM emblazoned across the upper levels of the stadium structure in giant scripted letters—it was awesome! Once over the threshold, and into the cavernous ground level concourse, you could look "through" the stadium superstructure and see the centerfield bleachers and the outer reaches of the playing field, along with the

Chapter 5

large monuments dedicated to famous past Yankees lined up in dead straight away center field (the three Yankees memorialized were Miller Huggins, Lou Gehrig, and Babe Ruth). And the smells! You could smell the peanuts, Cracker Jacks, hot dogs, cotton candy, and cold beer…and it all blended together perfectly—it was an experience you never forgot!

As you progressed up the "walking ramps" to the upper deck levels, a view of the complete field unfolded in front of you with every step you took. In slow motion you saw the infield, the dugouts, the whole outfield from right field foul pole to left field foul pole, and the brilliant green carpet of a playing field. On this day it was all in dazzling sunlight—the colors were brilliant and I'll bet that many, many young boys could still describe the sights and smells of their trip to a hometown stadium in the same detail I just did—it was that kind of special!

Our seats were amazing! We were seated in the first row of the mezzanine section right behind the press box, manned by none other than the world famous Mel Allen, Phil Rizzutto, and Red Barbara. We all looked at each other knowing we were likely sitting in the best seats in the house—holy cow! All of this was directly behind home plate so we could see all the action, and we anticipated having a chance to catch a foul ball hit directly back at the press box.

Midway through the game, when the Yanks were coming to bat in the bottom half of an inning, Maris was due up second and Mantle would follow him, "how about that" (a famous Mel Allen saying), and so up steps Maris into the batter's box and he uncorks a blast into the upper reaches of the upper deck in right field. And as if that wasn't exciting enough, Mantle quickly steps into the batter's box, fouls off a couple of pitches, and then POW…he hits a towering shot, which from our vantage point looked like it would carry over the large stadium lights in right field and sail completely out of the stadium. It didn't go out of the stadium but it did hit midway up in the stadium lights—the sportscasters called the shot "Ruthian" (the Babe used to hit them like that). Back to back homers by the M&M boys—something to remember!

Pretty exciting stuff, but the "highlight" of the day was yet to come. Long about maybe the seventh inning, a blazing foul ball comes straight back at the press box causing all those in the vicinity to take cover. Well my 9-year-old brother Jim, a future Army Airborne Ranger, is right behind them, but instead of moving out of the way, he moves to the ball and in a split second and in grand style, he stretches out his right hand and BAM—gets hammered with a 110-mph bullet that careens off his hand back 25 rows into the crowd. As Jim nursed his now scarlet red right hand, one of the announcers yelled something like "nice try

Chapter 5

kid, but bring a glove next time"—it was a highlight for the day akin to "shooting your eye out"!

Maris eventually broke Babe Ruth's record by hitting 61 homers in 61, while Mantle hit 54 homers in a

Me on the big bike with my brother Jim on the little bike, Silver Beach, New Jersey, about 1957.

The "Fox Den" in Silver Beach, New Jersey, five doors down from the ocean.

shortened season for him as he had to sit out September due to an injury. For the record, together they hit 115 homers between them. A record that stands to this day!

Our family's one extravagance was that we owned a bungalow, and I mean a bungalow, at the Jersey Shore, which my parents bought in 1954. In the first six years of owning the place, they rented it out for eight of the 10 weeks during the summer "high season" just to help pay the mortgage and taxes. During those years, our family would normally go to the shore for two weeks in August and weekends in the fall, maybe the most beautiful time of the year at the Jersey Shore!

After 1960, we would go to the shore for the entire summer from the day after school closed until the day before school opened. What it all meant for me was that I virtually spent six full summers, from 1961 to 1966 (age 13 through 19), at the shore. Those were good times with many fond memories and some friends for a lifetime. All of it was my dad's plan to get my mom, my brother Jim, and me out of the city of Newark during the summer months. And while the three of us were at the shore full time, my dad would commute from the beach to work a few times a week while staying in our city house on the other nights. Good plan, Dad—thanks!

One fond memory with a "friend for a life" happened during the summer of 1965. My friend, Dominick

Chapter 5

My friend, Dominick Mussolino (left), and me, with the Alfa Romeo in the background, just before we left on our adventure to meet "Jabba the Hutt" in Atlantic City, New Jersey, 1965.

Mussolino (yeah really, Mussolino), who had just graduated from high school, was "provided" access to his father's "brand new" Alfa Romeo Spider, an Italian sports car convertible (a two-seater type, with no room for anything else, ugh!). As a result, we two amigos decided to take an overnight trip the 70 miles or so down the New Jersey Parkway to Atlantic City. This was before that city became the gambling capital of the East Coast. In 1965, it was a little threadbare and just a gilmer of its former self, a period that had lasted some 70 years from the late 19th century.

Our plan was to leave Silver Beach early on a Saturday, get to the "city on the ocean" by about noon, find a cheap hotel, settle in, and hit the beach first and then the "joints." I don't think we were old enough for most of the joints, but we were game! You know that saying about "the best laid plans"? Well, our plans sorta fell apart after spending almost five hours in beach traffic, top down, blazing sun, 90-degree temps, no sunscreen, and no good radio reception for a drive that should have taken a shade over an hour and a half.

Not to be discouraged, however, we made it to the city and spied what looked like a "cheap" hotel a block away from Atlantic City's epicenter, the Steel Pier. To our surprise, Frank Sinatra was performing that weekend right adjacent to the "diving" mule—they really had a mule that would jump from a 50-foot high platform into a large tank of water. I suspect PETA would not approve of that today, and I can't say I would disagree!

Anyway, into the dimly lit, creaky, narrow hallway of the Orville Hotel, which had been built in the 1890s, we marched, looking to make contact with the "desk manager" and register for a single room with two beds and, if possible, a separate shower. Well, we met the manager, who was sitting on a high-backed stool in a "cubby hole" of an archway that served as the registration desk.

She was sitting under a single yellowed light bulb that dangled over an unkempt head of red hair, wearing thick gold-rimmed glasses and lots of necklaces, and sporting yellow teeth that clenched a cigarette holder with a lighted Pall Mall, non-filtered. She must have weighed in at nearly 400 pounds, and when we got to her "perch," she asked us, in her best gravelly voice, what we boys were "looking for."

Chapter 5

Almost simultaneously we blurted out that we needed a room with two beds and a separate shower! She stared at us over her glasses, and with what seemed like a chuckle, said the rooms only had double beds and the shower was down the hall and was shared with possibly 14 other "boarders." Dominick and I looked at each other, gave each other the "seagull" salute, and told her we would take it, as long as she could give us a room on the street. She agreed to that—likely because we drove such a hard bargain—really, on the street!

We then asked about the price and when was check-out time, etc. At that she asked us if we were college boys. Dominick immediately said that he was going to be a college student in the fall semester, to which she said, "Good for you, that will be $6 cash." She then turned to me and said, "How about you?" I said that I wasn't a college boy. All true, I hadn't started "night" college yet. She looked me up and down and said, "Better for you, that will be $3 cash." Dominick never mentioned anything about being a college boy in my presence again. She gave each of us a key, and we bounded up the stairs to the third floor, laughing and "ribbing" each other all the way.

When we entered our room, we couldn't help but notice a big "round" of rope attached to a big swinging bracket mounted to the wall. The "bitter end" of the rope was affixed to grommets located on each side of a four to five foot long and maybe three foot wide thick leather type strap. This entire contraption looked medieval or worse, and our minds were racing with what this thing could be used for in this smallish room with one double bed. Well, it turns out it wasn't what you might think. Instead, it was a "fire escape" circa the late 1800s—really. One would sit in the leather seat and then you would be swung out the window and lowered to the ground by someone working a crank mechanism. I don't know who would lower the person who did the cranking, as there might not be anyone left on the floor to assume the duties! We both guessed that saving at least 50% of the guests was better than nothing and left it at that.

We had a great adventure that weekend. Two young guys out and about trying to experience a different slice of life on our own and away from our "safety zone"—and the time just flew by! Over the years I have thought about that adventure many times, and while "Star Wars" was still a distant 20 years off, I think my friend Dominick and I had a close encounter with "Jabba the Hutt" in real life!

In the fall of 1965, I started evening classes at Seton Hall University on the Newark campus. I dove in with accounting I, world lit, western civilization, and public speaking, which totaled a shade over 12 semester hours, qualifying me for a student deferment from the draft. I

Chapter 5

plowed along through winter and spring of 1965 and 1966, working during the day and attending classes four nights a week. Time flew by and things were good, but I started to realize that majoring in accounting was not for me.

Midway through the spring semester, I found myself drowning in profit and loss statements, balance sheets, and accounts receivable and payable ledger entries. The realization that night school was going to take six full years, or maybe even longer, to complete seemed staggering at the time, and while the tuition and books offer from the company was wonderful, it all didn't fit into what or where I wanted to be. Mind you, I didn't know what or where I wanted to be, but I pretty much knew that accounting wasn't going to be the what and an office environment forever wasn't going to be the where.

In the background, Vietnam was grinding away, and I was starting to see guys my age either enlist in the service of their choice or wait it out and surrender to the draft if it came to that. About mid May 1966, I was becoming more restless, as I knew I didn't want to pursue a degree in accounting and, if that was the case, I would have to inform the company of my intentions to not continue on in school, which would mean the end of my "scholarship," loss of my student deferment, and maybe the loss of my job!

One Friday afternoon in May, in fact, the Friday before Memorial Day weekend, I went to the Armed Forces recruiting office in downtown Newark, which was located on the corner of Green and Broad streets, across the parking lot from where my dad worked at the Newark Police Department. I wanted to speak with an Army recruiter about helicopter flight school opportunities I had read about. Anyway, when I walked through the recruitment center, the Army, Navy, and Air Force recruiters were all out on "appointment"—translated, that meant getting away early for the Memorial Day weekend.

So, without hesitation, and because he was the only one there, I stopped by the Marine Corps office and spoke with the recruitment sergeant for a good half hour. Turns out, the Marines did not have a program like the Army's Warrant Officer helicopter flight program, nor did the Navy or Air Force. The Marine sergeant assured me, however, he could get me into Marine aviation through the enlisted ranks, and if I enlisted they could pretty much guarantee my choice of specialties and assignment after basic training at either Camp Lejeune, North Carolina, or Camp Pendleton, California. He went on to tell me that if I signed a letter of intent to join the Corps that afternoon, he could guarantee me Camp Pendleton as my basic training assignment. I guess Camp Pendleton was a more ideal place to get your ass kicked for 10 weeks because of the temperate California coast weather, compared to the hot, humid, swampy conditions

Chapter 5

experienced at Camp Lejeune during the summer. So, if you did the good sergeant a favor and signed up that afternoon, he would do you a favor and ensure you did your basic training at the crown jewel of the Marine Corps training facilities.

All I had to do was sign the letter of intent—"should I or shouldn't I"—return the following Monday with my birth certificate, and I would be off and running. I did think about it, and little did I know what a pivotal point that was in my life. Without question, fate was looking over my shoulder! Joining up would have definitely gotten me out of the accounting arena and out of the company, and I would have been embarking on a completely new adventure or worse. I thought about it for three minutes and told the recruitment sergeant that I'd think about it over the weekend while at the beach and that he would likely see me back on Monday morning. I then departed for the weekend to the Jersey Shore.

While there, I told friends I had visited the recruitment center and I was considering joining the Marine Corps. They thought I was nuts, not because it was the service or specifically the Marine Corps, but because the summer was coming up. The consensus was that if I was inclined to join the Marines or another branch of service, then I should wait until summer was over and enjoy the time at the beach during the upcoming 10 summer weekends. After a few beers, and further discussion, that seemed like a good idea, and so that became my plan.

I didn't return the following Monday, and I didn't enroll in the summer session for night school. I also didn't inform the company of my thoughts on joining the service in the September 1966 timeframe. The way things played out, it didn't matter. Because I set this up as my course of action, I was playing Russian roulette with the draft. I wasn't afraid or overly concerned about being drafted, but if one was drafted then you were put where the service wanted you, and in most cases that meant rifleman, military specialty code, 11B, Infantry, and likely Army!

Well, I didn't think I'd be drafted between June and September, so I just went on about my merry way thinking all was well and that I would enlist in some branch of the service in September 1966. In fact, I was looking forward to enlisting, and I never thought the government would be efficient enough to catch up to me in less than 90 days. Wow, was I wrong!

As an aside, the Marine Corps recruitment sergeant with whom I talked to in May 1966 called my home for a follow-up (hello, almost a year later) and spoke to my dad about me having expressed a desire to join the Marine Corps. My dad replied that I had considered it, but right at the present, June 1967, I was about to graduate from Army

Chapter 5

Officer Candidate School (OCS) as a 2nd lieutenant of infantry and was on orders to attend the Army's Rotary Wing Flight School at Ft. Wolters, Texas. The sergeant wished all the best and gave my dad an enthusiastic "Hooo...rah"! I ended up where I initially wanted to be, but arrived there in a much different way, and was now on a path to being a commissioned officer—2nd Lieutenant, Infantry, U.S. Army!

Chapter 6
Wow, I Really Did Get Drafted

Chapter 6

I saw it protruding from the mailbox as soon as I turned onto Leslie Street. I had just finished driving up from the Jersey Shore early on a Monday morning, you know, after the weekend, en route to work at Standard Bitulithic. It was a large manila envelope with the Selective Service moniker emblazoned on the upper left portion of the envelope. The Selective Service was, in essence, the "draft meisters" who oversaw running the process of selecting and notifying men who would be called up in the monthly draft and placed into military service. It was the draft notice that I didn't think would catch up with me so quickly after losing my student deferment. After all, it was only Monday, July 18, 1966, a mere 52 days after deciding to take a chance on the possibility of not being drafted before September, the month I thought I would be enlisting in a branch of service. How could any branch of the U.S. government be so efficient?

After digesting the news, I drove to work at Standard Bitulithic and, by chance, met Mike Washington walking through the parking lot. Almost simultaneously, we blurted out to each other that we had just been drafted by "Uncle"—you know, the government! Never had we ever given any thought to both of us being drafted on the same day. After we were over the "holy shits, what do you think of that," we went in to see Vinny and related to him what was happening. Another round of "holy shits." Our colleagues joined us in Vinny's office, and it was like a party until it wasn't like a party anymore. After a while, and I suppose because the Vietnam War was raging, I think people didn't know whether to wish us well or to feel sorry for us. A lot of young men were being killed every week, and it was being documented every night on the TV news. After taking stock of the entire situation, it was more a somber occasion than a happy one.

After things calmed down, Mike and I both agreed to work for one more week and then take the following week off. Vinny was appreciative that we didn't depart the next day because, with both of us leaving, it put a good-sized dent in the payroll and accounting office. Toward the end of that week, Mr. Landers, the company president, took all eight of us from the front office out to lunch at his country club (can't remember the name) and it was a really nice event. There were very kind words for Mike and I, along with a two-week severance check with a little extra bonus and the promise of having our jobs back when we satisfied our military obligation. How nice was that? It was sad too, as it was the last time, save for Mike, that I saw most of them. Mr. Landers passed away in the fall of 1967 while attending a son's basketball game at St. Benedict's Prep in Newark. I was home on a short leave prior to flight school, and I visited the funeral home. That too was sad. Mr. Landers was a good guy who died much too soon!

Chapter 7
So, It Was Settled— You're in the Army Now

Chapter 7

My reporting date to the Armed Forces Recruitment Center in Newark was Monday, August 1, 1966. It would become a day that I, and I'm sure anyone who went through that drill, will never forget. It was also the day I was launched on a life-long trajectory that would be guided by acts of fate, pure accident, and happenstance, in ways that still amaze me. The first significant fateful act was not enlisting in the Marine Corps but allowing events to guide me while not knowing I was being guided. Sometimes life just unfolds in front of you, and so it's probably not so bad to just let it…unfold! What did Forrest Gump say: "Life is like a box of chocolates, you never know what you're going to get." Doesn't hurt to be a little prepared, though, recognizing you can't anticipate everything life throws your way, but it's less painful if you have at least thought about some of the "what ifs."

My dad and I drove up from the Jersey Shore early that Monday morning, and he dropped me off at Green and Broad streets in Newark at about 0645 hours—the 0 stands for "O my God, it's early"—for an 0700 hours reporting time. I was carrying a gym bag with a change of clothes, towel, shaving kit, couple extra pair of underwear, and pen and paper. That was it, along with $50! I wouldn't need much money as "everything" from here on in was to be picked up by Uncle Sam. The monthly pay as a Private E1 in the U.S. Army was $88, before taxes! It's

So, It Was Settled—You're in the Army Now

hard to imagine and to think, but I never felt like I was literally broke.

Shortly after arriving at the recruitment center, our group of about 175 underwent roll call to reconcile the list of those who were officially summoned to take part in the festivities with those who up to that point were AWOL (absent without official leave). Yeah, the military jargon starts early, and we were only 15 minutes into our time in service. In summary, it was good to have been on time. Those who arrived later, about 20 guys total, got the real rush approach of hurry up, hurry up, hurry up, and wait, and then hurry up some more. They seemed to be out of sync the entire day, and when it ended, they just appeared to be in raggedy shape. I saw my friend Mike from Standard Bitulithic, but with all the commotion all we could do was acknowledge each other.

The first big item on the morning's agenda was the induction physical. All inductees, still in civilian street clothes, were instructed to strip down to our undershorts and bring our clothing with us. It was an interesting drill if you'd never disrobed with 150+ other guys all squeezed together in a room meant for 90. You could tell that some were uncomfortable. Some guys had probably never undressed in "public" before. I had been a Boy Scout, you know, summer camp skinny-dipping, high school athletics, and "pick up" basketball at the Ironbound Newark YMCA.

Chapter 7

If you wanted a shower, you stripped down and stood in line to get into the group shower room. Once in, you hoped you could find a working shower with a smidgen of hot water dripping out. No privacy there but, at that time, all part of growing up and, unbeknownst to all, it was good training for what was coming in the future.

Once the mass disrobing drill had been accomplished, we were broken out into sections of about 35, and each section started out at a different point in the physical process so as to have everyone doing something over the next two hours or so. The physical consisted of tests of eyes, hearing, lungs, reflexes, heart, blood, extremities, hands and feet, male privates with cough, and the first finger wave/prostate exam for, I suspect, most of us. All were conducted for the most part in front of the group. This whole process is the start of losing one's sense of individual identity and the start of morphing into something bigger than one's self. Sometime later, the realization of being a member of a team would take hold—the whole point of basic training and what follows, as in military service! It was a little different than what I suspect takes place now, although I hope not.

Once completed and declared "fit for service," we were moved into a different area where we were instructed to get dressed. Under the watchful eye of a couple of recruitment sergeants, we assembled into four lines of about 40 guys each. After forming up and straightening the lines, we were called by name and assigned to a service like so—recruitment sergeant yelled out FOX, FRANCIS M, ARMY! Bada bing, pretty straightforward, you're in the Army now, with no room for negotiating.

Once all present had been assigned, we were asked to come to attention and raise our right hands, and with that we were sworn into the Armed Forces of the United States with the mission to "protect and defend the Constitution of the United States against all enemies foreign and domestic."

Declared "fit for service" was sort of a joke in that the demand for men was so great that it was said anyone and everyone was found fit for service as the military really only needed warm bodies. Contrary to this "urban/suburban" myth, however, on my induction day, a number of men were found to be unfit for service and, in fact, they were separated from the group. You know, bone spurs, flat feet, eyesight issues or maybe heart palpitations, parents well connected, conscientious objectors, or whatever.

If memory is correct, within our group we had two men who identified themselves as being conscientious objectors. I'm not sure if they were ever truly separated that day, or whether they had to endure a process of re-evaluation and went on to serve in non-combat-related positions such as medics or perhaps chaplains' assistants.

Chapter 7

Note: Serving as a medic or corpsman can be as tough as it can get. A portion of these "specialists" serve in the field with infantry units and they go into combat situations arm and arm with their colleagues. The "red cross" emblem emblazoned across their armbands is no guarantee of not being shot at and many medics have died while attempting to save other wounded men. They are a brave band of brothers—watch the movie "Hacksaw Ridge," and while it is a movie, it is a true story focusing on a real person who in fact lived it!

My recollection of induction day is that the overwhelming majority of those of us being drafted went to the Army. About a dozen went to the Marines, and a smaller number went to the Air Force. I don't think, on that day, any were pushed to the Navy. This made sense, if that can be said of anything associated with the "draft," as it was the height of the Vietnam War and the Army's needs were the greatest. We were nearing 550,000 troops of all services on the ground in Vietnam, with Army troops nearing 425,000! So hey, it was nice to be wanted!

After the morning's activities concluded, our group was issued a meal voucher for the cafeteria-style restaurant across Broad Street, where we could get the blue plate special for lunch. This was in the days of the 35-cent hamburger with fries and a pickle along with a 10-cent

So, It Was Settled—You're in the Army Now

Coke. So off we all went. I think we were instructed to be back by 1400 hours.

After lunch and back in the recruitment center, the group designated for assignment to Ft. Dix, New Jersey, of which I was one, and happy for it, would be boarding buses at around 1800 hours for the trip to Ft. Dix, our basic training site. I was happy to be going to basic in New Jersey, a mere 90 miles from home in Newark and a long 50 miles to the Jersey Shore. I had heard that new inductees and recruits of the week before had all been shipped to Ft. Jackson, South Carolina. I was very happy I missed that one. It was very hot and humid in August and September with up-to-your-armpit swamps and flies the size of bumblebees. It's amazing how, in the big scheme, the small things evolve into big things for which one can be very thankful or maybe unthankful for—the box of chocolates!

While waiting for the bus transport, we thought we could watch TV in the lounge area of the building. Not so fast GI—TV was only for those men who had volunteered and enlisted. Those who were drafted would have to wait in another much smaller waiting room that had no TV. Who says the service can be unfair?

That was the first in a series of reminders about the difference between being a lowly draftee versus a volunteer enlisted member. We each had different service numbers too. Draftees were designated as US, meaning a selective

Chapter 7

service designee (drafted), followed by an eight-digit number, such as 51976827, which was my number (US51976827). Those who volunteered for enlistment were given an RA designation, meaning Regular Army, followed by an eight-digit number. To be RA was to be held in higher esteem by the recruitment and training cadre of the day, and it carried over to the basic training arena.

On being given a number: once issued, you had to commit it to memory and loudly recite it when asked by drill cadre or you wouldn't be admitted to the mess hall (dining area) for meals. I'll bet that all new members to the Army recited that number to someone for admittance to something a thousand times in a relatively short time. You memorized it pretty quick, and it's something that never leaves you, like riding a bike or typing, believe it or not. Years after being given that number, someone asked if I remembered it and, without hesitation, I said loudly US51976827—and I hadn't recited that number in 25 years!

The bus trip to Ft. Dix was boring and tiring, as it was a hot New Jersey late afternoon in mid summer. No one knew anyone and, frankly, I don't think anyone was looking to make new friends during this particular bus ride. On top of that, all of us had been up since the crack of dawn in order to get to the recruitment center on time. It was a quiet ride. My friend Mike and I ended up on different buses because

So, It Was Settled—You're in the Army Now

of the alphabet, me being an F and he being a W. We missed each other a lot during basic because of alphabetizing. So onward we plowed through central New Jersey, three charter buses bringing 150 FNGs (look it up) to a very different and new phase of our young lives. Our average age was 20 years old, I was 19 years and 4 months!

Arriving at Ft. Dix at around 2100 hours, the scene was chaotic and just like you see in the movies. Drill sergeants screaming, people moving but not knowing where to go or what to do. And hey, nobody knows what the command "fall in" means—don't we start learning that stuff tomorrow?!

And so it went. First order of business after assembling the group into three long lines was to route step (civilians marching in a gaggle) to the nearby mess hall. Remember the US/RA thing? Well, it was about to manifest itself for the second time that day when the drill sergeants in charge started to ask your name and whether you were US or RA. As you stepped up to the mess hall, you recited your name and your status, US/RA, in as loud a voice as you could muster or else you were likely to be sent to the back of the line to grow a pair! I never had a problem with the loud part; I always had an outside voice. RA guys were let in first. No hard feelings; it was just a reminder, after all, that they had joined! After a rather late meal in the mess hall, we were marched back to the temporary barracks for the night.

Chapter 7

The set-up in the barracks was spartan. First off, they were WWII buildings that had been repainted, cleaned, and fixed up to a very limited degree. The latrine (bathroom/shower area) was clean but very dated. It was OK but there was no hot water per se, more lukewarm than anything. The shower area was a gang shower, which was an open room with six to eight showerheads. There was no privacy to speak of, but it got the job done.

There were two rows of 20 metal frame beds, meaning sleeping arrangements for 40 men on each floor of the barracks building. Each bunk bed had a wooden footlocker and a metal wall locker at either end of the bed that could be secured with a padlock. I'm not sure many of us had thought to bring padlocks, and the Army wasn't supplying any of them, so most went to bed with whatever valuables we had unsecured.

Barracks "buddies," Ft. Dix, New Jersey, 1966. That's me kneeling on the right.

Once back in the barracks building, our temporary drill sergeants told us we had an hour to get squared away, which meant personal gear stowed in the lockers, toilet/latrine needs taken care of, and, yes, get a letter off to mom, dad, sister, brother, wife, or girlfriend. I had my writing stuff, so I actually got a quick note off to my mom, dad, and brother. I didn't say much other than hello, everything is OK, and I'll be more explicit the next time—love to all! The sergeants set up a drop box at one end of the barracks to collect the letters, and they ensured getting them into the postal system. They, the Army, were taking care of us! My letter arrived at home, as I recall, prior to the next weekend, in about five days' time.

Prior to lights out, we were all introduced to the practice of posting a fire guard. The posting of a guard for the entire period after lights out was made up of a number of us new soldiers who would each serve a one-hour stint at some point during the night. A duty roster was drawn up and names were selected randomly and assigned to the shifts. I was not selected for duty on my first night in the Army, and I was thankful as it had been a long day and I knew we were in for an early wake-up call. We needed six men for the entire evening spanning the period from midnight, when lights would be out on this night, until 0600 hours the next morning, as the wake-up call would be at 0530 hours. After an hour-long duty watch, the fire

Chapter 7

guard would then find the soldier who was to replace him on watch, wake him, and provide him with the flashlight and the instructions for turning in a fire report. The biggest challenge of the hour-long duty sometimes was finding where the next man up was sleeping. It was no small task when not familiar with anyone on the floor.

The fire guard was just that, a fire guard who would walk the barracks during his hour-long shift and alert and wake up the entire barracks if a fire broke out. The likelihood of a fire breaking out seemed somewhat remote, but it had happened in the past and having someone up and awake while all others are sleeping had saved lives. In addition, part of this drill on the first night in the Army was to burn into the mind of each one of us that some kind of guard duty is a constant and quite serious part of military life. Guard duty in a combat zone could be a life or death event.

0530 comes around really quick when hitting the rack sometime after midnight. With not much warning, and in what seemed like the middle of the night, our barracks was descended upon by a four or more drill sergeant cadre, all yelling various things about getting up and getting a move on. We were notified that we had 30 minutes to formation on the company street (most of us didn't know what the company street was—turns out to be just what it sounds like, the street in front of the barracks). So, throw your gear

So, It Was Settled—You're in the Army Now

together, hit the latrine to shave, shower (no time), or splash a little water in the face and under the pits, then out the door and into the company street.

Still in civilian clothes, we were off to the mess hall for a speed drill breakfast with some nominal harassment. Remember the RA/US thing—well that was in play again along with some drill instructors asking everyone to recite their eight-digit serial number (12345678) along with the appropriate US or RA prefix. Most of us hadn't memorized our service numbers, so those among us who had figured out the game realized if you wanted breakfast with time to eat it, you needed to quickly rattle off any eight numbers in order to pass GO into the mess hall. The drill instructors didn't know what your specific numbers were, so what the hey!

The lesson here was that you had to be quick on your feet and able to adapt in order to move through it. Although I didn't think up the "any eight numbers thing," I picked up on it pretty quickly, and on that day it gave me and others about 10 more minutes in the mess hall to enjoy a "leisurely" breakfast amid the chaos. The alternative to passing GO into the mess hall was heading to the rear of the chow line to memorize eight numbers, real or otherwise!

Out of the mess hall and into a sort of formation of about 40 per grouping, we were marched to a large

Chapter 7

warehouse-type building that had a barbershop at one end, uniform issue stations for both work and dress attire including shoes and boots, another eye exam, dental exam, ID card issue point, dog tag issue point, and a sundry item station for belt buckles, hats, and cloth name tags that were made up and sewn on while you waited.

Much like in the recruitment center, we were broken into smaller groups and sent to different stations so that the whole place was bustling with newly minted GIs (Army for "government issue," meaning the men were now GIs). Haircuts were in order and, without exception, we were all shorn of whatever locks we had right down to the skin, well below crew cut level! I wasn't bothered by that as I had worn my hair in a crew cut during high school and afterward. Some of the rock and rollers, however, were crushed, but that only lasted for about two minutes!

There wasn't much time to think about what was happening while dragging a newly issued duffel bag jam packed with all the new stuff you were acquiring. This entire activity for about 160 newbies took the better part of three hours, after which we were marched back to the barracks and instructed to get into our new uniforms and get back out onto the company street for the march over to the mess hall for midday chow (Army for lunch). We were a sorry looking bunch. The all-new olive drab uniforms had not been washed or pressed, and they had a strange smell of newness, and in the hot August sun of a New Jersey summer in the pinelands, they didn't wick very well.

Chapter 8

Army Basic Combat Training

Chapter 8

Following chow, we were instructed to get all our gear and board the six Army olive drab cattle cars (Army for trailer truck with large windows and a step-up, side-entry door) waiting in the company street for the short ride over to the newly built 3rd Brigade training area. Our group was to be the first set of trainees housed in this new complex of barracks, classrooms, physical training facilities, mess halls, and chapels. All the buildings were brick and modern looking, and the new facility would have the capacity to train and graduate roughly 1,500 trainees every eight weeks.

This new complex of buildings was far and away much nicer than the wooden barracks of the WWII era in terms of creature comforts. The new barracks were air conditioned with eight-man rooms, and they had a community college feel about them, whereas the WWII barracks looked and smelled like what we all expected, with metal bunk beds, no air conditioning, and rifle racks placed right down the middle of the barracks floor. That's what an Army barracks was supposed to look like. The smell of gun oil was ever present as was the scent and feeling of thousands of newbies who had gone before. And because of it, you couldn't quite lose sight of why you were actually there, you know, to be trained as a soldier! In the new barracks, the rifle racks were concentrated into one room at one end of the building. It was probably planned that way

Two weeks after being drafted with my brother Jim (left) and dad (right), at Ft. Dix, New Jersey, 1966.

for better security, but it took something away from the overall feel of the place.

While I was in the first two weeks of training, I literally ran into someone I had gone to high school with—my friend Richie Silva, who had been drafted about six weeks prior to me being drafted and who was about to graduate from basic. Prior to his graduating and leaving Ft. Dix, Rich and I met at the beer garden that was set up on Sundays adjacent to a parade field in roughly the center of the training brigades. He took me on a tour of his barracks—real Army as I mentioned. I, in kind, took him over to our barracks complex and was almost embarrassed about our comfortable living style versus his.

Chapter 8

The old timers would call our area the "black" boot Army versus the "brown" boot Army of their day. Black boot was a derogatory term, implying we would turn out to be a bunch of puffs, unlike the "tough" men who had gone through training in the brown boot era of WWII up through the Korean War and the early days of Vietnam. The stark conditions they encountered toughened them up, mentally and physically, and got them ready for adversity and learning to do without, whereas the comfortable amenities provided us would set us up for expecting more of the same. It's hard to tell, but I understood it in theory. Ask soldiers who served on Okinawa in WWII if they expected to get a shower at the end of the day (or even week) and air-conditioned hooches and PXs. Never happened, GI; however, that mindset was prevalent throughout Vietnam with the exception of the ground combat units. What did we do to ourselves?!

The beer hall, on the other hand, was a tradition that had been ongoing since at least WWII, or so we were told. The beer was 3.2% by volume of alcohol, and the Army allowed 18 year olds to consume within the confines of the beer garden. Although the beer was of lower alcohol content than "real" beer, as the soldiers called it, it could work you over in the hot August sun or sweltering tent of the beer garden area. The "gardens" were only open on Sunday afternoons and only for about three hours. It drew a large crowd and a lot of guys slept it off until reveille the next morning!

My friend Richie went on to advanced individual training (AIT) at, I believe, Ft. Gordon, Georgia, to some sort of signal school. Then it was on to Vietnam where he served a one-year tour honorably and without injury. During his tour, he ran into an Army chaplain and our former high school athletic director from St. James High School, Father (Captain) Al Arvay. He was saying Mass on a makeshift altar in the middle of nowhere on a mountain top in South Central Vietnam. What a small world we live in!

When coupled with the other two training brigades at Ft. Dix, a total of roughly 4,500 trainees would be graduating every two months and heading out for AIT, designed to provide specific specialty training that a volunteer enlistee likely signed up for or training randomly assigned by the Army. Some would go right from basic combat training to advanced infantry training, also at Ft. Dix, with likely assignment to Vietnam as an infantry rifleman, military specialty code 11B.

Yes, Vietnam was building up with additional Army divisions being fielded, as in the 4th Infantry Division, 9th Infantry Division, Americal Division (Infantry), 5th Mechanized Infantry Division, 101st Airborne/Airmobile Division, one brigade of the 82nd Airborne Division, and the 173rd Airborne Brigade, not to mention the 1st

Chapter 8

Cavalry Division, along with increasing numbers of artillery, aviation attack helicopter units (1st Aviation Brigade), 5th Special Forces (Green Berets), and engineering and communications units.

Air Force and Navy units were also in build-up mode with the addition of such military assets as the Battleship USS New Jersey along with the entire U.S. 7th Fleet, while B-52 bomber missions were being flown against targets in North and South Vietnam from as far away as Guam. All told, the number of boots on the ground would amount to 575,000 during the time I served there in 1968–1969.

Losses were mounting and U.S. public support for the war and respect for the military, read confidence in General Westmoreland's "strategy," was on the wane and fast eroding, and it continued in a downward spiral throughout the late 1960s. What were we attempting to achieve in Vietnam? Stem Communist aggression—seemed to make sense. Was Ho Chi Min bent on establishing a totalitarian regime or was he a "freedom fighter" who had been fighting against the Japanese invaders and French "colonialism" in an effort to "unify" his country—it was never very well explained, nor was an "end game" strategy ever articulated to the American people. Were we there in order to achieve "our" goals—democratic principles—or economic opportunities—oil? Keep reading!

For the next 18 weeks, it was one training cycle after another with Basic Combat Training (BCT) lasting eight weeks, followed, for me, by a two-week leadership training course, and culminating in eight weeks of AIT. The first few days of basic training consisted of physical training (PT) in the early morning, followed by breakfast, followed by close order drills (marching in column and formations), drill commands, the proper way to wear the uniform, the proper way to salute, the proper way to address superiors, the proper way to shine your boots/shoes, the proper way to care for your individually assigned/personal weapon, the proper way to take your meals (like in manners), and so on. I'm sure you get the idea. There's a proper way to do everything in the Army, even the most menial of things that unknowingly add up to one's performing every task the proper way—the Army way! In a different part of the world, and under different circumstances, doing it the Army way could save soldiers' lives, not to mention your own.

PT was vigorous and was conducted as the first event of the day, every day, and consisted of calisthenics, overhead bars, jogging, timed running (the mile), the obstacle course (running, jumping, low crawling, roping, and running, running, and more running), just to name some of the games we played. These activities were all performed in combat boots (not so good on the feet), fatigue uniform

Chapter 8

pants with a pistol belt and canteen, tee shirts, and fatigue cap. At times, PT was conducted in full or partial combat gear, including steel pots, "fanny packs," personal issue weapons, which for basic trainees was the M-14 rifle, and even one's entrenching tool attached to the pistol belt. We never walked anywhere either. Everything was done at what was called "quick time." It wasn't running or jogging, but it was a notch up from walking. Kept you in shape!

August 1966 was essentially a five-week month. The end of the fifth week would be followed by Labor Day, which was and is still celebrated as a three-day weekend unofficially marking the end of summer vacation season and the start of the traditional school year. So, bright and early on Saturday, September 3, 1966, our training company was rousted up at "o'dark thirty" and marched out to the PT fields, which were near the cantonment area. Our uniform was fatigue pants, plain tee shirts, combat boots, and fatigue caps.

Once there, our field first sergeant (commonly referred to as TOP across the Army, as he is the unit's ranking/"top" sergeant) presented a challenge that went something like this: "Any of you studs that can attain a total score of at least 450 (500 was a perfect score) on this PT test, along with completing the mile run in under 6 minutes, 30 seconds will be awarded a weekend pass that will start today, Saturday, at noon and end at lights out on Monday evening. Those of you who remain on post for the weekend will pull KP (kitchen police), fire guard, and area policing as needed throughout the training brigade area. Questions? No questions—OK. Good luck!"

So, the real challenge within the challenge was going to be the 6 minute, 30 second mile in combat boots on an uneven, somewhat gravelly, rutted track, which would be run after completing/passing the other four events that made up the total PT test. Just by comparison, world-class athletes were running miles in just under 4 minutes with ideal track conditions, sans combat boots, no other events scheduled, and many years of training under their belts.

Well, what this meant for me was that if I could meet the requirements laid out by TOP, I might be at the Jersey Shore before 1400 hours that afternoon, which would give me a full 48 hours plus at Silver Beach. That was all the motivation I needed. I passed the PT test with an aggregate score of over 450, while running the mile in, I believe, 6 minutes, 12 seconds. About 90 men of the 220 in the unit were awarded the three-day pass. Another 75 or so guys scored a cumulative 450 or better, but they came up shy in the mile run. So, like I mentioned, the mile run was the challenge. It felt good to "win" something after being challenged.

After making it back to the barracks, skipping breakfast, and changing into a clean uniform, it was off to

Chapter 8

the Greyhound Bus stop on Ft. Dix to catch a bus to Pt. Pleasant. After almost a one and a half hour bus ride up NJ Rte. 70, I debarked the bus near the center of Pt. Pleasant. From there, I walked out to the Rte. 88/Rte. 35 intersection and began thumbing a ride south on Rte. 35, the shore road. In pretty quick fashion, two girls my age, and nice as they could be, driving daddy's new Mustang convertible, destination Seaside Heights, gave this soldier boy a lift to West Colony Road in Silver Beach. It took three minutes to walk home from there.

I knocked on the screen door, and when my mom looked up and saw me standing in the doorway, she about fainted. No one knew that I would be home at the beach for the weekend. My parents did not have a phone in the bungalow, so I couldn't alert them and, remember, there were no cell phones. After hugs and handshakes, I went into the kitchen. It was only 1245 hours, and I had almost two and a half days of a three-day pass remaining—what a good feeling!

I had accomplished a lot in just six plus hours. You know the commercial the Army used to run about getting more done before noon than most civilians get done all day? How true! My day so far: early wake up, road march to and from PT test site, complete the test, clean up, 75+ mile bus ride along with a nice seven-mile hitch down the beach road—all before 1300 hours. That's a full day in itself, and half of the day remained!

Army Basic Combat Training

New Jersey is an interesting state to travel through. Although small, it is very diverse with distinct climates and ecosystems. The coast, or the Jersey Shore, as we referred to it, consists of 170 miles of beautiful sandy beaches and salt marshes behind the barrier islands extending well inland. The northern part of the state is mountainous and includes the Delaware Water Gap to the west and the Palisades on the Hudson to the east, with many secluded lakes and seemingly undisturbed old growth forest in between. The south central portion of the state contains pinelands similar to the southeastern United States but with very different flora and fauna.

So, when you departed Ft. Dix, you were in the pinelands, an area that closely resembled the pine forests of Georgia, red clay and all, and it was isolated to the point that it did not feel like other parts of New Jersey. For roughly 20 minutes you would travel through a part of the state that most people would not believe was actually New Jersey if they had been blindfolded and taken there. The kick was that you were only 90 minutes away from the New York metro area with its 10 million residents and 60 minutes away from Philadelphia with its multi millions of residents.

Because the state is sandwiched between Pennsylvania and New York, it has always had an identity problem. People tended to identify with New York or Pennsylvania,

Chapter 8

not New Jersey. This was/is likely because many of them commuted to cities in those states for work, and to me they tended to adopt character traits of one place or the other.

Such was the case with professional sports teams and New Jersey residents. If you lived in northern New Jersey above the Barnegat Inlet, then you tended to be a New York Giants, Yankees, Rangers, or Mets fan, but if you were from south of the same inlet, you were likely to be a fan of the Eagles, Phillies, or Flyers. This point was brought home to me loud and clear in the 1990s when my wife and I went to Cape May, New Jersey, for a long weekend in mid September. Turns out, the Mets, my team, were in the thick of a pennant race, and I thought we would be able to watch a Mets game at a sports bar in Cape May while bar/restaurant hopping. No such luck! All that was on TV was either Phillies baseball or Eagles football. No matter where we went, it was the Phillies or Eagles, and no one cared about the fate of the Mets! I was shocked and not very happy that I couldn't catch some of the Mets action in New Jersey. Then it dawned on me—we were way south of the Barnegat Inlet and although still in the Great State of New Jersey, we were in Philly cheesesteak country!

So, now that you've had the short course in New Jersey geography and sports demographics, let's move back to Basic Combat Training. A real "highlight" of basic training was going to the rifle range for weapons qualification.

Actual firing was preceded by learning about the M-14, which was the Army's standard issue rifle at the time, including how to assemble and disassemble, clean, oil, and generally maintain it. Most of us trainees likely had never handled a firearm before, so it was a new and profound experience. This wasn't a "for-fun" exercise, as the M-14 was a "killing" machine and the reality of that kind of hits you right between the eyes. We all became very familiar with our individual weapons as a result of sleeping with them during the days leading up to and heading out to the firing ranges. It was good training, and we were learning how to be riflemen—the backbone of the Army!

After learning how to care for the rifle, which took place in a classroom in the cantonment area, we started a five-day marksmanship qualification course that terminated with our attaining marksman, sharpshooter, or expert marksman status. For our group, marksmanship qualification began on a Monday morning starting in the fourth week of basic training. Mid August in south central New Jersey can be sweltering hot, and this year was no exception!

Temperatures hovered in the low to mid 80s early in the morning and moved into the low to mid 90s by afternoon. In all, the heat index was above 100 degrees with no shade in sight. An earlier wake-up than normal with breakfast on the fly was followed by a three-mile road march with steel

Chapter 8

Me (third from left) with Mike Washington (to my left) at basic training, Ft. Dix, New Jersey, 1966. Mike and I were drafted on the same day, August 1, 1966.

pots, butt packs, first aid pouch, rifle with four unloaded magazines, and two canteens of water. It was roughly three miles out in the morning and three miles back in the early evening each day while qualifying. They were long, hot days!

The first two days centered on zeroing one's rifle, which is the process you go through in order to make you, the shooter, an integral part of the weapon. Because everyone sees things a tad differently, if you just randomly picked up a rifle and fired it at a target, everyone would likely have a different result. So, zeroing the rifle has the shooter match his eye's sight picture of the target to what the rifle is actually pointing at and hitting. On a 25-meter range, with the rifle sight set at the neutral position, the shooter will start out by shooting three rounds at a target that is overlaid with small equidistance squares.

The object of this drill is to get a tight shot group whose closeness to target center can then be applied to the rifle sight by moving the sight picture x number of clicks to the right or left, then up or down. Essentially, you are calibrating your eyeball through the rifle sight to the target then recording what becomes your target sight picture by counting how many equidistant target squares with right/left, up/down clicks on the rifle sight. This process is repeated until the shot groups are dispersed in the center (bullseye) of the target area. Once both instructor and shooter are satisfied that the results are consistent, then the shooter records how many clicks up and across it takes for him to strike near target center. Once achieved and acknowledged, it is said that your rifle is zeroed and you need to remember how many clicks right/left and up/down it takes to get to the target center or else all this work will have been for naught. This also means that zeroing is exclusively between you and a particular rifle. Anytime thereafter, if you should be assigned a different rifle, you would need to go through the zeroing process in order to achieve maximum effective results with that rifle.

At the end of each training day on the rifle range, all the trainees would "police" the firing line to include the firing pits and pick up all the brass shell casings and any "live" rounds that were scattered about. After sorting

Chapter 8

out the "live" rounds from the "spent" casings, all trainees then went to an area and cleared their personal weapons by sliding the bolt open to check the chamber for any unexpended ammunition, releasing the bolt and "slamming" it home, and concluding by pointing the weapon into a sand-filled 55-gallon drum and discharging it.

If you had properly cleared the weapon, when you discharged it into the sand-filled drum, the trigger would harmlessly click with no resulting ammo discharge. The bolt would then be set in the open position and the trainee would address the nearby NCO as such: "Sergeant, Private Fox reports NO BRASS OR AMMO," after which you would be cleared to join your unit formation for the march back to the barracks—a long, hot day!

And so it went for the remainder of August and September 1966—constant physical conditioning, spirit of the bayonet in concert with hand-to-hand combat, radio/telephone procedures, intro to map reading and calling for fire, history of the U.S. Army and the United States, the soldier's code of conduct, road marching in full combat gear, the grenade toss, familiarization with chemical warfare and introduction to the proper use of a gas mask, and an introduction to night operations replete with a live fire low crawl through a booby-trapped, 75-yard long, very muddy piece of Ft. Dix.

Somewhere toward the end of basic training, all trainees were being notified of what the Army was going to do with them, such as send some off to cook school, or combat engineering school, or infantry, armor, or artillery school, or aviation or vehicle maintenance school, or maybe even chaplain's assistant or medic school. Although this all seemed random, it was probably determined, in some way, shape, or form, by how one did on the aptitude tests that were administered to all of us during the first week of being in the Army at Ft. Dix.

I was called out of an evening formation at about the fifth week with maybe eight to 10 others. We were informed by our field 1st sergeant that we had tested well enough to be considered for Officer Candidate School (OCS) and, if interested, as a first step, we would "interview" with our company commander. If that interview went favorably, we would then meet with our battalion commander. He would conduct an overall evaluation and render a "go/no go" edict. If you were a "go," accepted the offer to attend OCS, and graduated as a 2nd lieutenant, then you would owe the Army an additional year of service, which would now make your total time commitment to the Army three years instead of the two years associated with being drafted. Those who were a "go" were given until the next day's evening formation to decide and either decline or accept. I, and six others, accepted

Chapter 8

the Army's offer, and so the next chapter in our lives was unfolding.

Why did I accept going to OCS as a 19-year-old who would graduate during wartime as a 20-year-old 2nd lieutenant of infantry if all went "well"? I thought it would be a challenging experience that would introduce me to things that I couldn't begin to imagine at the time. Also, I thought it would perhaps be good to re-enter the civilian workforce after having served as a commissioned officer—it might open up some opportunities that might not have presented themselves otherwise. The pay was better and, frankly, I felt proud to have been offered the opportunity to serve in that capacity. The extra year in service didn't matter. The big catch was that I would have to attend Infantry OCS and there was a war going on, and the preponderance of casualties were infantry soldiers. So, it was something to consider but, hey, I was 19 and, you know, bullet proof.

After all was said and done, it was an opportunity that would provide a chance for self-improvement and serve as a real first step into the next part of life. I also didn't have any better offers. It seemed a very good opportunity at the time and, unbeknownst to me, it put me on a collision course with what was to be my fate! Another one of life's lessons—weigh out the pros and cons with the best information available at the time, make a considered decision, don't be afraid to take the chance, and then drive on!

After basic training, I attended AIT (Infantry) at Ft. Dix, which was good on a couple of levels: 1) the training was good, infantry stuff, more PT, various individual and crew served weapons training, land navigation, small unit tactics, advanced first aid, and so on, which all in all was good prep for infantry OCS; and 2) coming out of basic, I was promoted from private E-1, lowest of the low, to private E-2, next up from the lowest. That was worth a little pay raise, maybe $28 a month, but, more importantly, I was eligible for weekend passes as long as I didn't come out on any of the weekend duty rosters. That being said, and being from New Jersey, I was able to get home about every other weekend over the next eight weeks. All was good and as things worked out in terms of training weeks, I completed AIT right around Christmas of 1966. As a result, I was able to take 10 days of leave at home before flying out to OCS at Ft. Benning, Georgia.

I had never been on an airplane before, so flying to Columbus, Georgia, the home of Ft. Benning and the U.S. Infantry, was the beginning of those experiences I could hardly have imagined a short time before. I had never been outside of New Jersey other than to New York City for Mets and Yankee games; West Point, New York, for a couple of Army football games; Philadelphia for an Army-Navy

Chapter 8

football game with my dad and cousins; a Phillies-Giants game with the Old Bridge Little League, which was rained out after two innings; the Ben Franklin Institute with my grammar school class; and a college graduation in Connecticut. I'd never been outside of a four-state area (New Jersey, New York, Pennsylvania, and Connecticut). So, here we go!

Chapter 9

Ft. Benning—
"I Am the Infantry,
Queen of Battle,
Follow Me"

Chapter 9

On a chilly day in the first week of January 1967, I went to Newark Airport to catch my first ever airplane flight, which would take me to Atlanta and then on to Columbus, Georgia, the home of Ft. Benning. In those days, service members were required to travel in uniform. I'm not sure why, but obviously it made it easy to spot other service members in your branch. While milling around the ticket area (way before 9/11—there were no formal security checks), I started a conversation with another Army guy who, as it turned out, was also going to Ft. Benning to attend OCS. His name was Mike Fisher. Because he and I were heading in the same direction, we buddied up and traveled together.

Mike and I ended up being assigned to the same company, 51st Company, 5th Battalion, OCS, which was

Home of the U.S. Army Infantry—Infantry Hall, Ft. Benning, Georgia, 1967.

Ft. Benning—"I Am the Infantry, Queen of Battle, Follow Me"

the original officer training unit from WWII. There was a lot of history, tradition, and pride in what was being accomplished there, like in turning out the best infantry "two LTs" that could be for the Army! The place was haunted by those who had gone before us. Think WWII and North Africa, Sicily, Italy, D-Day (Normandy), the Battle of the Bulge, and finally into Germany. And let's not forget the Army's participation in the island hopping campaign in the Pacific Theater, the liberation of the Philippines, the taking of Okinawa, and the prep for the push to Japan.

To that point, our battalion commander, a lieutenant colonel, was in fact a 1944 OCS graduate who later participated in D-Day operations and crossed the Rhine River into Germany. Now, at likely the same age as most of our fathers, he was completing the cycle mentoring new officer candidates for a different type of war.

My new friend Mike was an intense guy who knew he wanted to be an Airborne Ranger and later a Green Beret. His dad was a retired Army major general, and he was up on that kind of stuff. I knew about Green Berets but wasn't entirely sure where Airborne Rangers fit in. I found out real quick, as Ft. Benning was also the home of the Army's Ranger and Airborne schools. All of us from day one in OCS were encouraged to become Airborne Rangers. It was omnipresent, and all we had to do was look out our barracks

Chapter 9

windows to see soldiers going through training and actually jumping from the 250-foot towers preparing to become airborne soldiers and maybe Rangers; the BEST of the BEST!

As time went on, 90% of my company volunteered to attend both schools. I volunteered to attend the three-week-long Airborne school thinking it would be a neat thing to do and that, because I would be in good physical shape after graduating from OCS, this was probably the best time to do it. All who applied, however, did not receive orders to attend. I did not, but 20 or 30 classmates out of a graduating class of about 130 did. In times past we were told that all OCS graduates, if they applied, were assigned to Airborne school, Ranger school, or both. It seems that my class had such a low number of graduates coming out on orders for Airborne or Ranger training because our graduation coincided with West Point's graduation in early June 1967. All of the West Point graduates were being sent to Airborne and Ranger school at Ft. Benning. The West Pointers essentially overloaded the Ft. Benning facilities for the two to three months after they graduated. Some of our guys were disappointed in not being selected for Airborne or Ranger school, but many were relieved. I was a little disappointed but not overly affected, as I would be going on to a four-month duty assignment with the 197th Infantry Brigade at Ft. Benning, followed by attendance at the Army's Rotary Winged Flight School located at Ft. Wolters, Texas.

Ft. Benning—"I Am the Infantry, Queen of Battle, Follow Me"

After one night in a neat and clean little motel on Benning Drive, with fine dining at the Waffle House next door, we called a cab for the ride to the 5th OCS Battalion HQ. Upon being dropped off curbside, we couldn't believe how beautiful everything looked, to the point that we simultaneously said something to that effect. The barracks were oldish but well maintained and freshly painted. All area signage was crisp and also freshly painted. The brass bell in front of HQ gleamed, as did the brass cannon that was displayed nearby. And then there was the landscaping. There wasn't a blade of grass out of place—it was all neatly and evenly trimmed. Lining the sidewalks there was a six-inch wide trough of gray pebbles with nary a weed to be seen! We would soon find out how all the sparkle was achieved and who did it.

After five to 10 minutes at the 5th Battalion archway, we were greeted by senior officer candidates, who were four weeks from graduation and being commissioned 2nd lieutenants. Their mission in life at this time was to get us in-processed, assigned to a platoon, and settled into a cubicle, followed by a fast lunch, because it was that time of day, and then placed on a work detail.

Guess who ended up trimming that beautiful grass with a pair of scissors? Yours truly! Oh, and the gray pebbles sans weeds; well, the way to ensure no weeds was to lift the pebbles out of the trough, pick the underlying weeds, rough

Chapter 9

up the dirt, and scoop the pebbles back into the trough. We had about 400 feet of trough and pebbles lining our barracks and needless to say it took a long time in the hot—yes, hot—January sun in southern Georgia. It sure looked good though when we finished!

Although we started out as two, others joined us after they reported through the battalion HQ. Something we all agreed with was that it wasn't really good to have reported in at mid-day, being as we could have reported in anytime within the 24-hour period encompassing the reporting date. We unseasoned soldiers didn't pick up on this until that day, so it was a lesson learned that went something like this: it might not always be so good to be early for things unknown in the Army. There was a group of soldiers who had learned this at some point before reporting for OCS, as we noticed an influx of folks reporting in after the dinner hour and after dark. This group, as we later found out, was composed of prior servicemen, some of whom had already had a tour in Vietnam and likely had at least two years of time in the Army—practical experience matters!

As a result of arriving later in the day, they missed the grass cutting and rock removal and replacement detail and most of the early evening hazing by the senior candidates, along with the barracks chaos that followed. Maybe it wasn't planned that way, but they appeared to be wiser than the newbies, meaning guys like me who thought being a

Ft. Benning—"I Am the Infantry, Queen of Battle, Follow Me"

little ahead of time would be a good thing and, you know, make a good impression. In a nutshell, they reported for duty within the allotted amount of time just before lights out and avoided the mayhem the rest of us endured. They knew the drill, even the newbies recognized that—so we live and we learn!

The first real day of OCS started at o'dark thirty (a lot of that o'dark thirty stuff going on in the Army—Ou…aaaah!), which comes out to be somewhere around 0430 hours, early, however you look at it. Morning formation was followed by a two-mile run and a low crawl down and across the infamous Raider Creek. From there, we went on to the statue of the Combat Infantryman in front of, you guessed it, Infantry Hall, where we recited the poem "I am the Infantry, Queen of Battle." It was a January morning in Georgia, and the temperature was frosty and probably right around freezing. We were all soaking wet and shivering to where you could hear teeth chattering. We "double timed" back to the barracks and prepared for breakfast and our first meeting with our company commander, Captain Danny Byard, a combat infantry veteran.

After breakfast, the entire company of 182 men formed a big semi-circle around one end of our barracks building and waited until the captain took to a makeshift podium. He was in his late 20s, with piercing blue eyes, a sharp military haircut, meaning "white" sidewalls and short on

Chapter 9

top, and he was loaded with what is called "military bearing." He looked every bit the Airborne Ranger former 1st Cavalry Division soldier his uniform identified him as. Like so many others during this timeframe at Ft. Benning, he had recently returned from Vietnam, where he served part of his tour as an infantry company commander.

His very presence commanded our full attention and, I suspect, everyone hung on virtually every word of his short talk, as I did. He only spoke for roughly five minutes, but I'm sure his remarks made a lasting impression on all in attendance. He stated that OCS would be tough and that all present would not be moving on for a variety of reasons; but for those who did, they would be trained to be the best 2nd lieutenants of infantry our nation could produce. He followed by saying that what we were embarking upon was serious business and that one day in the not so distant future our nation would entrust us with a platoon of 44 American men, infantry soldiers all, who would trust us with their lives. We needed to be ready for that, and so he implored us all to pay strict attention to the smallest of details taught here, because often it's a series of small things that make the difference between life and death in combat!

He made reference to his service in Vietnam and stated that, in his opinion, most of us would likely see action there, and so with that in mind keep these thoughts in your "headlights." He emphasized the importance of teamwork;

Ft. Benning—"I Am the Infantry, Queen of Battle, Follow Me"

loyalty to each other, family, and nation; and having a sense of those who sacrificed and went before us from these very barracks. He finished by stating cooperate and graduate, and then in his best infantry voice, he called the first sergeant to POST, and after rendering the hand salute, he commanded TOP to take charge of the company! It was a sober message as to the real reason why we were here. The first sergeant led us away and started the cadence song of We're 51st Company, OCS, Infantry, we're one day in, we're stepping out, we're on our way and MOVING UP!—which was to be sung with GUSTO!

The remainder of this day consisted of being issued books and instructional material, receiving additional sets of fatigue uniforms, arranging for laundry cleaning services, signing for a personal weapon (the M-14 rifle), and receiving an issue of TA-50 gear for field use. A lot happened, and then it was dinnertime. Remember the first night in the Army and the first day in basic training? Well, this was the same drill—you couldn't get into the mess hall until you answered a military-type question asked by senior candidates from the next barracks over.

Questions ranged from who the commander in chief was to how do you spell "lieutenant." The how do you spell "lieutenant" question stumped a fair number of candidates—remember, i before e except after c. So, if you stumbled with your question, you were directed to "give me

Chapter 9

25" (push-ups) and report to the back of the line. One of our guys got stumped, but didn't let on, and without hesitation, answered by saying, "Sir, yes sir, 'lieutenant,' and I spell it 'L-T-period' sir!" He got into the mess hall with that response for showing initiative and creativity, according to the senior candidates. Pretty cool response, don't you think?

OCS was six months of fast-forward with never enough time, it seemed, to get done what had to be done, along with everything else that needed to be done. There was a lot going on, and the faster you learned to manage your time and determine what was really important, the things that would eat you up if not attended to, the better. A friend of mine at the time stated it this way, "Slay the dragon closest to you." Good lifetime advice!

And so it went, day in, day out. Our academic courses ran the gamut from close order drill, to the law of land warfare, to small unit tactics, to heavy infantry weapons training, to call for fire, to coordinating close air support, to airmobile operations (something being conducted in Vietnam everyday), to weapons and vehicular maintenance programs, to a heavy dose of land navigation and map reading. Most all was geared to jungle warfare relative to the Vietnam environment and dwelled on platoon- and company-sized infantry operations.

Although, thinking back, we did have a "short course" on the employment of "low-yield" tactical nuclear weapons. There's nothing "low-yield" about nuclear weapons. The employment of any "low yield" nukes would likely wipe out most medium-sized cities and cause sufficient radioactive fallout that would be carried "downrange," contaminating air and water resources that over time would cause "radiation sickness" in humans and livestock, culminating in death.

A lot was crammed into a relatively short period of time, but it was well presented by combat veterans who had firsthand experience and who seemed intent on getting the real "poop" to us so that we didn't have to learn it the hard way, as some of them likely did.

On top of the military training, there was a big dollop of good behavior/good citizenship introduced into the syllabus. We did receive instructions on how to take meals in a civilized manner—you know, don't talk with your mouth full, please pass the butter, don't spread your butter with the butter knife, place it on your plate, napkin in your lap, cut your food, and place the knife across top side of your plate, pass the bread basket around the table, and leave some for your buddy!

We also received a few classes on the history of the U.S. Army, the U.S. Constitution and our republican form of government, voting, money management (how to manage your pay so as to not overspend yourself into trouble—very practical for some), and in general being a credit to

Chapter 9

yourself, your nation, the Army, and your parents! All good stuff then and now, and I hope it is still being emphasized in today's Army.

At two points in the six months of OCS, we had formal military dinner/dance receptions. These events occurred at the 11th week and then again at the 18th week. The 11th week event was called a military dining-in. That is an event where all the male officers—and there were only male officers in infantry units at the time—would have a formal meal together. The proceedings got started with all junior officers in training going through a senior officer/distinguished guest receiving line so as to properly introduce themselves. This would be followed by a cocktail-type reception and then by an announcement of dinner to be served. After taking positions at your assigned table, the posting of the national and unit colors (flags) by a formal Color Guard would commence. The colors would be paraded into the event area where they would be placed in full view for the remainder of the evening. It's a solemn event with all in attendance standing at attention while in one's own way paying respect to the flag while remembering all those who fought and died for our country.

At the end of the evening's events, the colors would be formally retired by the Color Guard and ceremoniously paraded out of the event area. During the course of the dinner, toasts would be made to the president, the chief of

Ft. Benning—"I Am the Infantry, Queen of Battle, Follow Me"

staff of the Army, our comrades, the nation, to any special guests in attendance, perhaps a Medal of Honor recipient, and to those who paid the last full measure of devotion to duty by giving their life for our country. Dinner was normally an elaborate event with multiple courses, wines, and dessert, topped off with after-dinner drinks and cigars. It was a fun and convivial evening!

The 18th week reception and dance was a bit more formal as this was the point where we were promoted to senior candidate level or, as we liked to refer to it as, 3rd lieutenants. There is no such rank as 3rd lieutenant in the Army, but if you were starting to feel like one, then you were pointing yourself in the right direction. It also meant we had six weeks to graduation, and we all were looking forward to that! This event was similar to the 11th week dining-in, but it was called a dining-out, which was to include ladies, and that meant we had to bring a date.

For some of the candidates, this would be easy, as we did have married officer candidates among us. They were set and in fact looking forward to the evening, as for many of them it would be the first time they had seen their spouses in four months! However, for those of us who did not have a "go-to" date, we had to make the necessary arrangements since being accompanied was mandatory.

How were a bunch of guys who had not been off the post at Ft. Benning in four months supposed to meet and

Chapter 9

ask a lady for a date? Well, the local Army ladies auxiliary sort of took the edge off by providing lists of eligible young ladies to candidates who requested them. I was one of the candidates needing assistance, as I knew no one in the immediate surrounding area. Mostly, the ladies on the lists were military dependent children ranging in age from 18 to 21 who had just graduated from high school or were now attending college. They also, for the most part, knew the score in so much as what the function was all about and why we needed dates—so that also took the edge off. The trick now was to make contact, and that was difficult because it was tough getting into one of the two phone booths on the ground floor of our barracks. Once you made contact, however, then you had to put the super sell on someone who didn't know you from Adam. It was a challenge, particularly because we had no idea of her likes/dislikes, background, or if she had any misgivings.

Something else I found interesting was the fact that most of the ladies involved were all southern ladies who, as it turned out, were deep rooted in southern U.S. traditions (a lot of southerners were career military at the time and their children leaned the same way, and there was still a south against north feeling a full 102 years after the Civil War). Having said that, it was manageable, but it was palpable to those of us from northern states, particularly if you carried a New York or New Jersey accent as I did. So,

Ft. Benning—"I Am the Infantry, Queen of Battle, Follow Me"

after three phone calls and with time running out, I persuaded an unknown lady to accompany me to our infantry "prom," New Jersey accent and all.

As it turned out, we had a fun time together with no strings attached and no expectations beyond dinner and the dance. Her dad was a retired Army Chief Warrant Officer who grilled me when I went to pick up his daughter, making sure I knew when she needed to be home that evening. Understandable on his part, to which I responded, "Yes sir, understand." First and last time any of us ever met, but it was memorable knowing that I took a completely unknown situation and turned it into a good happening. She and I had fun together, a bit awkward but fun with a little pomp and circumstance thrown in and, yes, I did get her home on time! It was a confidence builder and, although it didn't feel like it at the time, it was part of the training we were receiving—given a situation, figure out how to handle it, and then work it into a satisfactory outcome!

The dining-ins and dining-outs were commonplace in the Army during my term of service (1966–1988), and I have many fond memories of such events in places like Korea, with the 2nd Infantry Division; Ft. Carson, Colorado, with the 4th Infantry Division; the Infantry Center at Ft. Benning; and the U.S. Southern Command in Panama.

Chapter 9

While stationed on the Army staff at the Pentagon, I looked forward to attending the annual Infantry Ball, which was conducted as a formal dining-out, meaning spouses were encouraged to accompany their officer husbands or wives to the event. Dress for the evening was mess dress Army blues for the service member and formal attire for the spouses. All the internal events of the dinner remained the same as previously noted for a dining-in—reception line, cocktail event, posting of the colors, toasts, and so on. The one significant difference was that the dining-out culminated with a dance accompanied by live music sometimes provided by a military band. The Infantry Ball in Washington would normally have military band members performing. These men and women were in the Army Band, referred to as General Pershing's Own, which dated back to before WWI (1917–1919). The band members were all world-class musicians who had to audition for positions in the band. Not all applicants were chosen, as the process was very selective! Their selection of music ran the full gamut from popular to military to classical. They were a highlight wherever they performed and they, to this day, are the ones you see performing at presidential events along with Sousa's Marine Corps Band.

A highlight, perhaps **the** highlight, of my OCS "career" occurred around our 16th week of training. In order to understand it fully, you have to know that it is ILLEGAL to

Ft. Benning—"I Am the Infantry, Queen of Battle, Follow Me"

have any food or drink in the barracks. That included snacks, soft drinks, candy, crackers—you get the idea. That kind of stuff was called "pogey bait," and to this day, I have no idea how that came about as a description for prohibited food/drink items. Some also referred to these items as contraband, and that made more sense to me.

Regardless, everyone at the barracks knew what it meant, and if caught with it in your possession, it would constitute grounds for being dismissed from the OCS program. Well, being as our 2nd Platoon, 51st Company, OCS, band of brothers were full of daring do, my platoon started organizing a "pogey bait" run once a week on a Saturday or Sunday night. Our preferred treats were pizza with a 16-ounce Coke! This became a very highly coordinated operation, because we now knew how to conduct fast, somewhat covert, perfectly timed, quick strike and recovery shenanigans, disguised to look like a quite normal end-of-day activity leading up to lights out! Everyone in the platoon was in on it, and during our time there, all participated multiple times at great risk. The risk being that we might get caught, which then meant we might get tossed from the OCS program, and that would not have been good.

Here's how it went: In the early evening of any certain night, one of our platoon squad leaders (leadership positions changed every week, so most everyone had a

Chapter 9

Me, as a soon-to-be 2nd lieutenant, Ft. Benning, Georgia, 1967. The 51st OC Company "set the standard," and the 5th Battalion was the original OCS training battalion formed during WWII.

hand in this at some point) would send around a note asking for how many wanted pizza and Coke. Whatever you signed up for had to be paid for up front with no change coming back. Once the order was tallied, a secret phone call (remember, no cell phones) was made to the PX pizza shop. They would agree to deliver the order to an area near the old steam plant, which was also the location of the garbage collection point that was used every night to dump the barracks trash. So, if we had an order in for 20 pizzas and Cokes, we would send two large 50-gallon trash cans out to the dumpster area accompanied by a five-man trash detail—four men to carry the large, heavy cans that would be packed with pizzas and Cokes and one man to act as a

Ft. Benning—"I Am the Infantry, Queen of Battle, Follow Me"

backup and road crossing guard with flashlight. All this looked pretty normal to the casual observer; nothing more than end-of-day activities. Well, we got pretty good at it and executed this maneuver five or six times without being detected, so all was good.

Here I am, and it's my turn to lead the trash detail out to the pick-up point. Everything went fine on the way out. We made contact with the pizza man, loaded up and paid the bill, and started back to the barracks with about a half hour until lights out. Our group hits the steps to the barracks and goes up the one flight to our bay, but before getting to the double door, we notice that our platoon bay is loaded with senior Blue candidates generally harassing our guys—holy crap, can't go in there with these pizzas, we'll all get busted out. What to do?

The only thing we could do was duck into the latrine/open shower facility and hope that no one smelled the pizza. The lids were tightly secured on the garbage cans, so we hoped that the wonderful pizza aroma would not be noticed. After about 10 tense minutes, which felt more like an hour, the Blue candidates started leaving our platoon bay and, so far, no one ventured into the latrine area. Then, as luck would have it, one Blue guy comes into the latrine to relieve himself. While doing his duty, he smells the pizza. We were discovered cowering in the shower area. We five figured it was over, but our Blue guy, after reading us the riot

Chapter 9

act and having us do push-ups ad nauseum, got around to asking us about how we made so many pizzas and Cokes happen at the same time with no fanfare. We walked him through the entire operation from taking orders, to paying up, to meeting the pizza guy, to stuffing the garbage cans with our stash, to hustling back to the platoon area in an orderly manner as if all was normal.

After laying out the plan for him, he chuckled in a way that made me think he wished his group had thought up something like this. Not wanting to get too light, he put his Blue face back on and told us we were taking one helluva risk as close as we were to graduation, and he reminded us that we could lose all we worked for if caught by an RLO (real live officer, aka, 2nd lieutenant)! He shifted again, and then commended us on a well-thought-out scheme of maneuver, wished us luck, and departed the area never to be heard from again! Two ships passing in the night.

He was a good guy because he didn't report us to his peers or to anyone higher in the chain of command. He could've really ruined our day. In the extreme, it also would have impacted the entire platoon, as in extra duty, demerits, or the dreaded "confined to the barracks" punishment for the remaining time left at OCS. But then again, why would he report us? After all, we were comrades in arms, all scheming in our own way to find a small amount of pleasure in beating the system a little. He got it!

After ensuring the coast was clear, we brought the pizzas into the platoon area and had a feast, accompanied by a lot of nervous laughter. We didn't heed his advice about taking risks, and so our platoon continued to execute this operation for the remaining time we had in OCS, changing up pizzas for the occasional hamburger and fries with a Coke. Life was good, and taking risks was what we were being trained to do!

Graduation events started for us with a 5th Battalion OCS formation, parade, and pass in review on a hot Thursday morning in front of the Infantry School at Ft.

OCS "buddies" and soon to be commissioned 2nd Lieutenants (L to R): Tom Grenisen, Mike Fisher, and Pete Gutherie with their ladies. Mike and I flew to Ft Benning together out of Newark in early January 1967. I met Pete in the in-processing center in Long Binh, Vietnam my 2nd day "in country." He was departing Vietnam after surviving a year-long combat tour with the 4th US Infantry Division.

Chapter 9

Brand new Army 2nd Lieutenants of Infantry —(left to right) Mike Callaghan, John Dorne, and me. We all three went to flight school and survived a flying tour in Vietnam.

Benning on July 6, 1967. The actual graduation ceremonies were conducted on July 7 in the auditorium of Infantry Hall. My parents and brother drove down from New Jersey to attend. It was a neat ceremony, and it was nice to see everyone after more than six months away with very little access to phone calls.

Those of us in the graduating class were all happy when the diplomas were finally handed out and the remarks were finished; no more concerns of "will we graduate" or will something come up at the last minute. We all walked out of there as brand new 2nd lieutenants of infantry with orders that would take us to various parts of the world, most headed to Vietnam within the next couple

Ft. Benning—"I Am the Infantry, Queen of Battle, Follow Me"

Graduation day, Ft. Benning, Georgia, July 7, 1967. (Left to right) My brother Jim, my mom, me, and my dad.

of months. Of the 182 that had started in our OCS class, 134 graduated.

Because of applying to and being accepted for Army flight school, I was en route to the Army's Rotary Winged (Helicopter) Flight School at Ft. Wolters, Texas. Our "final" orders, upon completion of flight school, had virtually all of us reporting to Vietnam. My report date to Ft. Wolters was December 1, 1967.

During the ensuing four months, I was assigned to the 197th Infantry Brigade, which was located at the other end of Ft. Benning. I reported to the brigade HQ on the afternoon of OCS graduation and was assigned to A Company, 58th Infantry (Mechanized), 197th Infantry Brigade. Immediately after signing in, I signed out on a two-week leave, which all OCS graduates were authorized to take. So with that, I headed north up I-95 to New Jersey

Chapter 9

with family, where I intended on spending the better part of the two weeks at the Jersey Shore, catching up with friends, playing some golf with my dad, and, in general, getting ready for what came next!

The next part of life came at me from a little different angle than I had anticipated. During my last two months or so of OCS, there was much civil unrest within the country. We OCS students were somewhat isolated, as we didn't have access to TV news or even printed news because of the sparse living environment in the barracks and because we were flat out busy with other stuff. Some of the unrest centered on the Vietnam War and the military draft, while another part revolved around race and living conditions, voting rights, jobs, and educational opportunities for Black Americans (civil rights and voting rights acts were passed during LBJ's administration). The myriad social, racial, civil rights, voting rights (for Blacks and Whites), and the undeclared war got conflated, and it became hard to tell what issue the protestors in the street were marching for—civil rights or anti-war/anti-draft or something else entirely.

I'd been home for about three days when a really ugly protest/riot occurred in Newark's Central Ward. It was the second week of July 1967, and the flash point occurred when two Newark police officers were accused of beating a Black taxi driver for allegedly resisting arrest after having

Ft. Benning—"I Am the Infantry, Queen of Battle, Follow Me"

been stopped for driving on a revoked license. A protest ensued at the Newark Police Department 4th Precinct, after which looting and fire bombing erupted on Belmont and Springfield avenues.

Shortly afterward, a Newark Fire Department captain was shot and killed while leading his firefighters in knocking down an apartment fire that, as it turned out, had been set by an arsonist. This incident was followed by the shooting death of a police detective on patrol in the Central Ward. The fire captain was a lifelong "Newarker" who was a star athlete at one of Newark's prep schools and was married with five children. So, with the shooting deaths of a fireman and a police officer, the situation turned south real quick with city and state police and later the National Guard being deployed to quell the violent outbursts, indiscriminate shootings, and looting (sound familiar?).

Well, my dad was a member of the Newark Police Department, in the detective division, but as a result of the riots, which would last for almost 10 days, all police officers were called off vacation and placed back into a uniform status assigned to the streets. The National Guard, New Jersey's own 50th Armored Division, was called in by the governor. They came to the city with armored trucks and track vehicles, and their presence was very visible.

Chapter 9

I remember vividly a video, taken by one of the local TV news crews, showing a 50th Armored Division armored personnel carrier firing a .50 caliber machine gun up the face of a 20-story apartment building where earlier both guardsmen and police had taken rifle fire from a mid-level window. This video was followed later in the news by scenes from Vietnam, machine guns, lots of yelling, and so on. It was the Twilight Zone, and at first glance it was hard to tell what was what. We're at war in Vietnam, and now we seem to be having a war in our own country.

About five days into the riots, I drove up from the Jersey Shore to meet a high school friend with the intention of going to a movie in Montclair (not in the combat zone). When I got off the New Jersey Parkway at the Lyons Avenue exit, I discovered it was manned by guardsmen in Jeeps with M-60 machine guns—the same guns I had been training on only a few weeks earlier at Ft. Benning. What a strange feeling!

When stopped, I identified myself as being a city resident, the son of a Newark police officer, and a newly minted 2nd lieutenant on active duty in the U.S. Army. They wanted to know why I wanted to come into the city, and I told them that I was en route to pick up a friend, who didn't live in the combat zone, and also to see my dad, who was then at our home a mere four blocks from the

Ft. Benning—"I Am the Infantry, Queen of Battle, Follow Me"

checkpoint. After it was all said and done, a National Guard lieutenant hollered over to a sergeant to escort me to Leslie Street. The sergeant complied, and there I was, just graduated from a U.S. military school being escorted through the streets of Newark, my hometown, by two military Jeeps mounted with M-60 machine guns—another very strange feeling! They took me right up to the door, and I introduced them to my dad. The whole thing was weird. So, on my way to Vietnam, via flight school, I had to make a low pass through a combat zone in New Jersey. It was hard to get your head around!

There were casualties on all sides, and in the end I believe 25–30 people were killed—police, fire, and civilians. About 5,000 city police, state police, and National Guard were deployed with upwards of 200 men being injured while 1,500 arrests were made. Newark's Central Ward had been gutted, and the migration from the city by Whites, and others, had begun. The city that had a population of about 450,000 never came back, and it's not back yet, 65 years later!

The two weeks at home flew by. I spent only half a day with my dad at the beach bungalow and zero time on the golf course. My mom and dad took the situation hard as they were "Newarkers" born and bred, and they had a hard time accepting what had taken place.

Chapter 10
First Assignment— Real Army

Chapter 10

Welcome to A Company, 1st Battalion, 58th Infantry (Mechanized), 197th Infantry Brigade, located at the Sand Hill cantonment area at Ft. Benning. I reported the last week of July and was posted to the 2nd Platoon. It was an interesting place in that the platoon was a little short handed—authorized 44 troopers but had 36 assigned. Of that number, 30 of them were recent returnees from Vietnam with very little time left in the service, and their "give a shit" quotient was way down. They were all good guys, but their time in service was virtually over, they had served honorably in Vietnam, and it was time for them to separate.

The unit's mission was to support the Infantry School through field demonstrations and presentations, firing range instruction, weapons qualification, transportation, and mess support when required. Individual platoons within the battalion would be tasked to perform operations such as a platoon attack on a fortified area with an artillery prep, followed by Bangalore torpedoes and backpack-mounted flame throwers as the grand finale! We could put on quite a show, and sometimes even the Air Force would put down Napalm in support of the attack—something about loving the smell of Napalm in the morning!

Our troops worked hard and long hours, and although most, as I mentioned, were very near being discharged from the Army, they soldiered on until the end, taking some satisfaction in knowing they had served honorably. Those who hadn't been to Vietnam had a different slant on their time in service. As they were not close to separation from service, they all figured that if, as draftees, they served at Ft. Benning for a certain period of time, then they likely wouldn't ever see Vietnam, as there wouldn't be enough time left in their enlistment period. They were a relatively happy group that didn't mind doing the chicken crap required in a support unit. They realized they had literally dodged the bullet and doing the chicken crap in the States was much safer than doing similar things in Vietnam—they weren't shooting at you in Columbus, Georgia—at least not in the late 1960s!

The Green Berets and Colonel "Duke" Wayne

During my four-month stint with the unit, we also supported the movie production of "The Green Berets," starring John Wayne, David Janssen, Aldo Ray, Jim Hutton, George Takei, Jack Soo, and others, which was being filmed at various locations on the Ft. Benning reservation. On certain days, our unit would provide vehicles and personnel as extras for whatever scenes were being produced that day or over the next few days. The movie production company went so far as to build a replica Vietnamese village within the training area of Ft. Benning. After movie filming ended, the village reverted over to the

Chapter 10

Army for incorporation into the training regimen for those going to Vietnam.

On one particular day, the production company was shooting scenes in our battalion area around the PX and the gym. All our company officers went to watch the movie making, and all of a sudden there appeared John Wayne, who looked and acted more like a full Army colonel than most real Army colonels did. Anyway, our company commander thought it would be neat to invite the actors to lunch in his mess hall, so he sent a note to the production company inviting "COL Wayne" and company for lunch the following day. To everyone's amazement, all the principal actors accepted the invitation! So, for the next 18 hours we went into WARP speed, shaping up the unit mess hall and working with the mess sergeant to come up with something special for the "troops." Enlisted men went so far as to volunteer to act as dining room orderlies just so they could get close to the man (John Wayne).

The following day, "COL Wayne" walked up the hill from shooting a scene nearby. He was in the "proper" military uniform, green beret and all, and with his fellow actors in tow and dressed in the set's uniform of the day. They walked into our little company mess hall looking like the real deal! Our company commander, a "real live" Airborne Infantry captain and combat veteran, "escorted" Big John to the head of the table.

To a casual observer, it would have looked like "COL John Wayne," U.S. Army, was holding court with a group of his junior officers. We had a great time, and the movie crew and "COL Wayne" were the best!

Pictures, you ask, does anyone have a picture of this event? Can you believe, there are no known pictures of our luncheon! Nobody brought a camera to lunch—shoot me in the head! Remember again, way before cell phones—but stupid! And to think, we were hosting a movie crew and still no photographers—like I said, stupid!

Yeah, Riot Control Duty in DC

Another little sidebar duty was riot-control training. Our entire brigade was placed on alert for possible deployment to control any number of anti-war/anti-draft marches that were occurring across the country. During September and October 1967, there was an announced "protest" march that was to take place in Washington, D.C. It was thought that as many as one million people might show up to participate.

That said, the military was put on high alert to "mitigate" the protestors while protecting the citizenry and any federal institutions that might have been targeted. The battalion I was assigned to, the 1st Battalion, 58th Infantry, was put on alert to prepare for deployment to the Washington, D.C. area if determined necessary. So for a

Chapter 10

week, we readied our gear, trained up on riot/crowd control formations, studied aerial photos of the Pentagon and the surrounding area, and liaised with an Air Force troop transport unit (C-130s moving down the line—Jody's got your girl and gone). The rumors, and you know how rumors go, were that if we were tapped to deploy to the nation's capital, we would have to depart from Lawson Army Airfield at Ft. Benning aboard four C-130s destined for National Airport in D.C. (actually on the Virginia side of the Potomac). From National Airport, the understanding was that we would road march the three miles up to the Pentagon and take positions as directed. In an odd sort of way, we were ready, and I think the consensus was that we wanted to go to D.C. and the Pentagon.

This was a big adventure for newly commissioned 2nd lieutenants, and this unit had a load of new and very "green" 2nd lieutenants. Most viewed this potential deployment, I think, as an opportunity to put some of our training to use and lead a platoon into the unknown. And even though it was a deployment to our nation's capital, a big city, on our own soil, it would require us to implement newly learned Army skills while moving as a self-sustaining tactical unit. The question on most everyone's mind, I'm sure, was how will I/we do. The sobering part of this entire event was that we would be deployed against fellow Americans; the possibility of someone being hurt and/or

2nd Lieutenants Frank Fox (me, left) and Spencer Carpenter. Spence survived a combat tour in Vietnam as an infantryman. We met by chance at an Army/Navy football game 30 years after this picture was taken. He walked out of a crowd and yelled, "Hey, Lt. Fox!" We had a great visit!

killed loomed large and none of us relished the thought of that happening.

Long story short, we did not deploy to Washington; however, we spent four nights at the ready, bivouacked at the STOL (short takeoff and landing) airstrip co-located with the 197th Infantry Brigade HQ area, sharpening our newly learned Army skills!

We did good, planned a unit movement right up to execution, and saw up close how huge the logistics of it all plays into all facets of the operation. Feeding, fueling, arming, caring for in general, and maintaining it daily—never ends! While we did not deploy, units from the 82nd Airborne Division, along with the D.C. National Guard and multiple military police units from around the country were deployed and they were fully engaged for more than two weeks. Momentum against the war in Vietnam continued to build, and the anti-war marches, with on-again/off-again rioting, lasted well into the 1970s.

The West Point Graduating Class of 1967

In mid August 1967, my Infantry Platoon was tasked to support the Tactics Division of the Infantry School to conduct an attack on a fortified area that consisted of concrete "pillboxes," "strong points," barbed wire obstacles, and "booby" traps linked together by a network of trenches located on a slightly inclined hillside. This event was a demonstration to be "performed" for a large group of recent West Point graduates, so everything had to be perfect! The day before the actual event, my platoon-sized unit conducted an extensive rehearsal using live flamethrowers, Bangalore torpedoes (used to blast lanes in the barbed wire obstacles), M-16 rifles, M-60 machine guns, and concussion grenades for effect. It was a long day, and we rehearsed the entire operation three times from start to finish.

Once the officer in charge, a major assigned to the Infantry School, was satisfied that all was good and to his liking, he released me and my men for the remainder of the day with orders to be back on site at 0630 hours the following day (another one of those o'dark thirty events). The "attack" would kick off at 0900 hours, so we had a good two plus hours to set up and get ready for the "students" to arrive.

First Assignment—Real Army

Our cantonment area was about eight miles from the demonstration area over heavily rutted tank trails that could be very muddy during rainy periods and very dry, hard, sandy, and extremely dusty (red clay dust like talcum powder) during hot, dry periods. August at Ft. Benning is a hot, dry period!

After arriving back in the battalion with my "band of brothers," my senior sergeant and I made final arrangements for Army vehicle transportation support for the next day. It was important to ensure we would have access to the motor pool and that the appropriate person would be on site to dispatch the vehicles. We had a good plan, felt well rehearsed, and were "guaranteed" by the battalion motor sergeant that all was in order and we could be assured that we would be heading down range at the appropriate time. All that done, we headed out for the night to get some sleep and get personally prepared for the next day's event.

Well, that "best laid plans" thing started to go astray, and events didn't turn out the way we planned—get ready to improvise?!?! My group of 50 or so arrived at the A Company area a little after 0600 hours. Our "field first" sergeant for the day took a head count and conducted a roll call—"all present or accounted for, sir!" Well, so far, so good. Along comes 0630 hours, the appointed time for our truck transportation to arrive for our pick up. No trucks—

Chapter 10

let's give them 15 more minutes. No trucks! Off I go with my sergeant to see what's up at the motor pool. Four truck drivers are standing around the locked gate waiting for the motor sergeant to arrive with the keys for the gate, which only he had. Without him, we couldn't get the gate opened nor could we get into the dispatch office to retrieve the necessary paperwork (of course) and the individual vehicle keys. No word on the whereabouts of the motor pool sergeant.

I looked at my sergeant, he looked at me, and pretty much in unison we each say, "FUDGE!" OK, so how are we going to convert this pending disaster into a success story? I ask my sergeant something like how many privately owned vehicles (POVs) do you think we can "rustle" up to load out our soldiers, ammo, weapons, and other miscellaneous equipment? He says, "Do you want to go to jail for transporting arms and ammo in POVs? Not to mention having nonmilitary vehicles out on the range roads." I said, "Well, I guess we'll have to decide if we want to go to jail for that or for not conducting the demonstration for the West Point class!"

That said, we agreed to "ask the men if some of them would volunteer to drive their vehicles loaded with soldiers and equipment out onto the rugged range roads to the demonstration area." I finished by saying, "Sarge, my decision, my responsibility, and I solely will take any whipping that's coming." So, six weeks after being commissioned a 2nd lieutenant, I might be facing a court martial at worst or at least a severe tongue-lashing and being branded a "loose cannon" for not having our shit together. It ultimately might mean I could lose my appointment to flight school. At the time, I didn't think much of it as we had to concentrate on getting this mission underway—we'll deal with the other stuff later!

We go back up to the company area, form up the men, and here we go: "Good morning men, we have a little problem. The motor pool is locked down and there is no sign of the sergeant in charge. Looks like we will not be getting our Army transportation. So, we need to move ourselves out to the range where we rehearsed yesterday, and we need to be there as much before 0900 hours as possible. We have about an hour and 45 minutes to achieve this. Will any of you volunteer your vehicles and drive out to the demonstration site? Be advised that this will not be condoned by the powers that be, and we might run afoul of the range MPs, but we'll have to give it a go."

Without hesitation, 20 hands went up, all owners of some type of pickup truck, and they all understood that they would not be reimbursed for their efforts or recognized in any way for an "above and beyond" effort. Didn't matter, and in fact, they were enthusiastic about contributing in an odd way to complete our mission. This was an attitude I

Chapter 10

witnessed a lot during the course of making a career of the military—a "can-do" spirit—and these guys were on the way downhill side of serving out their time in the Army and didn't have to volunteer for anything—and everybody understood that!

So here we go. Seven pickup trucks of all colors led by a white VW Beetle, the command vehicle, mine, headed out of our company area at 0730 hours en route to "attacking a fortified area"—it goes without saying that we were ready to attack anything by then.

We arrived at the demonstration site about 0820 hours to a "howling mad" major who couldn't believe we showed up in civilian vehicles looking like something out of "Hogan's Heroes." After "locking my heels" (standing me at attention) and while "dressing me down," he directed my sergeant to park our vehicles well away from the gathering West Pointers. He didn't want to give any bad impressions,

Me at Ft. Benning, Georgia, with M-113 track vehicles at A Company, 1st Battalion, 58th Infantry, September 1967.

First Assignment—Real Army

whatever that meant, and he reminded me that we were late. We had roughly 45 minutes until show time, and that meant the major couldn't run us through a quickie rehearsal. He wasn't happy with that. Oh well, the good news was that we made it on time and the show did go on—on time and without incident and the West Pointers never suspected anything had gone wrong.

We wrapped up the demo site, loaded up our vehicles, and returned to our A Company area to clean and check weapons, get a well-deserved lunch in the mess hall, and close shop for the day a bit early. A very happy ending until I was summoned by Major Greene, our battalion Executive Officer, to meet him in his office. I reported in, and he then proceeded to grill me real hard on what took place leading up to our setting out to the range area in POVs. I told him about the locked-down motor pool and that I didn't see any other alternative for getting my group on the move.

Major Greene informed me then that the motor pool sergeant in charge had been in a fatal car accident on his way in that morning. Making the decision to form a "civilian convoy" resulted in my group being the only one of five groups with similar training tasks that made their commitment on time! On my way out the door, Major Greene told me it was a good decision and, while unorthodox, it got the job done—it's called improvising and it might come in handy for me at some time in the not

Chapter 10

so distant future. I acknowledged his remarks to me with a firm, "Yes, sir, thank you." So it looks like I will be going to flight school after all!

Chapter 11
Off to Flight School

Chapter 11

On January 7, 1967, John Steinbeck was in Pleiku, South Vietnam, where he flew aboard a UH-1 Huey helicopter with D Troop, 1st Squadron, 10th Cavalry. He wrote the following about the HELICOPTER PILOTS:

"I wish I could tell you about these pilots. They make me sick with envy. They ride their vehicles the way a man controls a fine, well-trained quarter horse. They weave along stream beds, rise like swallows to clear trees, they turn and twist and dip like swifts in the evening. I watch their hands and feet on the controls, the delicacy of the coordination reminds me of the sure and seeming slow hand of (Pablo) Casals on the cello. They are truly musicians' hands and they play their controls like music and they dance them like ballerinas and they make me jealous because I want so much to do it. Remember your child night dream of perfect flight free and wonderful? It's like that, and sadly I know I never can. My hands are too old and forgetful to take orders from the command center, which speaks of updrafts and side winds, of drift and shift, or ground fire indicated by a tiny puff or flash, or a hit and all these commands must be obeyed by the musician's hands instantly and automatically. I must take my longing out in admiration and the joy of seeing it. Sorry about that leak of ecstasy, Alicia, but I had to get it out or bust."

—John Steinbeck, January 1967

Flying High Deep in the Heart of Texas

My tour of duty with the 58th Infantry and Ft. Benning came to an end the week before Thanksgiving 1967. My orders were to report for rotary winged flight training at Ft. Wolters, Texas, the Tuesday after Thanksgiving. My company commander wanted me to stay with the unit until the day after Thanksgiving and then start my journey, but I declined so I could have time to visit with family in New Jersey. I drove up from Ft. Benning, arriving home in Newark the weekend before the holiday, and visited with family and friends, former work colleagues, high school coaches and teachers, and former girlfriends. Much had changed in the almost 16 months since I went into the Army. Most of my friends and former acquaintances were off to college, engaged to be married, or otherwise occupied, so being back at the old stomping grounds wasn't much fun. Besides, I was anxiously awaiting my next step in life. Fate and I were still on a collision course, but I couldn't tell, so all was well—ignorance is bliss!

After an incredible three-day drive from New Jersey out through Pennsylvania, Ohio, and Indiana, then along the famous or maybe infamous U.S. Rte. 66 and whatever new sections of President Eisenhower's Interstate Highway System that had been completed, I arrived in Mineral Wells, Texas, home to Ft. Wolters, the Army's primary Helicopter Training Center. It was one heck of a trip, as I

Chapter 11

had never been any further west than Philadelphia. I spent nights in Indianapolis, Indiana, and Norman, Oklahoma, but they were mere pit stops along the way, as I had to hustle to make my reporting date. So, it was hit the hotel and early to bed/early to rise, and then spend 10 hours a day behind the wheel of my VW. I cooked right along at 70 mph all day on the interstates, never missing a beat!

I was assigned to the Purple Hat class that was to start formal orientation for flight school classes a few days after signing in. While processing into the Ft. Wolters system, I met a friend from OCS who was also assigned to the Purple Hats, and he and I rented a trailer home together out near the Mineral Wells Airport, which also served as one of the three area Army heliports, this one being named Downing Army Heliport.

House trailers were about the only thing available as far as temporary housing went. As the Vietnam War evolved, the need for helicopter pilots grew exponentially to where there were about 600 new pilot trainees coming to the area every month. Mineral Wells just didn't have the permanent housing available to accommodate that many newcomers, so some entrepreneurial locals started trailer parks for those needing housing. It turned out to be a very lucrative market for them as the Army maintained a flight school there until 1972.

Because of the lack of housing, and because the Army is required to provide housing for all its people, we were paid $480 per month above and beyond our basic pay. That was a princely sum at the time and almost equal to our monthly pay. On top of that, we received flight pay of $125 as part of our regular monthly pay. In total, 2nd lieutenants were making over $1,000 per month before taxes. You saw a lot of Corvettes in and around the flight line. I drove a VW Beetle—dumb—and to this day I'm not sure I know why I didn't convert to a Corvette Stingray! You should have seen some of the poker games at the Officers' Club (O Club) on the 15th of the month—per diem pay day! Life was good, even though Vietnam was looming just around the corner.

My roommate was Wayman Hedrick, and he too was a brand new 2nd lieutenant, having graduated with me from Infantry OCS the previous July. After the initial week of flight training, we acquired another roommate, Alan Gilles. He was also a recently graduated 2nd lieutenant, but he was from the Air Defense Artillery OCS at Ft. Bliss, Texas. We were a good group. We helped each other out, hung out on weekends, shared rides to our morning formations, cooked a little or went out together, and yes, even studied together. We all graduated from flight school, and we all went to Vietnam, winding up in different units.

Chapter 11

My other roommate, Al Gilles, was KIA in Vietnam as a result of hostile fire while conducting helicopter combat assault missions in support of special operations forces. Al died in February 1969 near the Laotian border after his aircraft was hit by ground fire in the engine transmission, causing it to fail in flight. There were nine men onboard, all KIA. Al was from California, married with a child. I lost contact with him after flight school, and he died before we could ever reconnect. He was a good guy, and very California cool in a good way. Interestingly, Wayman and Al flew with different units but they were co-located at the airfield in Pleiku. They saw each other frequently, and it was Wayman who told me about Al's death when he visited me and the 192nd Assault Helicopter Company while we were both serving in Vietnam.

On the first day of flight school, after pre-flight discussions and inspection of the aircraft, you went and flew with a flight instructor pilot. It was a big deal for me as I had only been on one other aircraft in my life, and that was the flight from New Jersey to Ft. Benning the year before. This helicopter, the Hughes TH-55, looked like an egg that had a stick protruding from the aft end with a small two-bladed tail rotor and a thin three-bladed main rotor. The whole thing looked like it was held together with adhesive tape. It sure didn't look like much, but sometimes first impressions can be very deceiving. As far as I was concerned, if the instructor had full confidence in this aircraft, then so did I.

Out the door leading to the flight line we went, and without further introduction or instruction, the instructor said to me, "Want to give hovering this thing a try?" "Absolutely!" was my response, and that's how it went. Hovering looks easyish when an experienced pilot is doing it, but it's anything but easy, and to work at hovering for half an hour, having never done it before, was exhausting. It took about three days to start getting the hang of it. If it took you longer than that, you might get set up for an evaluation check ride—meaning if you didn't get the hang of it soon, you might be terminated.

On the morning of my third day of hovering, my instructor set the helicopter down on the ground, looked at me, and said, "Think you can keep this thing in the state of Texas?" I said yes. He took his hands off the controls and said, "OK, you got it!" The next 20 minutes or so was devoted to showing him that I had the hang of it—I passed and went on to the next phase. It was tense, but I believe all members of my flight section passed the hover test and then went on to receive instruction in general flying skills, such as landings and takeoffs, straight and level flight, climbing and descending turns, autorotations, running landings and takeoffs, and cross-country flying, which occurred near the very end of the formal course.

Chapter 11

The ground school portion focused on ground map orientation and air navigation, maintenance, weather, flight planning, and general aviation science. In what seemed like no time at all, the big day came. After 10 hours or so of actual flight time with an instructor pilot, we would be nominated to fly solo, meaning alone, around the airfield three times, making the landings and takeoffs and coordinating our flight via radio with the tower operators. This was another significant point in our training, as you needed to solo between the 10 and 15 hour level, according to the syllabus, or else face being set back a class or worse—being dropped from flight school.

I believe we had six or seven classmates of 39 in our section who needed some additional time beyond the 15-hour level, and of that group, three were sent back into another class. I'm not sure if they completed the course as we all lost touch. I soloed at between the 10–11-hour level and was technically the third one in my section to solo. That didn't mean I was more skilled than the 30+ guys behind me. It just meant that along with having the requisite amount of flight time, and having displayed to my flight instructor that I likely wouldn't kill myself, he was ready to sign off on letting me solo. Being the third guy to solo happened because I was scheduled to fly third in the first group rotation of the first morning of solo flights.

Off to Flight School

Our instructor would sign off on our being "qualified" to solo, but we weren't just turned loose and directed to report to such and such aircraft. It was more structured and safer than that. We first went on an instructor-accompanied flight. After about an hour, the instructor said something like, if you feel ready to solo this beast then I think you can handle it. We both looked at each other, and I said I think I'm ready! The instructor then climbed out of the aircraft, closed the door, stepped out from under the rotor blades, looked at me, and gave a thumbs up. He then turned and went into the tower building.

It was sure lonely in the cockpit without him! After settling my head down, I went through the pre-takeoff checklist and called the tower for clearance to proceed to the departure helipad. Request for clearance was granted, and I picked the aircraft up to a three-foot hover and moved to the helipad—by myself! That was spectacular. I moved that thing at a hover the length of the staging area and I didn't waver, meaning crash, and I felt confident in what I was doing! It was all likely attributable to good training and good learning, and it is amazing how, and you hear this often but it's true, what you've been trained to do kicks in and it seems to happen automatically. It seems to be there when you need it!

From there, I was cleared for departure for the purpose of conducting three laps around the helicopter stage field,

Chapter 11

which consisted of three takeoffs and landings with what was called cross wind, downwind, and base leg turns. Throughout my flight, my instructor got on the radio from the tower and provided encouragement while critiquing my angle of descent and rate of closure during approaches to a landing. In essence, he was keeping an eye on me and just hearing his voice was reassuring. All the instructors were like that—all good guys who had flown helicopters in combat in Vietnam and they were all on their game. All went well during my solo ride but, rest assured, it was a cottonmouth, white-knuckle flight with a little something else all puckered up! But ah, once completed it was a really good feeling.

Wow, I accomplished something that in my wildest dreams I never thought I would have had an opportunity to do! As a younger guy, I read a few books about WWI-era American aviators who flew with the French L' Fayette Escadrille, like Eddie Rickenbacker and Frank Luke, both of who became "fighter pilot aces." I was enamored by their aerial exploits, and somewhere in the back of my brain I harbored thoughts of doing something like that.

It turns out I didn't have the right schooling. A college degree would have been needed. But I remained interested in airplanes and people around aviation in general. In fact, one of my favorite ways of passing time as a teenager on a weekend was to take the #107 public service bus from the Newark/Irvington line to Newark Airport to hang out on the observation deck. In the early 1960s, commercial jet aircraft were coming on line and it was fun to watch landings and takeoffs. So the dream of flying was stuck in my brain. I was able to pursue flying in the Army because at the time you had to be a high school graduate, which I was, and you had to pass the flight aptitude test, which I did. So here I was, on the threshold of stepping into a long-time dream of flying and, to boot, the Army was willing to pay me to do something I really wanted and liked doing. I hadn't given much thought to flying helicopters, but hey, that's where the action was in the 1960s and it was the way of the future for Army aviation. Vietnam was a "helicopter" war, and I wanted to be part of it!

After soloing, we all got thrown into the pool at the local Holiday Inn by our classmates after first being carried through a crossed rotary wing archway, which boasted that "through these portals pass the world's best trained helicopter pilots." It was probably a true statement and it was a fun tradition, but it was December, and on this day, it was sleeting in Mineral Wells—not a real fun experience. It was a great way, probably, for some newly minted solo pilots to get pneumonia or worse, but no one was thinking of that and no one was complaining as we were happy to have "soloed." It would have been a lot better to solo in

Chapter 11

June, July, or August—it's hot, hot, hot during those months in that part of Texas. Something tells me they likely aren't doing those kinds of "traditional" things anymore—little more sensible than we were...who knows!

Well, life was a fast-moving train. Since December 1, 1967, I arrived at flight school, went through orientation, learned to hover, flew the machine straight and level, and earned my helicopter solo wings. Sometimes the Army gets a lot done in a relatively short period of time.

On December 17, the flight school shut down for the Christmas holidays, something that was done across the entire stateside Army. I went back to New Jersey and spent the holidays with family and friends. My commercial flight back home was uneventful except for the New York Airways helicopter flight I took from JFK Airport to Newark Airport, where my dad picked me up. New York Air operated a variant of the CH-46 helicopter between the New York City airports, which included Newark, midtown Manhattan, and Wall Street. The midtown heliport was atop the Pan Am building, 800 feet above street level. That was some kind of approach and landing on the rooftop, and it was exactly what we were being taught in flight school. On this evening it was even more difficult because there was a light snowfall with windy and icy conditions. Flying over Manhattan during the holidays was a sight to see if you knew where to look, and I knew where to look. The Statue of Liberty, Rockefeller Center, 5th Avenue, Central Park, the Empire State Building—Christmas in New York used to be spectacular!

The holidays literally flew by and classes resumed the first week of 1968. After two weeks off, we underwent a quickie refresher course and rode with an instructor for the first two hours before being cut loose for solo flights. It was a good idea as a little rust set in over the break, and it was reassuring to get "re-certified," so to speak. The remaining six weeks of this phase in training consisted of improving basic flying skills. Some of the time was devoted to flying with your instructor, but a greater amount of time was devoted to flying solo and doing traffic pattern work, takeoffs, landings, flying from the main heliport to the stage fields (short cross-country trips), and constantly going over in-flight emergency procedures, which included simulated engine failure followed by autorotation to a selected landing area.

The autorotations were real—the instructor cut off the engine but left it in the flight idle position for safety reasons. Even though the engine failure drill was simulated, it was about as real as you could make it. When the engine was chopped, it got real quiet and a lot of things had to be done quickly. That training thing again—you react and don't even think about it. We never took them all the way down to a field or road unless the instructor chopped the

Chapter 11

engine in the sterile environment of a stage field that had flat asphalt landing areas. Autorotation was the emergency procedure for an engine failure. If the engine fails on a helicopter, the blades will quickly stop turning unless you drop the collective to the floor, which takes pitch out of the blades, making them flat and allowing them to spin at or near operational rpm speed. This allows the pilot to fly the aircraft down to the ground.

In training, if the student pilot experienced an engine failure, we would drop the collective, which controls the blades to produce up and down movement, to the floor immediately, pull back on the cyclic, which controlled fore, aft, and sideward movement, and establish a 60-knot flight attitude, enabling the aircraft to be flown all the way to touchdown without power. At 50 feet above the ground, the pilot flared the helicopter nose up and held that flight attitude until approximately 10 feet above the ground. The pilot then levels the aircraft and pulls the collective upward, adding pitch back to the rotating blades, cushioning the helicopter onto the ground. Additionally, the pilot would "work" the pedals right/left to control the pitch in the tail rotor blades, maintaining directional control and ensuring the aircraft would not tip over. There was a lot happening all at the same time and it was over in a flash.

Is That a Scarlet Knight I Hear?

The daily routine during flight school started with a morning formation of all student pilots in training. All the sections would assemble in a big horseshoe formation, all sporting different colored hats to make for easy identification. I was in the Purple Hat section. At the start, the battalion adjutant would call the mass formation to attention and take the report, normally all present and accounted for, after which he would remand the flight sections over to the student section commanders to oversee the day's training activities.

From this point, the sections would go single file to Army olive green-colored, school-type buses that would take us either to ground school classes or to designated mini-heliports for training. While moving to board the bus one day, I heard a New Jersey accent in the line next to mine—a fellow in the Orange Hat class had the distinctive mid-Jersey "speech defect" that I was familiar with. I sought him out and, in the brief amount of time we had before getting on the bus, I found out that he was from the New Brunswick, New Jersey area. We exchanged phone numbers—remember, no cell phones.

Later that week we arranged to meet at the O Club. It turns out Fred Eckert was a recent graduate of Rutgers, and he had been the quarterback of the Scarlet Knights football team. What was interesting about that was I had attended

Chapter 11

the Rutgers/Army football game at West Point in the fall of 1965. When I told him I saw him play and mentioned that I thought Rutgers had lost that game in the waning seconds, Fred gave me a play-by-play overview of the last four minutes of the game. A well-executed drive, which started deep in Rutgers territory, culminated with his tight end dropping the potential game-winning pass in the end zone alone as time ran out with not an Army defender in sight. Fred recalled the whole sequence, as he said, in color, and he was still seething at the thought of having lost that game.

Final score: Army 27–Rutgers 24. In those days, a Rutgers win against Army would have been big for the program. Fred finished his training at Hunter Army Air Field and, while he was behind my class, we did get to spend time together when I lived in Savannah at the beach house and enjoyed the emerging lively night scene along the riverfront.

After I graduated, and while I was on leave prior to departing for Vietnam, Fred got in touch and wanted me to meet him and two other classmates at Newark Airport the Saturday of the Rutgers/Princeton football game. I picked them up, and we proceeded to the Princeton stadium. The significance of this game was that Princeton and Rutgers played the first organized college football game, and I believe this game was the 99th meeting of the two teams.

Rutgers won this game, which spawned a big party back at Fred's old football frat house on the Rutgers campus. He was not only a football player, but also an ROTC cadet who received his commission upon graduation as a 2nd lieutenant of artillery. Because of him being a star athlete and a recently graduated member of the on-campus military community, Fred was well remembered by many across the campus. As a result, our group was at the epicenter of the party scene—and the party lasted until daylight! All good things must come to an end and so, groggily, we band of brothers rallied at Fred's family home in New Brunswick for a quick meet with family and neighbors, followed by breakfast served up by Fred's mom and sister.

Fred graduated from flight school the following month and went on to Vietnam, where he flew Cobra helicopter gunships with the 101st Airborne Division's Screaming Eagles. I later found out he served two tours in Vietnam and spent a career flying with the New York Army National Guard, attaining the rank of colonel before retiring. Fred attended my wedding in Annapolis, and I attended his in Savannah.

Over the years we kept in touch and met a few times at events such as his sons' college lacrosse games whenever they were playing near Annapolis. They both played for Harvard at the same time, and on one occasion I met Fred at U Penn's Franklin Field in Philadelphia. I climbed up

Chapter 11

into the catwalk near the stadium's roof top because Fred was the team videographer and, you know, that was the best place to get the big picture. So there we were, a couple hundred feet above the playing field, freezing our tails off on a cold, damp, and windy day in April 1996 or 1997, sipping a little brandy, for medicinal purposes of course, and just chattering away like the long lost friends that we were! Again, I'm always amazed at that military bonding thing—it's easy to slip into meaningful, and not so meaningful, conversations with friends from long ago just like you had been with each other last week.

The years passed, and we were living in a marina/condo in Annapolis. I became friendly with a guy named Doug Divelbest, who I later found out was a former Air Force pilot and a graduate of Rutgers. While having cocktails at Doug's place one evening, I discovered that he played football for a couple years while at Rutgers, but left the team in his senior year because of his academic load and ROTC requirements. The conversation then drifted to Fred Eckert, the quarterback. When I mentioned Fred's name, Doug almost fell out of his chair and told me that in his junior year he was Fred's center on the football team—talk about a small world! It was Doug who later told me that he had found out through other classmates that Fred passed away shortly after retiring and moving to Florida. He was in his early to mid 60s and departed our company way too soon!

Army "Solo" Pilot— You Are Cleared for Bigger Adventures

In mid February 1968, my class graduated from the Primary I phase of helicopter training to Primary II. It was at this point that our training relocated to Dempsey Army Heliport, about 25 miles west of Mineral Wells in a place called Palo Pinto, Texas. The town consisted of maybe six buildings at an intersection with a stop light on the highway going west to Abilene. It was pretty desolate but great for helicopter training with many lowland landing areas along the Brazos River coupled with cliffside "pinnacle" landing areas higher up along the river.

This phase built on the basics of Primary I and turned the training into a real-life adventure. What I mean is that it was during this phase that we started making landings into riverbeds, mountaintops, wooded confined areas, and sloped areas. We not only flew solo, but also we started flying these exercises with other student pilot classmates in sort of a tandem solo event. We had to learn to trust each other, and it was getting us used to what the future held—two relatively newbie pilots flying together in Vietnam.

Along with this came the feeling of really having achieved something—being in charge of an aircraft, the flight planning, the conduct of the flight, and accomplishing the mission, even if it was only to fly to a

Chapter 11

small Texas town some 50 miles away. We were on our own, honing good training, our own instincts, and everything that went with it into action. It was also the training phase in which we would be conducting daylong and nighttime cross-country flights with specific routes and destinations. It really was an adventure!

Way Off Course—Almost!

Well, my adventure almost came to an abrupt end. It didn't, though, and this is where the twists and turns of fate entered and steered me in a lifelong direction. Here's how that happened. At the start of Primary II, our class was taking aeronautical chart and tactical map reading courses in the ground school portion of flight school. This was part of the overall flight planning and execution portion of mission prep and completion.

Well, for me, I thought that things were fine, and I even liked the map exercises. And to boot, it was the only subject I aced in OCS with perfect scores, and that included a nighttime compass course. The aeronautical charts were easier to read, and you didn't have to be concerned with contour lines, hilltops, eight-digit coordinates, the declination diagrams, the degree of offset, and so on. And it was flying stuff, which was the whole reason for being there, whereas the tactical map was infantry stuff, and I thought I had it covered based on past history—aced that one!

Next up were the comprehensive tests that followed the completion of each academic segment. I passed the aeronautical chart and flight planning exam without a hitch—off and running! Next was the tactical map exam minus the compass course. I flunked it! After review by the academic staff, it was determined that there must have been an abnormality associated with the test map sheets as 11 of 39 students failed the exam. We were all notified that because more than 25% of the section failed, the academic staff recommended that all concerned should/could take the test again.

Three days later, I failed the test again—me and six others. I was shattered to say the least and embarrassed beyond belief to the point that I didn't write or call my parents for a whole month. I was released from flight school but remained at Ft. Wolters, awaiting orders, likely for Vietnam as a grunt. I figured the processing out of Ft. Wolters would take four to six weeks. Dream over, so I thought, but this actually started an interesting chain of events that changed my life's trajectory—I didn't know it while it was happening, but it happened anyway!

Shortly after failing the exam for the second time, I was informed by the Student Battalion Commander that I would be assigned to the O Club at Ft. Wolters, to assist, as necessary, the club's chief financial officer. I essentially drew the daily working account money from either the post bank or the club's safe and distributed it to cashiers within the club system and the Class VI store (Army for liquor/package store). At close of business, I totaled and balanced the cash on hand amount against the morning's draw for the club and the Class VI sales. And do you know what helped me at this point? It was having worked accounts receivable and payable and balancing the corporate bank accounts when I was with Standard Bitulithic. It's funny how some seemingly small things you worked through in the past help in the bigger scheme—the experience factor!

A couple of weeks into my club act, as I came through the front door of the club on the way to the accounting office, I noticed about 10 young women who were starting to set up tables and some decorations for a luncheon. The luncheon's theme was meeting your husband for rest and relaxation (R&R) in Hawaii: what to wear, what to do, planning travel arrangements, how to deal with your husband who has just flown in from a combat zone and who might be a little tense, and the myriad of things that one needed to take care of before traveling to paradise.

There were guest speakers from the Army, travel agents to assist with making arrangements, a psychologist, and some clergy members. Because all the student pilots were on orders for Vietnam, once in Vietnam all married personnel would be eligible to get one government flight

Off to Flight School

from Vietnam to Hawaii any time after having served six months in-country. It was something that the pilots and the spouses looked forward to—a chance to see and be with each other for five days of some kind of normalcy. Anyway, because I knew how to make coffee in the club's kitchen and had access to soft drinks, I asked the women if they would like some refreshments. All replied yes, so I went about firing up the 10-gallon coffee pot and went back to helping with some ladder moving and decoration placement.

The scene, I'm sure, looked like something out of a before high school prom afternoon. You know, the group that always gets stuck with the set-up and makes everything look good and run smoothly. For me it was a little change of scenery, and it was fun working with the student wives. You know, Army pilots and future pilots have the best-looking wives in all the Army and maybe the services—bar none! I watched the luncheon from across the club floor and afterward I assisted some of the attendees with getting stuff out to waiting cars and vans. That said, all of the ladies involved in that day's activities quickly faded from my mind, but I remembered it as a fun day!

It was all in a day's work at the O Club, killing time and awaiting orders. I never ran into any of the women I encountered that morning save one, and she and I discovered our encounter about a month later at a social

Chapter 11

event when the fickle finger of fate reached out and grabbed me by the back of the neck!

The first part of fate hunting me out occurred on a Friday afternoon after I had been working at the club for about a month. I received a call from the Student Battalion personnel officer, who told me that a recent "in-depth" review of the map exam had been conducted as a result of some 60+ student pilots in the last three classes failing the test. Because that was a very high attrition rate, just above 25%, within a group of students who had excelled in all other phases of the training, the academic board reviewed the exam in its entirety to include examining the printed map sheet extracts used during the exam.

What they determined was that on a random number of map sheets used during the tests for plotting coordinates and determining en route waypoints, the print had been offset, meaning it was printed in error, which in turn caused a sizable error in calculating positions and/or locations. Bottom line was that you could, in fact, be doing the calculations correctly, but you would always come up with the wrong answer.

For me it meant I was offered another opportunity to take the revised test if I wanted. All I had to do was to get in to see the Student Brigade's chief of staff ASAP. I immediately made an appointment with him and met him later that day. After my interview, I was cleared to retake the test the following Monday. Enter the next piece of fate being the hunter!

Word that the 60 or so students who had failed the map exam would be allowed to take the test again quickly spread across the post. Some of these officers had already received orders and were no longer at Ft. Wolters, and, therefore, they did not get the opportunity to make a decision on whether or not to retake. Their stars hadn't aligned and their dream was lost—funny how that works—missed by a day, never meant to be. They were in the same situation I was in but for whatever reason, they received orders to who knows where within two or three weeks of being released from flight school. They likely never even found out that they could have retaken the exam. For me, I was still waiting for orders after four full weeks—fate…who knows!

After being told by the chief of staff that I would be given another shot at the test, I went back to the club to close out and collect my stuff and my thoughts—I couldn't believe it! While there, a guardian angel came up to the cash window looking for me. It was a friend from my class, 2nd Lieutenant Nicholas (Nick) Swidonovich.

Nick was a big guy from New York City whom I instantly liked the first time we met at the beginning of flight training. We were in different sections of the same class so our schedules were not in sync, which meant we would normally only see each other at the O Club or at a

Chapter 11

mutual friend's trailer home. It was always fun. Nick kept things moving.

So Nick says to me, in a thick New York accent, "Hey, I hear you have been offered another chance at the map exam." I said yes, and he asked if I was going to retake. I said yes and that I was scheduled for Monday, three days hence. Nick also said, "I think you have a birthday soon, right?" I said, "Right, I'll be 21 tomorrow!"

He said to me, "Well, here's the deal. Meet me at my trailer in an hour with all your map stuff. We will be going over to 2nd Lieutenant Mike Wilsey's place to set up a study group for tonight, tomorrow, and Sunday. Mike's wife will make a batch of spaghetti for tonight, and tomorrow night the four of us will go to dinner in Fort Worth for your birthday dinner. No getting fired up, just dinner in celebration and 'maybe' a drink, and then back to study."

I was incredulous! My past association with Nick had been purely as two ships passing in the night. It was always fun but short in duration. He was willing to give me the next two and a half days of his life to help me—someone he hardly knew. It was the kind of thing I encountered all the time in the Army. People who hardly knew each other would commit to one another and then maybe never meet again. In Vietnam, some lost their lives committing to others like this. It still amazes me.

Off to Flight School

Being with Nick, Mike, and his wife that weekend was hard work with a big dose of fun ladled into the mix. We studied everything front and back more than once. Nick was a mountain of a guy of Russian descent with a Gronkowski look about him. And he was a no-kidding-around taskmaster when he had to be.

I passed the test on that Monday morning, and although I didn't see it at the time, fate was still on the hunt for me. I was reinstated back into flight school and into a class that was five weeks behind the class I washed out of. Needless to say, I was ecstatic and very much looking forward to getting back in the cockpit. I called my parents that afternoon, relieved and happy to be back!

Nick and I remained friends for the duration of flight school, and although we were no longer in the same class, we caught up with each other at Hunter Army Airfield in Savannah, Georgia, for the advanced phase of helicopter flight school. While at Hunter, Nick and I lived about three blocks apart on Tybee Island, about 15 miles east of Savannah. My place, which I shared with three others, was party central for anyone from flight school who wanted to spend a day at the beach, drink daiquiris, and grill steaks, burgers, and dogs on the weekend. Nick and his roommate, Shimo, a Japanese American who was also in our flight class, often frequented our place. Because we all knew that we would be in Vietnam for a year following flight school,

Chapter 11

we celebrated Halloween, Thanksgiving, and Christmas of 1969 all during the summer of 1968. Many good times!

Nick and Shimo graduated from flight training in late August 1968, and that Labor Day weekend, Wayman Hedrick and I flew up to New York City, where we met Nick for a night of carousing. Wayman had graduated with Nick and was from Birmingham, Alabama. I'm not sure he knew what carousing was all about, but he was a quick learner. Very late that Friday night, we left out of Manhattan for the Jersey Shore, where we met my dad at the bungalow in Silver Beach. We talked a bit and my mom made us all breakfast at the ungodly hour of 4:00 am, after which Nick left to return to New York City at around 5:00 am that Saturday morning. I remember him turning right out of East Colony Road onto Rte. 35 North like it was yesterday. I never saw Nick again. He was shot down in Vietnam and KIA on January 9, 1969, a mere four months from the short time we spent together in New York and less than a year from the time he took me under his wing for a weekend of mentoring. I have thought often of Nick throughout the years and have not forgotten what he did for me—two ships passing in the night!

Nick being killed was a shock. If you had to pick, you would never have thought Nick wouldn't make it back home. He was big, outgoing, a little New York loud, and full of confidence—not in a hundred years! Shimo was also shot down while serving in Vietnam and lost both of his legs. I never saw Shimo again, but I believe he lived in Hawaii. Another good guy!

Wayman stayed with me for the Saturday and Sunday of Labor Day weekend at the Jersey Shore, and we had a blast! For one thing, Wayman thought he was moving amongst Martians, as New Jersey was so much different than what he was familiar with in Birmingham. We partied up and down the coast, hitting the beach bars from Seaside Heights to Belmar.

Our favorite turned out to be Murphy's Sea Bay Inn in Normandy Beach. There was great Irish music and lots of happy people, many of whom were girls our age—and it was all so far removed from flight school, Vietnam, and the possibility of dying. Wayman had such a good time with the "Irish stuff" that he sent my mother a St. Patrick's Day card for a whole lot of years afterward, something I didn't know about until my mom mentioned it sometime in the 1980s. Wayman Hedrick—solid citizen and good guy!

New Guy on the Bus

The very next day after passing the test, I reported to the class leader of the Brown Hat class, and he welcomed me and assigned me to a section by alphabetical order. So, here we go again, and unbeknownst to me, fate was on the prowl!

Chapter 11

Every morning the flight school classes formed up in front of the Student Battalion administration building for roll call and instructions. Once released by our section commander, we did an about face and peeled off in single file to board the buses headed to the flight line or ground school classrooms. My story regarding the map reading saga had preceded me, and regardless of the way things broke, there was a certain stigma attached to having been set back into another class. Boarding the bus was awkward. This class had been together now for almost two months, so the members had bonded amongst themselves, which meant that any new guy was pretty much on his own and no one asked me to join them, save one person who was sitting by himself.

That person was 2nd Lieutenant Thomas Jones, and he nodded and motioned for me to join him. I did, and we immediately struck up a conversion as if we had known each other for some time. Tom broke the ice for me, and he made me feel very comfortable and accepted. Over the course of the next few days, Tom and I became seatmates, and he introduced me around to the other members of the class. He had attended the University of Maryland and, like me, recently graduated from Infantry OCS in September 1967. Tom was very well liked and admired. He was a good student and was married with a child on the way.

Toward the end of that first week, Tom invited me to a happy hour gathering at his trailer for the upcoming Friday evening after classes. I accepted the invite and arrived at the appointed time, joining a few more students, some married, some single, and some not from our class. Tom and his wife Kathy were the perfect couple and great hosts. She made everyone feel at home and introduced folks who otherwise hadn't met before. Kathy turned the 10 by 40 trailer into a comfortable home with some nice touches, and all the single men in attendance wanted to know if she had an "eligible sister." Unfortunately for us, she was an only daughter.

During the course of the evening, she and I discovered we had met before. Would you believe she was one of the women who was part of the decorating detail for the R&R luncheon? When we decided that we had, in fact, met before, she said something like, oh yes, yes, you were the "nice young" lieutenant who made coffee and brought out soft drinks to the working women (she recalled it being a Coke for her). I wasn't sure I liked being remembered as the "nice young" lieutenant, but it was probably better than not being remembered at all. It didn't matter, she was fun to talk to and her being pregnant made for interesting conversation—how she felt, when was she due, what were she and Tom hoping for. The women in attendance were interested in baby clothes, a baby shower, and what will you do when Tom is overseas? At the time, she was almost four months pregnant and due in August 1968.

Chapter 11

Having been reinstated into the flight training program caused me to find a new place to live, as my current roommates would be graduating in about six weeks and I would be staying on at Ft. Wolters until my new class graduated. During the search process, another friend recommended I contact 1st Lieutenant Don MacIntyre. He had just lost a roommate who elected to drop out of flight school. So Mac and I met and decided we were a good fit. Not only were we a good fit, but we also had a lot of fun together.

One highlight during our time together was buying a pair of Triumph motorcycles and spending the next couple of months riding our bikes in and around Mineral Wells. Now, talk about an easy way to kill oneself! Driving a motorcycle at 70 mph with no protective clothing and only a skimpy helmet that barely met the safety requirement was one sure way of accomplishing that. Flying helicopters was a safer bet.

Well, one Sunday late afternoon, probably in early May 1968, we were coming back from a hill climb when we decided, rather abruptly, to stop at a roadside Mexican restaurant. We came roaring into the parking lot, engines snarling and making loud bap, bap, bapping noises, shifting frantically into lower gear, powering down, sliding and skidding in the gravel parking lot—you get the picture. Amidst the commotion, and for whatever reason, I think I

The Triumph "Tiger Cubs" responsible for the chaos at a Mexican restaurant near Mineral Wells, Texas, May 1968.

goosed the throttle, causing my motor to jump the curb hard and the front wheel to hit the restaurant's plate glass window, shattering it into ten thousand pieces.

It happened so fast that to this day I'm not sure what the exact sequence of events was that caused it. The only thing I clearly remember was the look on people's faces as I hit the window and the glass exploded. I'm sure they remember the look on my face too. The good news was that no one was hurt and my insurance settled with the owners. Nothing else came of it except that I developed a new-found respect for motorcycles and gravel parking lots!

Another adventure Mac and I shared was a fast trip down to Nuevo Laredo, Mexico, which was about 450 miles from Mineral Wells. I'm not sure how we decided to do that, but we left early afternoon on a Friday after only having a half-day of classes. When I got back to our trailer, Don said to me, "Hey amigo, you no hafta know

Chapter 11

how to read a map to be in Poncho Villa's bandidos," whatever the hell that meant. Anyway, off we went down U.S. Rte. 281, which runs the complete length of Texas north to south.

We arrived at the border around 10:00 pm and found a hotel to collapse in after the almost 10-hour drive. We made like "touristas" the next day and decided after an hour in Mexico that it was a terrible little border town, so we went back to Laredo, Texas, on the U.S. side. We spent the rest of our time bar hopping up and down the main drag of town and decided that the U.S. side wasn't much better than the Mexican side.

We started back to Mineral Wells early on Sunday morning with a planned stop at the Alamo and the LBJ ranch. The Alamo was neat, and we made the rounds in an hour and headed out of town in search of LBJ's place. Lyndon Baines Johnson, aka LBJ, was the sitting U.S. president at the time, and he was from the hill country of central Texas.

We found the ranch, did a quick walk through, and, by coincidence, ran into a flight school classmate from my original class who was in the San Antonio area visiting family. 2nd Lieutenant Doug Howard was a soft-spoken, nice guy from Oklahoma. I would see him occasionally in the O Club at Ft. Wolters and we got along. He was very interested in me being from the New York/New Jersey area and my strange accent. His accent was called a drawl, and I was very interested in that. We would both laugh at each other's speech impediments! That brief encounter at the LBJ ranch on a pretty Sunday afternoon was the last time I would ever see Doug, as he had less than 24 hours to live. He was killed in a mid-air collision at a training site the very next morning!

Life is very fleeting and everything can change in a second, literally a heartbeat. Mac and I were shocked at the suddenness of it all. Not sure I know why, maybe it was Doug's easy, likable way, but through the years I have thought of him often. I would've liked running into him again.

Hey College Boy—You Have a Big Mouth

My next adventure included a high school friend from Newark, Dave Whitaker, who at the time was attending college in Dodge City, Kansas, a "mere" 550 miles from Mineral Wells. Dave called me one night and said he had 10 days of spring break coming up and what did I think if he came and visited for five days or so. It sounded OK to me, so late on a Saturday afternoon in mid to late April 1968, I drove up to Love Field in Dallas to pick him up, and then we drove all the way back to Mineral Wells to "freshen up" before returning to Dallas to hit some of the "honky tonks."

Chapter 11

"Hey college boy, you have a big mouth." My high school buddy Dave Whitaker (left) and me.

This was in the days of the "blue laws" concerning the purchase of liquor and beer and the private club industry that "grew up" within the framework of those laws. Sounds crazy, and it was. The only way to buy a drink was to go to a "private club," pay a significant cover charge to get in, bring in your own "brown bag" of liquor, then pay an additional amount for "mixers" such as ginger ale or Coke. The liquor had to be purchased in advance at a state ABC store, or in our case at the Ft. Wolters Class VI Store (Army for liquor store).

Another "blue law" trampled on our evening of fun in the form of a midnight curfew on Saturday. All club operations ceased because we had entered into Sunday, the Lord's Day! I'm all good with the Lord's Day, but we were unknowing and unaware of this "blue law." New Jersey didn't have this type of system, at least not in the late 1960s. So for all our trouble, we hadn't even been able to settle into a club before it was closed for the evening. We didn't even have a drink, nor had we had one while back in Ft. Wolters. So now that it was about 12:30 am, we found an all-night type diner and had a hearty very early morning breakfast, grits and all! With no other place to go but back to the Mineral Wells area, we started out of the parking lot and that's when our evening really started!

I had no sooner pulled out of the parking lot than a police cruiser hit its flashing lights and pulled us to the side. An officer approached my side of the car and asked for my driver's license and registration, which I provided. He then proceeded to ask what I was doing in Texas, being as I had New Jersey tags on the car. I told him I was in flight school at Ft. Wolters and that I had picked up my high school friend just a few hours earlier.

Everything was pleasant until he noticed we had a "brown bag" in the back seat. The officer asked to see it, and when I handed it to him, he discovered the seal had been broken open, which would seem to indicate that we had been drinking that evening. In fact, that was not the case as the bottle had been opened likely the weekend before while at home. This was a big problem in Texas, and likely in most states, as you cannot have an "open" container in the passenger section of a car.

Chapter 11

We were asked to get out of the car, put our hands on the roof, and spread our legs. At that, my friend Dave starts mouthing off about the cops not being able to treat him in this manner because he is not the operator of the vehicle. You know, my civil rights are being violated—I know about this stuff—I'm a college student! His civil rights were being violated and so were mine, but under the circumstances I really didn't give a crap. I was more concerned about getting thrown out of flight school. So as Dave kept challenging the officer, I was telling Dave, in very low tones, to shut his bleeping mouth. I had a whole lot more to lose than he did and down at the street level, a college kid blabbering about the Constitution and one's civil rights didn't carry much weight with the "cop on the beat."

None of it fazed the officer, who by this time had been backed up by another officer who fell right in line with what was going down. Together they paid zero attention to my friend's protests and proceeded to take us both down to the station, which was a dual-purpose firehouse and police station. My car was impounded, and we were placed in a jail cell where we remained overnight! In addition, we were relieved of our belts, our wallets, our shoes, and whatever else we had in our possession.

We were never told what we were being put in jail for. I suspected it was for an open container of liquor in the passenger compartment of a motor vehicle. We were never given a breathalyzer test to determine intoxication, never read our Miranda rights, and only after much pleading on my part (you know, "Officer, my dad is a policeman in New Jersey and I'm a lieutenant in the Army," and so on) was I given the opportunity to make a phone call—to my roommate, McIntyre.

The long and short of it was that I was stopped not for "probable cause" but for having New Jersey tags on my car (you know, I was a much despised "Yankee") and a U.S. Army post decal in the front window (indicating I was member of the "Yankee" army). The open container was fortuitous for them and all they needed to make the stop and subsequent "arrest" appear legitimate.

The next morning we were released without ceremony and without appearing before a judge or anything. The officers decided our punishment would be to forfeit our bottle of liquor and $60 of the $100 we had on us. They also indicated that in my case they would be sending a report to the military authorities.

No report ever followed, and I was very happy for that as the military would have likely turned it into a "federal" case. The consequences would probably have ended in me being relieved from flight school, for the second time! No official follow-up report further indicated this was all a sham. So off we went with my friend mouthing off about bringing a lawsuit, to which the officers responded almost in unison, "Hey college boy, you have a big mouth," and me trying to determine if we had enough to get the car out of hock!

Turns out they were all in on it, including the tow truck guys who charged us the remaining $40 we had to secure my car. If this is how they treated two White guys who were decently dressed, clean shaven, one in college and one in the military, imagine how Black, Mexican, Asian, or maybe Catholic people were treated when they were stopped for merely driving while being different!

BBQ—Along the Red River in Texas

Over the next few months, we were all busy with the business of learning more advanced flying skills, some limited instrument training (read turn and slip indicator, attitude indicator, and magnetic compass—pretty basic stuff, but necessary), day and nighttime cross-country flights, and last, but certainly not least, nighttime autorotations.

One of the highlights of this training period was an all-day cross-country flight that took 32 helicopters on randomly assigned and variously spaced missions from Mineral Wells to some points south and east of Dallas, then north and east of Dallas to the banks of the Red River that separates Texas and Oklahoma. I was assigned to fly the first two legs of the cross-country route with my new friend, 2nd Lieutenant Tom Jones, which gave us a further opportunity to "professionally bond"—we had a good time flying together!

The entire flight broke for lunch after landing in a pasture, which was followed by a grand ole Texas BBQ provided by the surrounding farmers and ranchers. It was a great day, and it was covered with great fanfare by the local radio station and newspaper. It all came about because one

Our primary helicopter trainer, the TH-55, at the great Texas fly-in BBQ along the Red River, Ft. Wolters, Texas, April 1968.

Fellow classmates at the fly-in BBQ, Ft. Wolters, Texas, April 1968.

Chapter 11

Night flying near the end of Phase II, Ft. Wolters, Texas, May 1968.

member of our class had grandparents living in the area, and they invited our entire class to a "fly in" BBQ. So, in the middle of what was becoming a very unpopular war, about 75 student pilots and staff were honored and spoiled by real people—real Americans near the Red River on the Texas/Oklahoma border! Most of the men were WWII and Korean War vets, and they made us all feel very appreciated and welcomed. When looking the site over, it looked like the whole community turned out to cook, serve, share war stories, and to just look over our helicopters. It was a neat sight as we had 32 helicopters and two light fixed-winged aircraft parked in rows in the cow pasture.

We also had pre-positioned four fuel trucks, two firefighting vehicles, and a water trailer. What the hell? That's what I thought too. Well, they sprayed water on the very dry pasture to keep the helicopters from kicking up too much dust and creating a hazard. Pretty smart of those Army guys—they thought it all through. Overall, it was a pretty big operation for a small farming community in North Texas!

Chapter 12
Moving On— Savannah Here We Come!

Chapter 12

As our training at Ft. Wolters was coming to an end, we were all in the "get ready to get ready" mode for our upcoming stationing at Ft. Rucker, Alabama (Mother Rucker, the acknowledged home of Army aviation) or Hunter Army Airfield, Georgia, a former Air Force base located in Savannah. When initially reporting to flight school, all student pilots were slated to attend the final phase of training at Ft. Rucker; however, Hunter had just recently opened up to reduce the student load on Ft. Rucker, so those of us who didn't want to go to Ft. Rucker were given an opportunity to formally apply for stationing at Hunter.

I didn't want to go to Rucker, for a few reasons, one of which was that the county was dry, meaning no alcoholic beverages. I didn't need alcohol per se, but it was nice to be able to have a beer in your trailer home. That sealed the deal for me, and I applied for Hunter. Savannah was near the beach and on the Atlantic, and that's where I wanted to be in mid summer versus lower Alabama. I thought the beach would be great as we were going to be there from Memorial Day weekend through the end of September. That was peak time at the Jersey Shore, and that's what I was gauging the Savannah beach against. What better time to be at the beach! I was thinking tiki bars and co-eds, when in fact Tybee Island, aka Savannah beach, was more like an old folks home with very limited nightlife. And as

Moving On—Savannah Here We Come!

far as I was concerned, the beach was nothing like the nice sandy beaches I was used to in New Jersey.

Most of my core group of friends applied for Hunter, which included Nick Swidonovich, who departed a month earlier; Bob and Sandy Hemple, friends from my days at Ft. Benning; Tom and Kathy Jones, the friend who took me under his wing and "re-introduced" me to his wife Kathy, whom I had met while awaiting orders after being dismissed from flight school; and Mike Callahan, an OCS classmate.

Don McIntyre was also scheduled to report to Hunter but because of a transportation screw up, which occurred while traveling back to Ft. Wolters after attending a classmate's wedding to an Air Force general's daughter, Mac did not report to Hunter. Ever notice how often in life those best laid plans seem always to go astray? In this case, the dedicated Air Force transport plane carrying the wedding goers experienced a maintenance problem and had to divert overnight to an Air Force base in South Carolina. This resulted in all aboard being a day late in reporting back to Ft. Wolters.

The upshot for Don was that he was summarily penalized by having his orders for Hunter revoked, much to my chagrin as we had big plans for the beach that summer. It worked out good for me, in spite of not having my roommate from Ft. Wolters with us, but I'm told Mac languished at "Mother Rucker." Some of the decisions

Chapter 12

made by Army command and staff make one wonder. The ridiculous circumstances surrounding Mac's revocation of orders was because he and four other classmates were traveling on a designated U.S. Air Force aircraft whose mission it was to return Mac and friends, and the bride and groom, to the Dallas/Fort Worth area. Unfortunately for all concerned, that didn't happen due to the maintenance problem. As a result, Mac, through no fault of his own, was sentenced to four months at Ft. Rucker.

So, after all was said and done, he and I, along with five or six other classmates, traveled in a convoy to Birmingham, Alabama, where we broke up as a group and took the fork in the road turning due south for Ft. Rucker or continuing on east to Hunter as I did.

The next time I ran into Mac was in the skies over Vietnam about a year later in the spring of 1969. I was leading a flight of Hueys on a combat assault mission and after talking on the UHF radio to the Phan Thiet AAF tower, Mac cut in on the frequency asking if the person on the other end of the radio call was "related" to Pancho Villa, whatever that meant. Not being sure of what the question was, as I had totally forgotten about our trip to Nuevo Laredo, I acknowledged, and said something like "no comprende."

He came back to me, with his best "south of the border" accent, and said, "Hey amigo, it's good to see you broke

Moving On—Savannah Here We Come!

away from Pancho Villa, but more importantly it now seems you know how to read a map." With that, I recognized the voice and knew that I was talking to Mac! We had a brief "God damn, is that really you?" type conversation and then it was back to work. It was an incredible encounter in the skies over Vietnam. I wouldn't see or hear from Mac again until the fall of 1970, when he dropped in unannounced and visited with me at Ft. Wolters after he returned from a second tour in Vietnam.

We hit the Savannah area on the Thursday before Memorial Day weekend. I made my way out to the Savannah beach area along with a couple of other classmates, Bill Mastraetti, Mike Nevin, and Jim Huisman. Together we found a house that was a half block from the beach and across the street from the infamous Black Lace Lounge. The house was a rather stark, four-bedroom, non-air conditioned, seedy, and threadbare place with only one bathroom but two showers and a big floor model TV—perfect for four bachelors. The beach, the bar, the liquor store, a pizza joint, and the ice cream stand were all within walking distance. What more could a guy ask for?!

The owner of the house also owned the Black Lace Lounge, and he rented the place to us for $100 per person per month. The thing that cinched the deal was he threw in a membership to the Black Lace Lounge. What a deal! We could now pay $2.25 a beer when other places along

Chapter 12

the beach charged 85 cents or less. The difference in the price paid was for the Black Lace's "world-renowned" nightly entertainment of start-up bands, belly dancers, sword swallowers, jugglers, and ventriloquists, to name a few of the acts; boa constrictors also come to mind. A real class place, that Black Lace Lounge, but nevertheless, home for the next four months.

After taking the Memorial Day weekend to settle into our surroundings, we started classes. We were now in the advanced portion of Army rotary wing flight training, and we would conduct flight training in the Bell Helicopter UH-1, which was universally known as the Huey and was, in fact, the helicopter used most extensively in Vietnam. It was powered by a Lycoming turbine engine, was fully instrumented, could cruise at 120 knots, although we typically flew them at 80–90 knots, and had hydraulically

Flying the UH-1 Huey helicopter at Hunter AAF, Savannah, Georgia, July 1968. Hueys were the primary trainer in this phase of training.

Having fun at the hover, Hunter AAF, Savannah, Georgia, July 1968.

assisted flight controls. After coming from the TH-55 basic training helicopter to the Huey, it was like getting into a Cadillac!

The first segment of this phase was devoted to instrument flight training in both air and ground classes. From day one, we students flew under the hood, which meant we had a cardboard shield placed up against the windscreen on the student side of the cockpit and we affixed a black plastic hood on our flight helmets. This arrangement had the effect of our not being able to see outside the cockpit. We had to keep our head/eyes inside the cockpit and rely on what the instruments were telling us about the aircraft flight attitude while maintaining a compass heading, "standard" left or right turns, climbing or descending turns, straight and level flight, and maintaining

Chapter 12

Me on the "stick" and keeping a tight formation, Hunter AAF, Savannah, Georgia, July 1968.

proper airspeed, in addition to monitoring a myriad of engine-related instruments. All this while also listening to three radios all tuned to different frequencies—the most important of which was the air traffic control frequency. It took a little time to sort out all the instrument cross-checking required, but once you developed a routine, it was amazing how fast you could adapt to whatever came up in the way of real or flight instructor-initiated emergencies.

Instrument training lasted eight weeks, after which all students had to take a check ride with an instrument-rated instructor. It was the biggest check ride of our fledgling flight careers. I passed on the first attempt, as did most of my classmates. A few had to re-check on certain parts of the in-flight test such as the instrument takeoff or published controlled approach procedures. I believe everyone made it, and then we were all off and onto "real" flying.

The remainder of our time in flight school was dedicated to learning how to carry sling loads, familiarization with and employment of gunships, formation flight, cross-country flying, low level navigation, hot refueling, and advanced night flying, which included night formations.

Our last two weeks in flight school were spent in an isolated location that was set up just like a tactical airfield in Vietnam, and we ran missions day and night just like the type we would be performing in a combat environment. It was good, realistic training that put everyone in the right mindset. My entire flight class was sent to Vietnam. Some, like myself, went home on a 30-day leave and then went overseas. Others went to gunship school and then overseas, while still others went to maintenance test flight school or heavy lift helicopter (Chinook) flight school. Regardless of where we ended up initially, we all served in Vietnam at some point in time.

The summer of 1968 was hot and humid in Savannah proper and at the beach, which was 20 miles to the east. It was so hot that being at the ocean was not even refreshing, as I had remembered it being at the Jersey Shore growing

Chapter 12

up. There always seemed to be a "hot" breeze off the Atlantic Ocean's Gulf Stream, which at that point along the coast was a mere two miles or so offshore. Savannah Beach was just south of where the Savannah River emptied into the Atlantic Ocean and, as a result, tons of fine sandy silt was discharged into the ocean where the mixing of currents caused the silt to wash down south along the beaches of Savannah. The effect it had on ocean swimming was that the silt was so fine it spread from top to bottom in the shoreline water column and it would cling to your body. The only remedy for removing the silt was showering. As a result, we rarely went swimming in the ocean. We mostly just walked along the shore. And as I mentioned before, the nightlife at the beach area was slow.

It didn't keep our group from having a good time though. Our place became party central for everyone in our class if they were so inclined to spend a day at the beach. All had a standing invitation to visit on the weekends and a fair number of our classmates with girlfriends or wives did just that. We had some married couples but mostly single guys partaking. For the summer of 1968, we had an interesting mix of White guys and girls, a couple of Asian-American classmates, a mixed-race couple, two Black-American couples, a single Black-American guy, local single women, a few of our instructor pilots with wives, three or four New Yorkers, and, as I found out later, a

Moving On—Savannah Here We Come!

homosexual guy who I went to OCS with who was a good friend. It didn't matter, all were invited, and we all had some great fun times together—good memories!!!

Saturdays at our place normally started a little slow as the occupants of the house were normally up late on Friday night. Things didn't start shaking until noon. It really didn't start shaking until Tom and Kathy Jones showed up with the Oster blender, normally around 1:00 pm. The blender was the magic machine that made literally thousands of daiquiris during our four-month stay in the Savannah Beach area. Bacardi was our poison of choice. Sometimes it was the Bacardi Gold, but most times just the run of the mill Bacardi Silver. It might have had something to do with the supply and demand of it all at the Class VI store or the local liquor establishment. The ingredients were generally pretty basic: rum, fresh lime juice or concentrate, and maybe a dash of sugar. Sometimes, when it was late and a certain ingredient was missing, we used anything that was available. At least on one occasion that I remember, we used Worcestershire sauce—can you imagine?! It's amazing what some people will drink in the spirit of having a good time. It was all in good fun though, and nobody got hurt and no marriages were broken up.

It's interesting to note that there was an unwritten rule when it came to the opposite sex in attendance. I'm not sure this was a universal rule, but it was prevalent in the

Chapter 12

military and was applied within our circle of classmates and friends. It went something like this: if she was married, she was off limits; if someone's date, well it was OK to be inquisitive. That was fair. It was not cool to be aggressive, however, but if you could arrange for a future date, that was OK.

A side effect of making so many daiquiris was the leftover bottles. For whatever reason, we started saving them by putting them in the floor-to-ceiling bookshelves that lined one entire wall of our living area. When we ran out of space there, we started putting them on the windowsills, above the cornices, atop the kitchen cabinets, and so on. When it was all said and done, I bet we had accumulated in excess of 500 bottles!

Fast-forward to graduation day when my mother came by our place as we were packing out. Upon walking in, the first question she asked us was where did all these bottles come from? My quick-thinking roommate said, "Oh, Mrs. Fox, they were left by the guys who had been here before us." I looked at my dad, and he just winked! My mother went on about what a carousing bunch they must have been—we all agreed!

I've mentioned before about fate being the hunter at certain points in my life, which then caused certain other things to seemingly happen in a significant way. Well, the summer of 1968 in Savannah was a continuous "fateful"

Moving On—Savannah Here We Come!

event. Tom and Kathy Jones, along with others, became regulars at our beach house normally on Saturday when we cooked burgers, steaks, or whatever. It was during this time that I got to know both Tom and Kathy better and considered them good married friends of mine. They were a good couple together, easy to talk to and good to be around. And on top of that, and at that point in time, all the single men and most of the women, married or single, as I recall, were interested in watching Kathy progress through her pregnancy. Likely because none of us had ever experienced anything like that, and it was a novelty and a special one at that.

While Kathy was very pregnant, she would organize the cooking and kitchen duties amongst us guys and the women on hand, most notably Margaret Newcomb and her husband along with some of the girlfriends in attendance. I distinctly remember having a Thanksgiving dinner midway through our stay at the beach that was to celebrate the Thanksgiving we would all miss the following year while in Vietnam. Kathy took the lead in that operation, and it was a chore because the beach house had little in the way of pots, pans, or other necessities for putting on a real meal with all the trimmings. Not to be deterred, however, Kathy and her "helpers" were very imaginative, and they did a great job bringing forth a turkey, with mashed potatoes, gravy, the traditional green bean casserole, a mainstay for

Chapter 12

many on Thanksgiving tables to this day, and, of course, the cranberry sauce—with the real berries!

For Tom and Kathy, their "carefree" days at the beach became numbered the closer she got to her due date, which was the beginning of August 1968. TJ was born on August 7 while we, as a student group, were undergoing night flight training. Kathy was attended to by her longtime friend, Linda McGill, who came down from the Washington, D.C. area to help out because of Tom's flying schedule. Well, TJ arrived with all 10 fingers and toes and was a big baby who had his days and nights mixed up, which later played havoc for the new mom and dad—read colic!

Aside from a rollicking case of colic, all seemed right with the world and the evening after Kathy gave birth, our flight school class was having a pool party at the O Club, which was located across the boulevard from the Hunter AAF hospital where Kathy would be confined for the next few days. During the course of the evening, some of our classmates' wives were inquiring about how Kathy and the baby were doing. No one in attendance knew, and Tom was taking Linda out to the airport and he wasn't expected to show at the pool gathering. I'm not sure how it happened, but some of my classmates' wives nominated me to go over to the hospital and "pretend" to be Kathy's husband so as to get a report on mother and baby.

Moving On—Savannah Here We Come!

I went and, after removing the nametag from my flight suit (remember, I had learned about conducting "clandestine" ops in Infantry OCS), presented myself to the corpsman at the front desk as the husband of Kathy and the father of TJ. The attendant didn't blink an eye and sent me right up to the maternity ward, something I hadn't expected nor did I really want, but hey, here I was.

From the ward's administration area, I was escorted into Kathy's room where I'm sure, under the circumstances, I surprised the "you know what" out of her. I'm sure she was thinking, what the hell is this guy doing up here! She was groggy, in and out of it, and still recovering from the anesthetic, but knew who I was and indicated that things were OK. I didn't get to see TJ but the nurses on duty gave me, you know, the "father," all good marks for TJ, who, as you would expect, was sleeping with all the other babies in the nursery. After our brief visit, I departed the hospital and reported back to our classmates that I saw Kathy and she and baby TJ were both fine. Mission accomplished!

TJ was formally introduced as the guest of honor at a beach house flight school Saturday cookout at about three weeks old. Lot of "oohing" and "aahing" was going on that day, and it goes without saying that he came by charming the crowd and enjoying a good time at a very early age—I think it's in his DNA!

Chapter 12

The remainder of the summer of 1968 saw us helicopter flight school students continue to master the skills necessary to become the all-around best pilots we could be. We practiced combat-type assault missions, and at one point we actually flew over to Ft. Benning, where we picked up and flew infantry officer candidates on simulated airmobile combat assaults. These missions were very much like the missions, employing the same type of helicopters, the Huey, that we would fly in Vietnam. Likely more than 90% of those officer candidates would be deployed to Vietnam, and they would fly into combat aboard Hueys. Some of us participating that day at Ft. Benning would probably, but unknowingly, meet again flying this type of mission for real, as part of combined air/ground operations in Vietnam.

Our training was realistic and it looked as real in training as it happened in the jungles and remote highlands of Vietnam. We also trained on a myriad of mission types we would be required to perform, like sling loading pallets of artillery ammo, fuel bladders, water buffaloes, rope drops for fast lining infantry troopers, low level navigation, and night ops. Time went by fast, and all of a sudden graduation was upon us.

One of the main highlights of flight school graduation was the helicopter fly-by, which consisted of 42 UH-1 Huey helicopters in six groups of seven aircraft flying in

Flight school graduation party with my dad, my mom, and me, Hunter AAF, Savannah, Georgia, September 1968.

Flight school graduation party. Me, kneeling, surrounded by two of my roommates, 1st Lts. Mike Nevin and Bill Mastretti. On the right is 1st Lt. Bob Henpel, a friend since Ft. Benning. I believe all in this photo survived a flying tour in Vietnam.

V formations, all manned by student pilots with a few instructors scattered throughout the flight. About 70 of our student colleagues flew in the formation and were selected to do so by a drawing of numbers from the flight commander's hat. I did not fly in the actual flight but I did fly the rehearsal the day before as a backup and on standby

Chapter 12

Graduation day with my mom and dad, Hunter AAF, Savannah, Georgia, September 1968. Wow, I got my "wings"... proud to be an Army aviator!

in the event an aircraft or crew was scrubbed from the main event for whatever might be the reason.

I did not fly in the "pass in review" formation, and so I had the pleasure of watching the fly over from the ground with my parents, who had driven down from New Jersey for graduation. All visitors formed in front of the former B-52 hangars at Hunter as the gaggle of 42 Hueys passed overhead at 500 feet and 110 knots, with decorative, colored smoke streaming off the skids of the 12 helicopters on the outer edges of the formation flight. It was impressive, and I was proud to have been part of every bit of it and happy to no end at having successfully completed the course and receiving the Wings of an Army Aviator!

That evening, the combined classes of commissioned officers, of which I was one, and the newly commissioned warrant officer pilots had a formal dinner dance in celebration of our collective accomplishment. My mom and dad were in attendance, and they were treated like royalty by my fellow classmates and the cadre of flight school staff and instructors. We have a couple of family pictures of my parents along with classmates, wives, and other parents in attendance at this event. Throughout the remainder of their lives, my parents happily talked about the events of that evening. The next morning, our class graduated and scattered to assignments all over the world, with the preponderance of us newly minted pilots heading to Vietnam.

Chapter 13

Beyond Flight School and Preparing for the Unknown

Chapter 13

Before breaking camp and heading for New Jersey, in my case, and Maryland, in Tom and Kathy Jones' case, Tom invited me to come to Washington, D.C. for a party he was planning for Columbus Day weekend at his parents' home. He had invited other family members and friends, including Kathy's mom and dad, college friends, growing up friends, and some other flight school classmates. I traveled to D.C., where Tom picked me up at the airport and showed me around the nation's capital, a place I had never visited, with quick trips to the Lincoln Memorial and up to the top of the Washington Monument, followed by a walkthrough of the Capitol Building with a stop in the Congressional Gallery (something you could do then as you could park your car and walk up the steps of the Capitol and into the building), and, last but not least, we cruised through the Library of Congress building. Wow, I got a lot done in a short time. Fantastic!

It was a great party. As it turned out, I was the only one from flight school who attended, likely because of the distances involved since most of our classmates were from the mid, far, or southwest part of the country. It was complicated. Well, I tended bar, and it was the perfect job to meet and greet all in attendance. I talked at length to Kathy's mom and her dad, Dave Thwaites. He was a retired U.S. Air Force lieutenant colonel and had been a fighter pilot during WWII, shooting down seven German aircraft.

He knew and appreciated what Tom and I had just finished, and so we had a lot in common to talk about.

The party came to an end, and we "younger" folks helped with the cleanup and had a nightcap before Linda McGill, Kathy's friend who had come to Savannah to help at TJ's birth, offered to drive me around D.C. to see it all lit up at night. We drove around until about 3:00 am, and then visited the Capitol Building, strolling through the rotunda and looking at the artwork and the incredible array of historical artifacts. It's still hard to believe you could do that at any time of the day back then. Those times ended for sure after the terror attacks of 9/11.

Linda dropped me off at the little motel (individual little buildings constituted single rooms) on Rte. 1 north of the University of Maryland campus. The next morning I caught the Greyhound bus en route to the bus terminal in D.C. to arrange for the shuttle to National Airport. The bus ride was an eye opener. The entire route into D.C. looked like a rundown slum. It was something like parts of Newark, but a bit more of a shock because it was, after all, our nation's capital, and I sort of expected more. Pretty naive!

About two weeks into our leave en route to Vietnam, Tom called me and told me that he and Kathy were going to spend a few days in New York City the following week, and he invited me to join them for cocktails at the Playboy

Chapter 13

Club followed by the Broadway show "Hello Dolly." Tom suggested that I bring a date so that we would be balanced out as two couples. I tried to arrange a date, but I had been out of circulation, locally, for more than two years and all members of the opposite sex I knew had moved on in life, attending college, moved out of the area, or got married. I had a date in mind, someone I had met the week prior, but I just didn't want to invest the time and effort knowing that in 10 days' time I would be traveling to Vietnam. I just didn't want to possibly start something that would tangle me up with another person, and vis a vis for the other person to get tangled up with me. I attended without a date and from where I "sat," we all had a good time—I think Kathy, however, would have preferred I had brought a date.

Oh well, my remaining time on leave just flew by and was consumed by getting ready. I said goodbyes to my parents while having a light breakfast in an airport café, and then boarded a cross-country flight at Newark Airport headed for San Francisco. It was a strange feeling, that we might never see each other again—very awkward. And without a doubt, my folks were well aware that my new profession, flying helicopters, was very dangerous and I'm sure they were worried sick.

They never showed it though, and they were very supportive and encouraging, at least outwardly. They were not happy that I was going to a war zone, but they were positive in their outlook and did not exhibit a gloom and doom attitude—that was good. I was anxious to go, but not in a hurry to leave. It was hard to get your head around the entire Vietnam War, which had now been going on for the better part of three years. Lots of young men were dying, with many more severely wounded and incapacitated. The United States was becoming more restless as time went on, and while I never thought much about those things, it was always there staring one in the face.

Chapter 14
Off to Vietnam

Chapter 14

So, here we go, 21 years old—my generation's WWII moment! I'm enroute to Vietnam by way of San Francisco, Hawaii, and the Philippines on October 30, 1968. I said goodbyes with hugs and some tears and departed Newark Airport at around 9:30 am aboard a direct flight to San Francisco. Flight time was about 5 hours, 30 minutes, which put me there at around noon. I met Tom Jones in the main terminal, and from there we caught a taxi into downtown San Francisco where we had reservations for two nights at the Fairmont Hotel on Knob Hill. We were settled in by mid-afternoon and began a sightseeing trip of the city—the cable cars, Lombard Street (the crookedest street in the world), the Buena Vista Bar (founders of the Irish coffee—who really believes that?), Chinatown, the famous waterfront restaurants, bars, and vaudeville dives. It was a great time and an eye opener for someone who had hardly ever been out of the great state of New Jersey!

The next day was Halloween, which didn't mean much to us, but throughout San Francisco it was manifest with many school children wearing costumes, some of which were very elaborate, like Chinese dragons, flying fish, and Asian-style headdress. Obviously, there was much Asian influence. It was very festive and colorful, and it was fun to watch it all go by!

It was in stark contrast to the Haight Ashbury section of the city, a hotbed for the 1960s counterculture movement, which was loaded with a mostly dirty looking anti-war and seemingly anti-life crowd of pot smoking groupies and students for life studying the social sciences.

We just made a low pass through that area, and then broke for lunch at the Top of the Mark, which was a restaurant and bar located on the top floor of the Mark Hopkins Hotel. From the bar, you had a spectacular view of the San Francisco Bay, the Golden Gate Bridge, Alcatraz Island, and points beyond. When we first walked into the bar/lounge area, the entire upper floors of the hotel were engulfed in fog, which obscured the view from the floor-to-ceiling windows. When the fog broke, there before us was the beautiful San Francisco Bay area looking sparkly in the brilliant afternoon sun.

We struck up a conversation with our very talkative and likable bartender, and when he found out we were headed to Vietnam, he took an interest in us and provided some adult beverages compliments of the hotel—most likely on him. He was a WWII Marine vet and understood what was going on with us. Anyway, with a little mentoring from him, and while looking out across the city, he pointed out all the other famous rooftop bars in San Francisco and suggested we try to visit as many as we could. He jotted down names and locations so we could taxi to them if necessary. We took up the challenge and wound up in a total of four world-class hotel rooftop bars and lounges that afternoon. We had a great time and met a lot of fun and interesting barkeepers, as most wanted to be remembered.

The day's events came to a close with our staggering through, and then becoming part of, a costume party in the main level of our hotel. We had stumbled into the Chamber of Commerce, or maybe a 49ers Club, or whatever, Halloween Party and met a lot of interesting folks who went out of their way to make sure we had enough to eat and drink—they did a good job and we had plenty of everything!

Morning arrived sooner than we wanted, but we packed out, grabbed a quick breakfast, and headed to the bus depot to catch a ride to Travis Air Force Base for our flight to Vietnam. While moving through the processing point, we started seeing some familiar faces—our former flight school classmates. Over the next couple of hours, about 70 of my classmates assembled at Travis for the flight overseas that was scheduled to depart at roughly 6:00 pm. In the couple of hours before takeoff, most of our group moved to the Air Force O Club annex, which was in the terminal building, where we celebrated various officer promotions.

It seemed like more than a few of our colleagues had been promoted to the next higher rank while at home on leave, and they had received their official orders while processing into Travis upon arrival. So we had some newly minted captains amongst us, and in the spirit of the

Military Officer Corps, we just had to celebrate the event with what is called a "wetting down"—surely you know what I mean. We did a fair amount of wetting down; it took the edge off and, after all, it was going to be a long flight!

Our chariot for the westward flight out and over the Pacific was a Boeing 707, Braniff Airways, Yellow Bird, Military Charter. It was an aircraft that normally held about 180 passengers for commercial flights but carried 220 when in the military charter configuration. Everything was a little tight. We started our rollout right at 6:00 pm with a full load of fuel and max passengers and cargo, read duffel bags, and we used every bit of the runway before we lifted off and started heading out over the Pacific. It was really quiet on the airplane, as everyone seemed to be coming to grips with what we were leaving behind and what was to come, and, I suspect, the feeling of would we ever see home again washed over all of us.

It was six hours to Hawaii for refueling and food supplies. Upon arrival, we were permitted to deplane into the airport with instructions of being back at the gate in one and a half hours. It was a nice break and, having never been to Hawaii, I couldn't get over the beautiful breezes and the scent of flowers wafting through the covered open-air concourse.

We arrived around midnight and things were pretty much shut down on the airport concourse, so Tom Jones

Chapter 14

and five or six other flight school classmates and I just walked around until we found that one last open bar at the opposite end of the concourse. We found it about the same time everyone else did. The two barkeeps were overwhelmed, but they fought the good fight and pretty much got something in the form of an adult beverage to everyone who wanted it.

Time flies when you're having fun, and before anyone knew it, we were directed to reassemble at the boarding area. Then it was back on the plane. The pilots fired up the engines, and shortly thereafter they shut them down. There was complete silence as we all listened to the engines winding down. Hey, we're not going on to Vietnam? War over? Not hardly! A few minutes later the pilot came on line and informed us that we had a fuel flow issue that required a maintenance check. I knew what that meant—we were likely going to be stuck on this airplane until the issue was resolved.

And as it turned out, it took almost two hours to remedy. Our "chaperones" would not let anyone off the plane and, needless to say, it was pretty uncomfortable on board with no air conditioning or even much circulating air. There was a lot of quiet mumbling from all aboard.

We were airborne again at about 4:30 am. Shortly after takeoff, the captain came on the intercom and told us all to relax and sleep if possible, as our next destination was Clark

Air Force Base in the Philippines and it was a 13-hour flight—a long time to hang in the sky and the Pacific is a big ocean!

We landed at Clark in the early afternoon of the next day. We had crossed the International Date Line, which meant that we lost a day in transit because we were chasing the sun across the Pacific. All told, we actually lost a day plus five hours as a result of time zone differences. We were permitted off the plane to stretch, and it was much welcomed. As soon as you stepped off the airplane, you couldn't help but notice how warm and humid it was. It took your breath away! The Philippines is in the tropics, as is Hawaii, but the noticeable difference in the comfortable/uncomfortable index is the humidity. Hawaii is temperate with little humidity, whereas the Philippines is jungle hot and very humid, hence much more uncomfortable than Hawaii.

From what we could see of the surrounding area, the Philippines looked pretty, with low-lying farmlands contrasted by 12,000-foot volcanic mountains all covered with lush vegetation and palm trees. Our total time on the ground was about two hours, and we spent our stretch time corralled in an isolated area of the terminal. I guess we were kept together so no one would consider going AWOL. After all was said and done, our next stop was Vietnam, and you gotta believe that was first and foremost on everyone's

Chapter 14

mind: "We gotta get out of this place, if it's the last thing we ever do!"

Clark Air Force Base was the biggest U.S. airbase in Asia. It had been under U.S. control through leasing agreements with the Philippines since early in the 20th century. It was bombed and overrun by the Japanese shortly after Pearl Harbor, only to come back under U.S. control after the Japanese were defeated in 1945. It was strategically important and coupled with the Navy base at Subic Bay, about 125 miles away, it was a huge military/industrial complex.

It provided the combined/coordinated base from which to project our nation's resolve in the region—think power projection for air, sea, and ground forces; intelligence gathering; high-end maintenance facilities; fuel storage; and logistical throughput capabilities. It had it all, and our presence there provided for a degree of stability in the Asian theater and sent a strong message of support for our SEATO Allies. In addition, the permanent nature of the facilities and ongoing operations provided countless job opportunities for the Filipino people, which had a positive impact on the Philippine national economy.

In 1991, the Pinatubo Volcano erupted, covering Clark in 30–60 feet of ash and pyroclastic flow. The base was abandoned!

Chapter 15

Vietnam, November 1, 1968: The Start of a Long Year!

Chapter 15

We departed early in the morning on the last leg of our trip. This was to be a "short" five-hour flight into Tan Son Nhut Air Force Base on the outskirts of Saigon, South Vietnam. It was another rather quiet flight, with some folks talking in low tones and others just staring out the windows deep in thoughts known only to them. I think everybody could probably have been accused of that. At about the four and a half hour mark, the pilot came on line and told us that we would be making landfall near Cam Ranh Bay, at which time we would turn south/left and fly the coast down to Saigon for our approach into Tan Son Nhut Airport. When we reached the coast, everyone was anxious to actually view Vietnam with our own eyes, and I think everyone remarked and agreed at how beautiful it looked from 28,000 feet. It was!

There were beautiful ocean beaches, lush green farmland with shimmering water-filled rice paddies, dark green mountains as a backdrop 20 or so miles inland, and rivers that sparkled in the sunlight. As time quickly passed, we could feel the pilots making throttle adjustments as our plane started to descend from altitude while aligning with the active runway. We were descending onto our final approach, and everything seemed pretty much like a routine commercial flight letting down into a controlled airport environment. However, it wasn't routine, and we soon felt this big aircraft pitch up and make a rather violent

Vietnam, November 1, 1968: The Start of a Long Year!

turn to the left out over the ocean. The airplane climbed back up to a "safe" altitude and made several circling maneuvers while, I'm sure, the pilot was awaiting additional instructions from the airport control tower.

It seems that while we were well out over the ocean and lining up with the runway, the military side of the base came under a short but intense mortar and rocket attack, and our pilot reported that he thought our plane had "taken" small arms ground fire. I'm not sure how that was determined though, as no rounds seemingly entered the cockpit or passenger compartment, and we did climb back up to an altitude above 10,000 feet, which is the magic flight level for pressurization of the cabin areas. If you had holes in the cockpit/passenger area, you would not be able to pressurize the aircraft, and I don't think that was the case. Whatever, and seemingly all in a day's work and, oh by the way, the mortar and rocket attack occurred at mid-morning. So much for only being attacked at night.

We landed shortly thereafter and were hustled off the aircraft into a processing point that had been quickly set up near what appeared to be the civilian side of the airport. The military side had experienced some damage during the mortar and rocket barrage and some equipment and small buildings were on fire, however contained. We probably didn't spend more than an hour at this location before

Chapter 15

being herded into military buses for the trip up through the outskirts of Saigon to the big in-processing center at Long Binh.

There was a convoy of 12–14 buses escorted by four to six military police vehicles that were manned with armed soldiers, some of who crewed mounted machine guns. So, with this type of security involved, I think we all felt somewhat secure for the trip through "friendly territory," i.e., the suburbs of Saigon.

Well, about 20 minutes into our trip, the first two buses were ambushed apparently by Viet Cong troops using rocket-propelled grenades and small arms fire. The lead military vehicle was incapacitated with casualties and the lead buses were damaged with casualties, as told to all through the "grapevine." The convoy was stopped for about 30 minutes, and us unarmed passengers offloaded and attempted to get out of any line of fire. For us, the ambush was over as soon as it started. The MPs in the convoy, however, called for reinforcements, and they then swept the area.

Shortly afterward, we re-boarded the buses and continued on our way no worse for wear. So, upon our arrival into Vietnam, we experienced a mortar attack at the destination airfield with our pilot suspecting his aircraft was under small arms attack, followed by an ambush of our bus convoy. It's gonna be a long year!

Vietnam, November 1, 1968: The Start of a Long Year!

We got off the buses at Long Binh and were again herded into another processing area, where we were assigned to a barracks building and a bunk. We secured our gear and headed to the mess hall for what seemed like a mid-afternoon snack, but in Vietnam it was almost a late evening meal; again, we lost a little time in the move west from the Philippines. I joined up again with flight school classmates and, together with Tom and a few infantrymen who had also been assigned to our barracks, headed to the transit O Club. Everyone had a turn at telling our side of the mortar attack/airplane diversion and the bus ambush. It's amazing how people who experience the same event all see it a bit differently, and everyone seems to come up with a different "here's what happened" description. And while sucking down a few cold ones, we listened to a USO-sponsored Filipino band sing Beatles songs damn near as good as the real Beatles. It was amazing how good the fake Beatles were. There were actually a lot of these "fake" Beatles bands roaming the country—and they were all really good!

Long Binh was called a reception center, and it served as a place to process replacement soldiers coming in and soldiers who had completed their one-year tour going out and heading back to the United States. What that meant for us newbies was that we would mingle with guys who were going home, so in effect, you had both ends of the

Chapter 15

spectrum; the brand new guy, who's very apprehensive and truly wet behind the ears, and the veteran, who knows the score and is ecstatic about making it out relatively unscathed. The veteran had a totally different demeanor—a little bit hard with a different kind of look than the newbies, who all looked nice and shiny and a little silly in their new, very baggy jungle fatigues. In stark contrast, the veteran, if he wasn't a rear echelon type, was all tanned up from many days in the field and his well-worn jungle fatigues seemed to fit him perfectly. They all looked to be 10 years older than the newbies, but most of them were not and in fact some were younger. All of this is attributable to having been a part of a lot of stuff that just a year before they would not have even thought possible. They had been involved in battles that we newbies had been taught about in OCS and flight school.

Such was the case of an OCS classmate of mine who roomed across the hall from me in the 51st Company and who I literally bumped into at the corner of the bar that night. His name was 1st Lieutenant Pete Guthrie. Pete was on his way home the next day after having successfully completed a tour with the 4th U.S. Infantry Division. He had been an infantry platoon leader, and in his last two months he commanded an infantry company. He had been wounded during a fierce battle with North Vietnamese Army regulars at Dak To, and he had seen action during the infamous Tet Offensive of early 1968. He had been in the field and in the fight as recently as yesterday morning and caught a helicopter flight into Long Binh for out-processing in the afternoon. He was tired and trying to adjust from being in a war yesterday to being on the verge of boarding a big jet airplane and running smack into severe culture shock within the next 15 hours. I could tell he was very different from the way I remembered him and older looking beyond his years, with deep sleepless lines across his forehead and dark circles under his light blue eyes. He also struck me as being savvy and well aware of his surroundings, and that, I noticed, was a trait shared by all who had spent many nights in the field in a combat situation. You became savvy and very aware of everything quickly, or else you lessened the chances of getting home safely.

Pete had been a college wrestler at The Ohio State University, and he was engaged to a girl from his college days whom I had met a few days before our graduation from OCS in July 1967. He was looking forward to getting home and getting "normal." He told me he didn't envy my arrival in the country at this particular time in the war. Combat activity was spiking up, and it was apparent to soldiers who had been there that the United States wasn't going to take it across the borders to defeat the enemy in detail. So what was the point? As he saw it, we would be in a war of attrition within the borders of South Vietnam for who

Chapter 15

knows how long. Savvy guy. This was November 1968, and the United States stayed in Vietnam until 1972–1973. North Vietnam waited us out and overran South Vietnam in 1975!

I never saw Pete again, but throughout the years I wondered how he made out and hoped he fared well while not suffering any of the post-combat action or PTSD maladies that affected many returning servicemen and women. As an aside, while I never saw Pete again, I did see his roommate, George Grotz, another one of my OCS classmates, give a briefing to onsite reporters while he was the FBI's special agent in charge of a high-profile child kidnapping in California in the mid 1980s. I just happened to turn the TV on, and there was George. He did a good job! The kidnapping, however, did not have a happy ending and it resulted in a homicide.

We're 51st Company, OCS, Infantry, we're one day in, we're stepping out, we're on our way and MOVING UP!

We hit the barracks for some rack time about midnight only to be rudely awakened a few hours later by the charge of quarters (CQ) runner. He was delighting in waking us newbies up with the flashlight-in-the-eyes drill, telling us of our assignments and providing us with orders. I did not get my orders that night nor did Tom, so we had at least another day to hang out in Long Binh. It was presidential election day 1968, November 3 in Vietnam as it turned out.

Vietnam, November 1, 1968: The Start of a Long Year!

The candidates were Richard Nixon (Republican) and Hubert Humphrey (Democrat). If you remember the MASH TV show set in the Korean War where announcements were always being made over the public address system for one thing or another, well, that's what Long Binh looked and sounded like: Attention in the Long Binh compound. Attention…will Sergeant Joe Bizots please report to the CQ's office ASAP, or Attention, Attention…the mess hall will be open at 1100 hours for serving the lunch meal, or better yet, Attention in the Long Binh Compound. Attention…tonight's movie will be "The Green Berets," starring John Wayne, David Jansen, and Aldo Ray. And so it went all day. And oh, by the way, really…"The Green Berets"!

Well on this day, election results were announced all day to the point where it got annoying: Attention in the Long Binh Compound. Attention…Richard Nixon is leading Hubert Humphrey by 1,033,423 votes, and on and on and on. Nixon won by a healthy margin. Who would vote for some guy named Hubert Humphrey anyway?

Later that night, Tom was one of those called out, along with others, and given orders to report to an Army aviation combat assault battalion in the south central part of South Vietnam. Tom and I said our midnight goodbyes, and that was the last time I ever saw Tom. He was KIA less than five months later on March 21, 1969. I read about his death in

Chapter 15

the Vietnam edition of the *Stars and Stripes* newspaper, and I was shocked and very, very sad. I didn't get over the feeling of deep sadness and loss for a long time. My thoughts and prayers were with his wife Kathy and baby TJ, who at the time was just shy of eight months old. Tom and I had become very good and close friends. I'm not sure I can explain it, but we just got along in a nice and easy way.

Another in-processing event that occurred with all newbies was the legal paperwork that included a final will and testament, arranging for monthly pay allotments to spouses, family, or financial institutions, and the opportunity to participate in the Soldiers' Deposit program, which paid a healthy 10% return on a deposit.

The last item on the paperwork trail was the opportunity to designate, by name, someone who was in-country, meaning in Vietnam, to serve as your escort officer in the event of your death. What this meant was that if you were designated by a fellow soldier, you would escort his body home and serve as a liaison for the Army to the aggrieved family. You would stay with the body until it was interred at the cemetery designated by the family. With that service accomplished, the escort officer would return to duty in Vietnam. I was designated by Tom to be his escort officer and in turn I designated Tom as my escort officer. I was never notified by the Army of Tom's death!

Vietnam, November 1, 1968: The Start of a Long Year!

I was plucked from the barracks on my third night at Long Binh and was assigned to the 17th Aviation Group in Nha Trang along with four others from my flight school class: 2nd Lieutenant Chris Fecher, 2nd Lieutenant Mike Nevin, 2nd Lieutenant John Jackson, and 2nd Lieutenant Jim Huisman. Nevin and Huisman had been roommates with me in Savannah, and Fecher lived down the street. So how about that, we're all going to the same aviation group. Turns out Fecher and I were assigned to the same aviation company—and we both lived through our tour, as did the others. Huisman survived a terrible crash while riding as a passenger and suffered severe back injuries, but he survived.

The five of us were then all further assigned to the 10th Combat Aviation Battalion at a place called Dong Ba Thin, which was on the mainland side of Cam Ranh Bay. The total complex was a huge multi-purpose seaport and airfield that also contained an Army field hospital and major supply, ammunition, and fuel depots, along with a U.S. Air Force fighter/bomber squadron and a U.S. Air Force CH-53 "Jolly Green" search and rescue helicopter detachment. It was a big 24-hour-a-day operation.

Settling In

Our stay at the 10th Combat Aviation Battalion was short lived, and all five of us were further assigned to units within the battalion. Fecher and I were assigned to the

Chapter 15

192nd Assault Helicopter Company and, along with a few newly arrived enlisted soldiers, we boarded a CH-47 Chinook for the 45-minute trip down south to our new home. We flew south down the coast at about 1,500 feet AGL a little out over the ocean to, I suspect, avoid ground fire.

From this level, Vietnam looked very pretty along the coast, but aside from the aesthetics, it also looked very primitive with very few cars or trucks moving along unimproved roads, old and dilapidated looking fishing boats or "junks," as they were referred to, and buildings that seemed to be constructed mostly of thatch and mud with the occasional two or three story block building. The larger villages all seemed to have an open-air market and a substantial-looking church or chapel, however rundown.

Approaching Phan Thiet, we could make out an airfield on a plateau above the city on the South China Sea to the south. The closer we got to the city limits, we could smell the pungent aroma of rotting fish, which would be turned into the "highly" sought after epicurean sauce named "Nuoc Mam." The Vietnamese loved it and put it on everything. It was Phan Thiet's major export item and was shipped from there across the region.

The Japanese had constructed the airfield and facilities during WWII. The cantonment area for our unit looked a little bleak, with row upon row of general-purpose medium tents that served as officer and enlisted housing. Each tent, and there were around 60 of them, was pitched on a wooden frame floor, which kept things dry and kept one's living area from becoming a muddy mess during the rainy season. Other units within our battalion, scattered throughout our area of operations, had wooden "hootches" with tin roofs and in some instances individual room air conditioners, refrigerators, and running water.

No such luck for this GI. We had four-man tents with a wall locker per, some wooden cabinets, maybe a desk made out of old ammunition boxes, and, if lucky, an electric fan left behind by the folks who probably departed just a few days earlier. No complaints—it was sorta what I expected sans wooden floors! The wind would howl from out of the southwest and deposit a fine red dust that adhered to everything you owned including yourself—it looked like red talcum powder.

The biggest drawback was that we took our water out of a water buffalo, which was a two-wheeled towed trailer that was filled up a couple times a day. That meant at any time the buffalo could run out of water, and there goes the morning shave! I figured out how to beat that—get it the night before!

Remember me comparing my friend Rich Silva's WWII "real Army" barracks to my college-type, air-conditioned barracks at Ft. Dix? Well, this time I got paid back with the

Chapter 15

"real Army" experience—not as real as sloughing through the jungle like an infantryman, but stark nonetheless. I hate to say it, but I liked the "feeling."

Showers were hard to come by, and you really had to plan for it as the water ran out quickly. We had a water tank perched on a 35-foot tower that maybe held 1,000 gallons of water. It provided water to three shower stalls and serviced 85 or so officer pilots. The first thing most of us would do if flying ended early, such as 1500 or 1600 hours in the afternoon, was to hit the shower. If your flight missions lasted until early evening, and often they did, then you were pretty much assured of not getting a shower. After two days of that, your body sweat mixed with the normal stench of our non-wicking NOMEX fire protective flight suits could really get you to stinking—no matter, you were taking buffalo showers drawn from the water trailers.

Even on a good day, there was no assurance of a hot shower. Hot water came from being heated by the scorching sun on a cloudless Vietnamese day during the dry season. During the "monsoon," or rainy season, the best you could hope for was a cool shower—no complaints, cool showers are better than no showers. The infantrymen we supported might go for weeks without a shower, and they bathed out of their steel pot. I remember picking up infantrymen after they completed a mission in the "bush" for 10 days or so. After they boarded, we departed the pick-up point and as we were reaching our altitude, the smell of body odor was so bad we flew the helicopter out of "trim" so we could get air rushing through the open cargo doors. It was really bad. So, being in an aviation unit was OK!

Sounds worse than it really was but once you got the hang of it, it wasn't bad. Reminiscent of the TV show MASH! What the hey—not bad for a combat zone and when I look back, I wouldn't trade it for anything. It felt like a real Army unit. Maybe you had to be there to understand that. It was a little primitive, no frills, hot dry climate, but it was as real as it gets and everyone, officer and enlisted, from all walks of life, got along to get along to get home!

It seems I no sooner got settled into my tent area than I was called up to the unit orderly room, where I was informed that I would be going back to the Battalion HQ at Dong Ba Thin the next day. The purpose of this assignment was to assume duties as a Report of Survey Officer (a formal investigation used to determine liability if deemed necessary) for missing military equipment from a sister unit located in Nha Trang about 125 miles up the coast from Phan Thiet.

I didn't like it, but I had no choice. Participating in reports of survey, accident reports, and Article 31 investigations were some of the extra duties you could expect to receive as a junior officer. It was all part of the

Chapter 15

duty description. I expected this would take about a week to 10 days to complete. What that meant to me was that I would be that much further behind in my flying assignment than my classmates who I'd reported into Vietnam with. The report of survey took exactly one week to complete, a couple days of traveling and sorting out the filing process, and then back to my unit.

This survey was pretty benign as things go; however, it was an action that I believe negatively impacted my career—yes, my career. It goes something like this: the survey was initiated because the commander of the 282nd Assault Helicopter Company, a major, loaned his Jeep with a full complement of radios (FM, UHF, VHF) and a limited amount of small arms ammunition to an officer who needed transportation to the departure processing point and finance center to pick up emergency leave papers and a partial pay. The soldier's dad had passed away and he was authorized 10 days' emergency leave to attend the funeral.

While parked at the processing point, the vehicle was stolen, most likely by members from the 5th Special Forces Group, U.S. Army, who were headquartered in the area. Now, this is speculation on my part, but the Special Forces were well known for "requisitioning" things their own way if they needed them. What that meant was the Jeep, in all likelihood, ended up performing services at some God-awful compound under the control of the Green Berets on behalf of and for the total U.S. Army! I suspect the Special Forces guys were toasting themselves for having scored a "big" one; after all, it was the aviation commanding officer's Jeep. And ironically, that commanding officer's aviation unit supported these same Special Forces guys almost exclusively on their combat assault missions along the Laotian border.

Long story short, my investigation found the commander liable, based on the evidence presented and the Army's guidelines for report of survey officers (he was extremely careless and should have had his driver take the soldier to the processing point and wait with the vehicle— and I know that hindsight is always 20/20). He could have been found pecuniary liable and subject to repaying the government. I did not recommend he be held to that "level" of liability, and I noted under "extenuating circumstances" that he was being a "Good Samaritan" in attempting to help one of his officers. And that, I believed, should be taken into account when determining liability.

I filed the report and never heard a thing about it until two days before I was to return to the United States— almost a full year from the time I finished and submitted the survey to the aviation battalion property book officer. It seems the report had been lost (most likely squashed by friends of the commanding officer from the 282nd Assault Helicopter Company), and the property book officer

Chapter 15

wanted to know if I had a copy that I could provide to him. I did have a copy, and I did provide it to him.

Fast-forward to Ft. Benning in 1971. The major (now a lieutenant colonel) who was the subject of the report of survey, sees me in the Infantry Hall and yells out to me. He then confronts me and "dresses me down" about my findings on that not-so-long-ago report of survey. It seems he was held responsible to some degree, and he obviously didn't like it. So we had words, and that was the last I ever saw of him.

Guess what happened in 1985—a full 14 years later? That major was then a colonel (survey incident didn't impact his career, did it?), and he was the "senior officer" on a Command Selection Board looking at Aviation Lieutenant Colonels, of which I was one, to be designated as Aviation Battalion Command selectees. Guess who didn't get selected for Aviation Battalion Command? All it would have taken was a "thumbs down," no questions asked, from the senior officer on the Command Selection Board.

I think it's possible that happened—what do you think? I'm not for certain that his being involved with that board made a difference; hell, maybe he completely forgot who I was, but he certainly was in the right place at the wrong time for me. In and of itself, the process is very selective and competitive, as there are many more eligible lieutenant colonels than there are available aviation commands—but we'll never know. I thought I was "in the running" as I had commanded a Mechanized Infantry Company at Ft. Carson, with 242 men and 25+ vehicles. I had 500+ hours of combat flying time, 350+ hours of aviation instructor pilot time, served as a deputy flight commander (student detachment) at Ft. Wolters, had been a provisional flight detachment commander and aviation unit executive officer while with the 2nd Infantry Division in Korea, and from 1977 to 1979, I was the aviation battalion logistics and executive officer of the 4th Aviation Battalion of the 4th Infantry Division. And while at Ft Carson, I was appointed a senior Army aviator, having accumulated in excess of 1,500 hours of total flight time while maintaining a current Instrument Flight Rating.

I thought I had a good background in aviation, and therefore thought I had a decent shot at being selected for command. At the time of the selection board, I was serving in the Pentagon on the Army staff in the Aviation Division within DCSOPS (a choice position within the Army staff). The one thing missing from my "resume" was that I had NOT commanded an aviation company-sized unit and, in all fairness, that, in and off itself, could have been the determining factor—but you know that box of chocolates thing!

Chapter 15

So without having had battalion command, one could hardly expect to go to the War College and at some point be considered for colonel. Again, no sour grapes, but it's amazing to me how that seemingly small incident from 1969 may have impacted me in the mid 1980s. Oh, and I have no regrets about my finding the major "liable" and noting that he was acting as a "Good Samaritan" whose actions should have been viewed from that angle—all of it was the right thing to do!

Back to my unit—I immediately fell into a good groove relative to flying and sorting through the myriad "extra" duties associated with being one of the junior officers in the unit. I was put on orders for the following extra duties: "perimeter defense officer," likely because I was a commissioned infantry officer; "aviator survival, escape & evasion officer" and "blood chit control officer," again, likely because I was infantry; and last but not least, the "awards and decorations control officer," I have no clue on this one. All were better than being the "rodent control officer"—no kidding, it had something to do with sanitation and keeping everyone from getting ill.

"Blood chit control officer" was interesting. The "blood chit" was a piece of silk that measured about 3 feet long and maybe 10 inches wide and was folded up so it would fit into a pocket on one's flight suit. It had an American flag embossed across the top and "instructions" written in, I

Vietnam, November 1, 1968: The Start of a Long Year!

believe, 20 languages, which in essence stated that the person in possession of this "chit" was an American service member and if he or she was delivered to American authorities, our government would pay $25,000 to the person(s) responsible for his or her rescue. That was a lot of money in that part of the world in 1969. These were also in use during WWII offering the same reward—a whole lot of money in the 1940s!

I received my in-country check ride the day after I returned, and thereafter I was assigned to fly missions with my flight platoon. The unit standard operating procedure required that all "new" pilots be paired with the "vets" for about the first 30–45 days in-country, so as to get the "lay of the land" and to be continuously evaluated by those who flew the missions with you. During this period, it wasn't unusual for the "new" guys to be assigned missions that would be of long duration with multiple takeoffs and landings with different types of load configurations to get the experience factor up.

My first real mission was with one of the senior pilots who was a captain. On that day, we were going to be the lead aircraft of a flight of 10 Hueys, which was going to be part of a larger operation that included a total of 36 Huey assault helicopters and 8 Huey gunships. The operation was centered about 50 miles northwest of our airfield in the mountains near Da Lat, a small city that at one time was

Chapter 15

the French provincial capital of Indo-China. We "inserted" a battalion of troopers from the 101st Airborne Division, along with artillery and 4.2 mortar support and a battalion of South Vietnamese soldiers from the 44th Regiment, Army of the Republic of Vietnam (ARVN) on what was termed a "search and destroy mission."

Our mission that day lasted 15 full hours, of which I logged 10.5 hours of actual flight time. I did a lot of the actual hands-on flying (real good training), and I was whipped at the end of the day. I literally crawled out of the helicopter in the "bent over" position and struggled to walk straight up. Man, it's going to be a long year I thought. It was great flying experience though, and it was amazing how quickly your senses become attuned to what's happening around you and how you seemingly become part of the aircraft. From an operations standpoint, the entire event was a complete success for the aviation elements as we did not suffer any casualties nor did we experience any maintenance issues and all aircraft returned to base safely!

And so it went for the first four months of my tour in Vietnam. I did a fair of amount of flying, with the missions varying between routine admin "haul anything and everything to anywhere flights," to sling-loading fuel bladders and water blivets, to C-ration and ammo pallets, to "combat assault" troop missions escorted by gunships and controlled by an airborne mission control aircraft

Vietnam, November 1, 1968: The Start of a Long Year!

monitoring from above. In addition, I was my flight platoon's mission scheduler and pilot flight time "monitor." Flight scheduler was just that, I assigned pilots to fly the missions sent down through the 10th Combat Aviation Battalion's flight ops section, our controlling organization located in Dong Ba Thin near Cam Ranh Bay. It was our practice to assign newly assigned pilots (affectionately known as "Peter Pilots") with a more "senior" pilot, known as a pilot in command or an accredited aircraft commander. In addition, our mission planners would factor in such things as daytime or nighttime; combat assault/extraction or admin/resupply (lots of takeoffs and landings); mountain, coastal, or "flatland" flying; and anticipated length of the total mission, keeping an eye on how many flight hours each pilot had accrued in the last 30-day period.

This linked into the flight time "monitor" responsibilities. We kept a running total of hours flown, and if a pilot reached 120 hours of flight time in a 30-day period, then we "grounded" him and set up an evaluation with our flight surgeon, Captain Jerome DeSimone, MSC. "Doc" DeSimone would conduct a modified physical primarily to check for exhaustion, despair, depression, judgment, eyesight, reflexes, and all the things that I guess lead up to PTSD, mission degradation, and an unsafe flying condition. The "normal" remedy for the 120-hour "disease" was to ground the pilot for three days. It was, in essence, a

Chapter 15

short term R&R, and in the case of my unit, meant that you could go to the beach below the cliffs that led down from our compound to the South China Sea.

We had a little beach bar and a "half" 55-gallon drum for a barbeque that was "manned" by a cook from the mess hall and always had burgers or hot dogs going. The whole experience was weird, as we had guard posts up on the cliffs with machine guns mounted and poised for action at all times. The beach was beautiful, and it was a good getaway and very close by—and included a GI lifeguard. Life was good!

Thanksgiving Day With all the Trimmings

I think we were all curious as to how our unit would observe the Thanksgiving holiday. After all, Thanksgiving is one of America's "favorite" events, marked at home by parades—think the Macy's parade in New York City—and the ushering in of the Christmas season. Well, what we did in Vietnam was Thanksgiving like at home, but with no parades, no college football games, and no TV. We did, however, have one very intense flag football game between the unit officers and enlisted men out on the "parade" field in front of the mess hall that was well attended; why not, it was the only entertainment in town! I can't remember who won but "winning/losing" wasn't the point—we were bonding as soldiers in a faraway place in an unpopular war

Vietnam, November 1, 1968: The Start of a Long Year!

and we had some fun "imitating" football players for an hour or so—followed by Thanksgiving dinner!

The day started early, with all scheduled flight missions slated to deliver Thanksgiving dinner in the field to all deployed members of the Task Force (TF) 3/506th of the 101st Airborne Division. We started our delivery runs at about 1000 hours when we were loaded up with marmite cans, which were hot/cold containers that stood about three-feet high and two-feet wide. On my aircraft, we had fresh cooked turkey with all the veggie trimmings, pies, soft drinks, breads, nuts, cranberries, condiments, ice cream, and a beer ration of two cans per person. Uncle Sam didn't miss a thing. And for the flight crews it was a real kick to deliver Thanksgiving dinner to the troops in the field!

For me it is one of the most vivid memories I have of Vietnam—providing a "festive" moment to infantrymen in the field who worked their asses off every day of their tour staring unthinkable horrors face on—I was commissioned an infantry officer, and although I ended up being an Army aviator, my controlling "branch" was infantry and I knew that supporting the ground troops was the reason we did anything and everything!

The look on the GIs' faces was priceless and one of disbelief—as in, wow, look at all this stuff out here in the middle of nowhere—with a beer ration thrown in. It was a good feeling for all our crews to be a part of providing a little normalcy to the guys in the field who saw anything but normalcy on a day-to-day basis. I don't believe a ceasefire had been called, but all the field units were ostensibly moved to "secure" high ground away from known hot spots so the meal could be served in "peace." After the "curbside" deliveries, we refueled, conducted trash pick-ups that afternoon, and then returned to base for our Thanksgiving dinner.

We all had the same "holy cow" look on our faces like the GIs in the field, I'm sure, when we went into our own mess hall. As we walked in, the cooks and bakers were all standing in a line wearing their "cooks whites" and looking happy, knowing what was to come. The senior sergeant cooks/chefs were similarly attired, but they were wearing the big buffoony chef's high hat, which was something we didn't normally see.

Looking back, the whole scene was like what you might see the last night of a nowadays ocean cruise—very festive with everything from soup to nuts to decorations to printed menus to a wine service with desserts. The cooks, bakers, and senior NCO chefs outdid themselves—they did a great job, but I think in the process it made everyone feel a little "homesick" on Thanksgiving Day 1968. And at this point in time, I had only been in Vietnam for just over three weeks!

Vietnam, November 1, 1968: *The Start of a Long Year!*

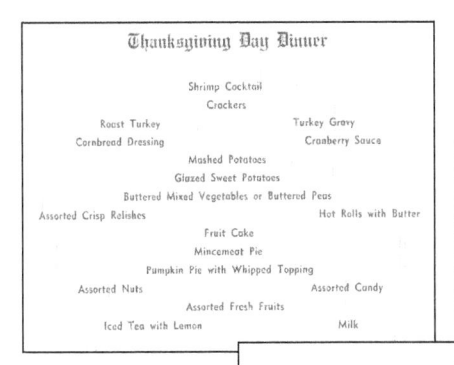

Thanksgiving Day dinner menu, prayer, and commander's message, Phan Thiet, Vietnam, 1968.

Christmas Eve in the Former French Capital of Indo-China

I had been with my unit for less than two months when, on December 23, 1968, I was assigned to fly as co-pilot on an "admin" mission to Da Lat on Christmas Eve. Da Lat had been the French provincial capital of Indo-China

Chapter 15

during the French colonial period, and it was the "bread basket" of Vietnam with a large French/Vietnamese population along with a large dose of French cultural and culinary influences. On this day, the mission was to provide support to the Da Lat U.S. MACV (Military Assistance Command Vietnam), essentially a mail and sundries run with the occasional passenger thrown in. Total flight time from our airfield was about 50 minutes, which meant that during the course of the day we would accumulate about four hours of flight time with six to eight takeoffs and landings and a planned ground control approach radar landing upon return to Phan Thiet—good training.

When the mission sheet was posted, our commanding officer, Major Paul Springer, talked to me about buying fresh veggies, fruits, pastries, and French breads at the local "French" markets in Da Lat so we could have something "special" for the Christmas Eve dinner that our mess hall staff was planning. He had arranged for the MACV guys in Da Lat to help us locate the stuff, and he gave me $500 worth of Vietnamese piasters from what's called the "unit fund" to purchase what we needed. We all thought that was good, and it seemed like a fun task for a "good cause."

While we were doing that, other members in our unit went into Phan Thiet and purchased spiny lobsters and shrimp from the fishing boats that came into the dock at mid-morning. Our mess hall staff would be cooking the

Vietnam, November 1, 1968: The Start of a Long Year!

"meat and potatoes" provided by the U.S. government—GI issue!

We landed at the MACV compound on a main boulevard in Da Lat at about 1000 hours and stayed close to the aircraft, prepared to assume a mission posture within minutes if needed. In the meantime, we watched the young French/Vietnamese women pass along the boulevard in groups of three and four, all wearing what I believe was the traditional "day" dress for women. It consisted of a conical straw hat, something that was worn throughout Vietnam whether strolling the boulevard or working in the rice paddies, black or white silky pants with a billowy leg, and a white silky tunic-type top that gathered at the waist and hung to the knee in "panels" that flowed whimsically in a breeze. It was very casual and likely very cool in the hot sun, and it was sophisticated looking to boot! All the women also had long, dark, flowing hair that complemented and completed the entire look.

Our "girl" watching ended abruptly when the compound's sergeant major woke us from our daydreams asking if we were the guys who needed an escort to the market to purchase the party fixings. I "owned" up to being the guy, so off we went to the Da Lat farmers-type market in what appeared to be the center city square. There was lots of hustle and bustle and haggling over quantity and prices—none of which I understood, so I

Chapter 15

relied on my good coach, the sergeant major, who spoke the language and knew the going rates. After 45 minutes or so, our mission was accomplished and back to the helipad we went.

Upon arrival there, we were directed to secure our purchases and airlift a security team of seven soldiers to a just-reported crash site of another helicopter. The report indicated that an aircraft transiting north to south over the valley east of Da Lat seemingly crashed into high-tension electric cables that were strung from the hydroelectric dam to a high point across the valley.

At the point of impact, the electric cables were 1,100 feet above the valley floor and unmarked with the familiar orange balls you see hanging from cables in the United States. Local aircrews were familiar with the cable site, and we were constantly reminded of the location whenever flying missions in the vicinity. They were also marked on the "local" aeronautical chart. The crew involved in the mishap, however, was unfamiliar with the area and totally unsuspecting, and with the cables at 1,100 feet, they were right at the flight level most helicopters operated.

The accident killed all nine aboard, including the command sergeant major of the Army's First Field Force who, according to the rumor mill, had completed his tour and was on his way to Cam Ranh Bay to catch the flight home for Christmas.

Vietnam, November 1, 1968: The Start of a Long Year!

We remained on the ground until a MEDEVAC aircraft arrived to recover the bodies and personal items, a task that took upwards of an hour and a half. The security team sorted through the wreckage, picked up the KY-28 Crypto box and M-60 machine guns with ammunition, and then boarded our aircraft for the return to Da Lat. On takeoff from the crash site, we made a climbing turn toward the power plant paralleling the power lines, where there remained, entangled in the cables, an 8–10 foot section of helicopter skid and cross tube—a thousand feet above the valley floor. It was a stark and terrible reminder that flying could have dire consequences even when not being shot at. That skid section remained dangling on the cables until damn near the end of my tour. It was removed when a series of big orange balls were installed on the cables across the entire length of the high-tension line—six months too late for nine fellow Americans.

En route back to Da Lat, we experienced an "intermittent" tail rotor chip detector light, which was attended to by the crew chief who removed and inspected the magnetic plug connected to the tail rotor gearbox. Inspection revealed a collection of fine metal shavings on the surface of the magnet. A follow-up inspection would be required after the magnet was cleaned off and reinserted into the gearbox. At that point, a 10-minute engine/drivetrain run up was conducted and the magnetic plug was

Chapter 15

re-inspected. A second look showed more metal shavings than the first inspection revealed. After that inspection, we called back to our unit asking for guidance from our maintenance officer. He recommended grounding the aircraft and said he would fly up on Christmas morning with a maintenance team to inspect, clean, and flush the tail rotor gearbox one more time.

What this meant for us was that we were in Da Lat for Christmas Eve with all the goodies we were supposed to deliver for the Christmas Eve dinner festivities. So now the question was: Where do we spend the night? You'd have thought the MACV compound could accommodate four U.S. air crewmen, but they claimed they couldn't. I think they thought we were a pain in the butt and that we would get in the way of their planned Christmas Eve activities. They were good enough, however, to "recommend" a hotel about two miles away, provide U.S. government ground transportation to and from, and they even had ARVN soldiers secure our aircraft inside the compound's fenced area. Real good of them!

OK, off we went to the "Hotel California," not knowing at all what we might be getting into but carrying M-14 rifles and crew-issued Smith & Wesson .38 pistols with a basic load of ammo. We probably looked a little silly, maybe very silly, but hey this was a war zone and strange things happened, even though Da Lat looked and felt "peaceful."

Vietnam, November 1, 1968: The Start of a Long Year!

The scene in the streets was festive and chaotic. People seemed happy. The main church, a Catholic church, was open and apparently conducting Christmas Eve services. The whole landscape was very unwarlike and even friendly. The same mood was prevalent in the hotel, which turned out to be a pleasant, albeit a bit threadbare, turn-of-the-century fine "oriental" hotel. Because of the holiday, rooms were a little scarce but they managed to put all four of us crewmen in one big room with two large beds. So it was two to a bed, and that was OK with all concerned.

We didn't have a change of clothes, so we stayed in the hotel and found our way to the bar area wearing our flight suits with shoulder holsters. Talk about standing out in the crowd! It was all very uncomfortable and awkward. Our rifles were checked at the front desk area in a "secure" room after we removed the bolts and retained possession of the ammunition. I'm not sure how smart all of that was really, but it was the "hotel policy" to check rifles, and after all, a Christmas truce had been declared. I don't think any of us knew that, but we agreed.

The bar scene was unreal—there were people from all over Asia and Europe and they seemed not to have a care in the world. What war? Some, both men and women, were dressed in their finest and looked as though they were very successful in life. Very weird. Remember the bar scene in one of the "Star Wars" movies with all the intergalactic characters milling about in exotic dress carrying oversized weaponry—well that's where I was on Christmas Eve 1968!

After we settled in at the bar, we befriended two other GIs in uniform, who also stood out in the crowd, and found out they were with a unit in the 173rd Airborne Brigade, which was located about 35 miles south of the city. One of these soldiers was a Black American of Jamaican descent with a very distinctive British-sounding, Caribbean-island accent. He was a sharp-looking airborne staff sergeant who had been sent to Da Lat to "collect up fancy food" and baked goods for his command's Christmas dinner—well, how about that, kindred spirits of sorts we were!

Our new friends wanted to know if we could drop them off the next day back at their unit. We told them it was all about what the maintenance team decided, but we were confident we could help them out. After a few Ba Me Ba 33s (Vietnamese beer), we said our goodnights and told the airborne troopers to meet us in the lobby at 0700 hours for the trip back to the helicopter. They cautioned us about the "friendly" atmosphere at the hotel and said, "You know, Da Lat is an in-country R&R center for the North Vietnamese, so keep an eye on your 'neighbor' and stay close to your sidearm because we are all likely sleeping with the enemy tonight!"

That was all we needed to hear. I hardly slept at all that night, and when I did, I had my hand on the Smith &

Vietnam, November 1, 1968: The Start of a Long Year!

Wesson. I think it could be said that we were suspicious of everything that went bump in the night that Christmas Eve, and it wasn't Santa we were thinking of.

0530 hours rolls around quickly, and so we started Christmas Day. About an hour after arriving back at the MACV compound, our maintenance aircraft, with "crusty" Chief Warrant Officer 3 Willie Sasser in charge, landed adjacent to our bird, and he immediately began the process of conducting a maintenance analysis concerning our "tail rotor" issue. When the inspection and gearbox flush was completed, Willie declared the aircraft flyable and offered to fly it with me back to Phan Thiet. Good deal I thought, after all, he's the chief maintenance officer who has probably forgotten more about the UH-1 helicopter than I now know about it! So, after we loaded up all our "party" stuff and two new "soldier" friends from the night before, we took off to the southeast heading for the coast.

The flight back was uneventful, and we even dropped off our two new airborne friends in a place called Bao Loc, which had a small base camp for units from the 173rd Airborne Brigade. The sharp-looking staff sergeant's name was Trevor Bennett, and he coordinated the comings and goings of all aircraft arriving at the 173rd's Airborne helipad, which meant that we would run into each other during the remainder of my time in Vietnam. And we did in passing—I always kept an eye out for him when we flew missions into his area. Whenever he saw us, he would always render a snappy hand salute as we departed his helipad and we would acknowledge him in turn.

A sharp guy—and would you believe, I met him again in the Navy commissary in Annapolis, Maryland, in the early 2000s, and I see him almost every week as he is in charge of the dairy products section at the ripe "young" age of 77. Why does he still work you ask? He says he has to keep it moving—God love him! We talk about politics, the weather, traveling, investments, property (he owns property in D.C., Delaware, and Florida), and the state of our military today.

He's still a "sharp" soldier who retired from the Army after attaining the highest enlisted rank of sergeant major. He has two stars on his Combat Infantry Badge (CIB), a combat star on his jump wings, indicating he made a "combat jump," along with the silver wings of a Master Paratrooper—all meaning he's been around. I still see him in the commissary, and I look forward to our short conversations. I consider him a good friend from somewhere out of my "intergalactic" past—so let's talk about a small world!

When we arrived at home base, our commanding officer, Major Paul Stringer, met us and was happy that the aircraft and crew were no worse for wear, but he was not happy we remained overnight in Da Lat; remember, we had

Vietnam, November 1, 1968: The Start of a Long Year!

Part of our living area at Phan Thiet, December 1968. Note the sandbags for "protection" against incoming mortars/rockets.

the party stuff. It all turned out well, however, as we quickly got the veggies, fruits, and breads to the "chefs" in the mess hall, and it was prepared and served for dinner on Christmas Day. Ho, Ho, Ho—Merry Christmas!

The days between Christmas and New Year's Day were always very special to me growing up. It was a time of visiting with family and friends and in general a happy seven days. This same period in Vietnam was pretty much just like every other day there. A three-day "ceasefire" had been declared and, as I recall, while there were some "hostile" incidents, it was mainly calm. It was a good time for a maintenance-intense aviation unit to get a leg up on performing/finishing scheduled maintenance and to think forward and anticipate unscheduled events through a series of "what if" drills. Our crews even did some touch-up painting of our aircraft just to pretty them up! All in all, nobody minded the three-day ceasefire, but it did make you scratch your head. If it was so easy to call for a Christmas ceasefire, why not call for a suspension of hostilities while working out ways to end the war?

The Night We Brought the "House" Down— New Year's Eve 1968

Along comes New Year's Eve and I get assigned to fly another admin-type mission up to our aviation battalion HQ in Dong Ba Thin. The purpose of our mission was to pick up four pilots and two enlisted crewmen new in-country and ferry them down to our unit in Phan Thiet. We arrived at Dong Ba Thin in the early afternoon, positioned our aircraft in front of my unit's liaison office, and checked in. We were told that it would be a couple of hours before we could return to home base because the "newbies" to our unit hadn't been completely processed through HQ.

OK, we then had time to go up to the Quonset hut-type club on the compound and order a burger with some fries. While there, some monsoon-type weather set in and lasted for hours, with big thunder boomers, 50,000-foot cloud tops, and lightning that put on a 4th of July-type show. All that said, our mission back to base was canceled as the weather forecast showed no let up in sight during the

Vietnam, November 1, 1968: The Start of a Long Year!

overnight hours. Well, here I am, déjà vu, all over again—guess I'm spending New Year's in Dong Ba Thin! Last week Da Lat, this week Dong Ba Thin—I'm gettin' around this country and I've only been here two months—rock on!

Getting a place to stay was no problem as our little liaison shack had 10 "transit billets" (military for beds) to accommodate unit members coming and going. So, we had that going for us, and then as luck would have it, starting at 2100 hours the O Club was hosting a Filipino traveling USO band that could literally sing any song and imitate any artist you could think of. Off to the club we went, four of us flight crewmen from the 192nd.

The O Club went all out that night with steaks to order and spiny lobster tails if you wanted to create your own surf and turf entrées. It was hard to believe—hey, pinch me, are we in Vietnam? You have to remember that the place was a Quonset hut and not very upscale, but they did have tablecloths with a little candle and real napkins set out on the tables that evening. They did a good job of making it special, and they even had holiday decorations. I think we all ordered the make-your-own surf and turf along with wine, Boone's Farm or maybe Lancer's or Mateus, real connoisseurs we were at the time, and we had a great time. The band was incredible, and yes it was true they could sing anything and pretty much impersonate anyone including the KING (who was the King you ask?—Google it—"thank

Chapter 15

you, thank you very much"), and they were good musicians! The only thing missing from the scene were women, except for three nurses from the Army field hospital at Cam Ranh Bay who were escorted by, we think, doctors with the rank of major. Oh well, we had a blast sans the women!

After midnight, the party started to wind down, so we had a nightcap, final final, and headed out the door to walk back to our liaison office. A couple of hundred yards down the road, an Army 5/quarter ton truck (something like a Jeep pickup truck, old style) stopped, and the driver asked where we were going. When we told him the airfield, he said jump in as he was headed in the same direction. After we settled in the back of the Jeep, we all introduced ourselves and found out that he was a major and the commanding officer of an airplane company (light fixed-wing aircraft) whose mission was to fly artillery spotter and liaison-type sorties.

We told him we were air crewmen with the 192nd Assault Helicopter Company. On that we all bonded and he passed us a bottle of Crown Royal, saying cheers and Happy New Year. We all partook in the bottle-passing exercise, and then we came to an abrupt—and I mean an abrupt—and crunchy stop. The front of the vehicle was pointed upwards at about a 30- to 40-degree angle and teetering a little side to side. We all piled out of the "wreck" and were groggily surveying the damage to the truck and

Vietnam, November 1, 1968: The Start of a Long Year!

the "object" we ran into. In an instant, and from out of the dark, we heard this very pissed off major, the commanding officer of the 92nd Assault Helicopter Company, a sister company of ours, calling us all to attention! It seems our driver, a major himself, had run over and destroyed the very pissed off major's personal "relief tube" (piss tube), which was between buildings, one of which was the angry major's quarters. We all came to attention, lined up, and, at the request of the angry major, sounded off with our name, rank, military occupation, and unit.

It went something like this: Sir, Frank Fox, 1st lieutenant, helicopter pilot, 192nd Assault Helicopter Company, followed by three more 192nd crewmen providing their personal specs. Well at this, the very angry major went into a tirade declaring that those of us from the 192nd were wild renegades, useless beyond belief, and disrespected his compound, his officers, and him personally. I was the senior officer from my little group, and I tried to explain to the very angry major that our group were merely passengers. The angry major didn't want to hear it and said that every time someone from my unit, the 192nd Assault Helicopter Company, came through Dong Ba Thin, they destroyed something in his area. He went on to "ban" us from his compound, saying he never wanted to see anyone from our unit again in his area, period! With that, he lit into the other major. When he found out that the other

Chapter 15

major was the driver and also an aviation commanding officer, he literally went into a state of shock and "double banned" the other major from setting foot in his area again.

It was sorta funny witnessing all of this; in fact, we interlopers from the 192nd, the "wild renegades from down south," took a fair amount of pride in having been associated with the whole affair—holy shit, we got banned. You think the Army will send us all the way back home?! Well after having been "banned and reamed," real good like, we helped get the Jeep down off the piss tube and said our goodnights and Happy New Years to the other major, our new friend, and went our separate ways—but the night wasn't over for the "renegades" from that unit down south!

Many a conversation in lots of aviation units around the world start out as follows, "No shit, there we were—flak so thick you could walk on it." On this night, however, we were on the ground walking back to our unit shack on the flight line when I ran into a friend from flight school who was assigned to the 92nd Assault Helicopter Company, the angry major's unit, whose company we just parted.

My friend was 1st Lieutenant Dan Ferguson, and when telling him what had just happened to us in a "no shit there I was sorta way," he couldn't stop laughing. Nor could his group, and so they "unbanned" us and invited us to join them in a moving party that was en route to a larger barracks-type, wooden, tin-roofed building that had a

Vietnam, November 1, 1968: The Start of a Long Year!

"pilots' lounge" located at one end. The party was up and running when we arrived, and these guys didn't need any help from the "renegades" up from the south—they had a few "renegades" of their own. Time was getting to be around 0200 hours or later on January 1, 1969. I only had 10 more months to go in Vietnam before my tour would be up—moving right along!

Our gathering was now to the point where about 15 guys, me being one of them, were standing on the bar hanging one arm over the wooden rafters that essentially held the building up. At the top of our lungs we were singing karaoke-style "We Gotta Get Out Of This Place" by the Animals, a song that was the national anthem for all Americans serving in Southeast Asia, when bam, bam, ear splitting crack, and then crash. You guessed it—the whole damn building collapsed inward under the weight of the 15 "rotor heads" on the bar singing their brains out (is that an oxymoron?).

There was tin roofing and wooden cross beams piled up four feet high. The water pipe to the bar burst and was spraying everywhere to the point that some of the more inebriated among us thought they would drown. Everybody who had been in attendance was knocked to the floor in the prone position. It was chaos for a while, and there was a lot of moaning and groaning going on under the debris— and that was good because it meant there were a fair amount of live ones crawling around. It took about 20 minutes for a "rescue" team to remove the large pieces so that people could start climbing out.

I was one of the last to ascend from the depths, and guess who was the first person I laid eyes on—you got it, the pissed off and very angry major who had banned me, and others, from his compound not two hours ago. Woe is me. After this I thought they might extend my tour in Vietnam. The major was so angry by then he could hardly speak. Anything he said ended up sounding like this: "#$!@%%$^&*^&^?(?#><+_- WTF!"

We all knew he wanted us to leave pronto—and we did! What a way to usher in the new year. By the way, no one was seriously hurt, probably because God protects drunks. There were some big bumps on heads and stitches for some, but the memory of having been there and participating was forever priceless!

The "Screaming Eagles," Task Force (TF) 3/506th, 101st Airborne Division (Air Assault)

During my year long tour of the duty in Vietnam, from November 1968 to October 1969, my unit, the 192nd Assault Helicopter Company provided airlift support to the TF-3/506 whenever they conducted combat air assault missions. This particular unit was the "band of brothers" unit that gained notoriety after "jumping" into France on D-Day during WWII.

Vietnam, November 1, 1968: The Start of a Long Year!

It was a proud unit with a rich historical legacy: Normandy, Carentan, Battle of the Bulge (Bastogne), Berchtesgaden, and Hitler's Eagle's Nest.

Lieutenant Colonel Manuel Alves, callsign Blackhawk 6, commanded the TF. He was a WWII, Korean War, and now a Vietnam War veteran. He oversaw ground ops flying in what we called the Command and Control (Charlie/Charlie) ship equipped with a huge multi-channel radio console provided by our unit along with a dedicated command pilot and crew. This aircraft would typically fly 700–1,000 feet above the action, and the commander would be constantly seeking intel and updates in a continuous attempt at "developing" the ground tactical situation.

When I became the aviation unit ops officer, in March–April 1969, I frequently flew this mission with Warrant Officer Jim Lynch, the dedicated command pilot, to assist in implementing any aviation support options the ground commander may have developed during the course of the operations. The Charlie/Charlie ship was always in the middle of it when TF 3/506 was "skirmishing," and as a result, a fair amount of enemy ground fire was directed at it.

The bad guys knew that this was the commander's aircraft and it would have been quite a "prize" to bring it down. Word on the street was that the Viet Cong would pay any of their soldiers/units a rich bounty for bringing down this bird. Lucky for us, no one claimed the reward

Chapter 15

A 192nd aircraft used by Lieutenant Colonel Manuel Alves (right), Commander of the 3/506 Infantry, 101st Airborne Division. Alves' callsign was Blackhawk 6, and the nose art reflects that. Sp4 Al Holland (left) was the aircraft crew chief.

during my time in-country. I say lucky because within two years, the Viet Cong had supplies of shoulder-fired, ground-to-air, heat-seeking missiles that would have significantly changed how we conducted ops, as the Charlie/Charlie aircraft would have become extremely vulnerable. Lieutenant Colonel Alves was a tough and demanding commander who was well liked by all. When he was in the area, and he was everywhere, you better be on your game.

Fast-forward to Ft. Benning, fall of 1971. While I was attending the Infantry Officers Advanced Course, then-Colonel Alves, who was chief of the tactics division, noticed me as a student in his class. He had me "stand to be recognized" by my classmates while he gave a brief overview of our Vietnam exploits together and me being one of his pilots. It was a very nice gesture, and I was floored

Vietnam, November 1, 1968: The Start of a Long Year!

that he would even recognize and remember me. The really good ones always remember the names and the places. I envy people who have that ability—even if I refresh and study the names, places, and circumstances, I still don't always get it right!

A couple of days before Christmas 1971, my wife and I had a chance encounter with Colonel Alves at the Ft. Benning O Club. We had one of those great two-minute conversations where you find out all about each other's lives, you know, kids, grandkids, how your golf game is working, etc. He told us he was traveling to California to be with his family over the holidays. He expected to be back at Ft. Benning in early January, and he said he would invite us over to his place on Colonels' row near the golf course for cocktails and talk.

We were excited at the prospect of meeting his family and seeing the inside of one of those big old "military" homes. It never happened, however, as early on New Year's Eve, he was killed by a drunk driver! I was shocked beyond belief—another good guy taken from the world much too soon. He had fought in WWII with the 101st Airborne as an enlisted man at the Battle of the Bulge, jumped into Normandy on D-Day, received his commission as a 2nd lieutenant in the field, fought in Korea and in Vietnam—and was killed by a drunk driver! Sometimes there is no justice!!!

Chapter 15

One of the aircraft being used by Lieutenant Colonel Manuel Alves experienced a hydraulic failure and crashed in Phan Thiet, Vietnam, 1969. Alves survived the crash, although one of his staff was killed. Alves survived Vietnam as well, but later was killed in an automobile accident in the United States by a drunk driver.

In-Flight Mission Change

On this particular day, February 12, 1969, we would be a flight of seven Hueys assaulting into three separate landing zones over a two-hour period. In total, we would offload roughly 50 troopers at each location for the purpose of conducting "search and destroy" ops against Viet

Vietnam, November 1, 1968: The Start of a Long Year!

Cong/North Vietnamese Army forces suspected of operating in the area. Escorting us throughout the course of the mission would be our very own Tiger Shark gunships, which were UH-1C Huey aircraft armed with rockets, mini-guns, and, in some cases, a 40mm grenade launcher. After an early morning mission brief by our ops officer, all crew members manned their aircraft to conduct pre-flight inspections, weight and balance checks, weapons systems checks, and communications checks.

I was the designated flight lead for this mission with a total of 135 in-country flight hours. At my direction, all seven of our aircraft requested and received clearance to move from our revetments to the airfield's mission-ready point. Once assembled in a staggered trail formation on the ground, the troops arrived marching out from their cantonment area in one company-sized formation of about 150 men in platoon-sized elements. It's impressive to see that many men under arms move in formation to the low, and in this case, relaxed cadence of their first sergeant. Left, left, your left, right, left, etc.

After coming to a halt, the first sergeant turned the company over to the company commander, who addressed the company regarding the upcoming mission and then turned the platoons over to the platoon commanders, lieutenants and sergeants. At this point, the troops were broken out into "sticks" of seven men per with each being

Chapter 15

assigned to an aircraft. The troopers boarded our ships, and our crew chiefs made certain all was secured and ready for departure. When all the aircraft commanders checked in with me giving a "ready up" call, I then checked with our gunship escort to confirm they were en route to the landing zone; they were. Yellow flight, our call sign, was ready, and I requested clearance from the airfield tower to depart north with a left break toward the mountains in the west. The tower cleared us to go, and we were on our way. We leveled off at 1,500 feet and settled in as a flight of seven in staggered trail formation for the 30-minute flight to the landing zone. En route, we were in contact with the airborne TF commander, Lieutenant Colonel Manuel Alves, and at that point we had a solid GO to insert his troopers into the mission-designated landing zone.

About 15 minutes out, our gunship lead contacted me and gave me a brief as to how the mission would unfold. They would arrive over the target before us and prep the area with mini-gun and rocket fire, making two complete passes. After the second pass, the Tiger Sharks would swing out, join up, and fly off our wing as we let down into a final approach.

One gunship would be off our wing and slightly out in front of the incoming formation of troop ships, laying down protective fire for our flight all the while being covered by his wingman, who also laid down suppressive fire, each one

Vietnam, November 1, 1968: The Start of a Long Year!

covering the other as they broke off the target. Adding to this crescendo of gunship fire, our troop ships would start peppering the areas immediately adjacent to the landing zone with machine gun fire from our internally mounted M-60s, commonly referred to as "door guns," two per troop ship. There was lots of suppressive fire coming out of our group, but as far as the crews were concerned, you never had enough suppressive fire.

All that said, on this day, about two miles out from touchdown, I received a call from "Blackhawk" to ABORT the mission and fly direct to a "new set of coordinates" where a South Vietnamese Army unit with American advisors was involved in an ongoing action about 25 miles from our current location. With this call, both our gunship lead, Captain Tom White, Tiger Shark flight platoon leader, and I ginned up a new "flight op plan" and proceeded to the "hot" area. We alerted the troops on board of the change in mission and kept them apprised of the ground situation as best we could.

The same sequence would be followed with the guns going in first and providing mini-gun and rocket prep, then picking us up a couple miles out. The only thing that changed was the guns had already expended a fair amount of their ordnance on the landing we "canceled." Now we were headed to an area that was declared hot and the unit in contact had taken casualties.

Chapter 15

As we got closer to the contact area, we could see smoke rising from the general area, which was the result of artillery fire that had been placed at the edge of a tree line where an enemy concentration was suspected to be dug in. From high above, Blackhawk directed us to put our seven ships in a long stretch of dry rice paddies marked with a colored smoke grenade at the far end of the designated landing zone. Within minutes, we were on short final and, while there was lots of smoke and the sound of gunfire, it was hard to tell if any of it was being directed at our incoming flight. If it was, it was ineffective as none of the aircraft seemed to be taking direct fire.

When we touched down, the troops "unassed" the aircraft in record time and set up a quick perimeter outward of 50 meters from the point of touchdown. As all this was occurring, the co-pilot and I saw and heard three explosions off the left side of our aircraft, but we couldn't tell if it was mortar, grenade, or RPG fire—didn't matter, we needed to get out of Dodge!

The situation in the landing zone was chaotic and confusing but organized, with friendly soldiers returning fire into a tree line and creek bed while unit leaders did what they do, putting troops in place, establishing fields of fire, supporting each other, distributing ammo, and taking head counts. OK, round one over with 50 troopers on the ground,

Vietnam, November 1, 1968: The Start of a Long Year!

which was a little more than a full platoon-sized element—big enough with enough firepower to take care of itself for now.

We were off the landing zone and heading back to the airfield at Phan Thiet for another pick up of troops for insertion into the combat zone. That pick up was uneventful as was the flight back to the fight. En route, we heard radio chatter, and there was plenty of it to the point of it being hard to determine who was on first.

What was clear was that there were U.S. casualties in the landing zone and the commander on the ground was requesting an immediate MEDEVAC for upwards of five casualties with what he determined to be life-threatening injuries. At that point, our flight was ordered to set up a 360-degree racetrack pattern, big circle, about one mile away from the landing zone to allow a MEDEVAC aircraft into the area.

Although it was acknowledged by the requesting unit that the landing zone was receiving sporadic fire, the MEDEVAC pilot did not hesitate to set up a fast approach into the area while instructing the ground commander to have the wounded ready for immediate up-load so as to limit his exposure time to enemy ground fire. Our one remaining Tiger Shark gunship (the number two ship was refueling) provided cover fire to an area forward of the landing zone during the approach phase.

Chapter 15

We could hear the radio transmissions between the MEDEVAC pilot and the ground commander, and the pilot was cool, calm, and collected. This wasn't his first rodeo! His voice and radio demeanor literally put all involved at ease, and this while we could literally see bits of his aircraft shattering out one side or the other presumably from small arms fire—honest! He touched down, and within 20 seconds the five casualties were loaded aboard and were likely back at a field aid station within 15 minutes. The whole event took about eight minutes from start to finish, and it was something to watch from where we were. I never met the pilot of the MEDEVAC but attended a brief awards ceremony the day following and witnessed him receiving a Silver Star for his actions. We later found out that all five of the wounded lived to be evacuated to a regional U.S. medical facility in Japan, in large part because of one very "brave" MEDEVAC pilot!

Well, we were up next, so as soon as the MEDEVAC had cleared the area, my flight of seven was cleared into the landing zone to deliver our "cargo" of nearly 50 more troopers. The landing zone hadn't been declared hot, meaning under continuous fire, but it was receiving and returning sporadic fire. Not an issue as we considered our mission essential for reinforcing the troops already on the ground and in contact. Our gunships joined up with us and started to lay down suppressive fire on areas designated

Vietnam, November 1, 1968: The Start of a Long Year!

by our troops on the ground. Our own door gunners were working "standard" suppressive fire patterns, covering close in tree lines, rice paddy dikes, and tall trees for suspected snipers, and all was going good until it wasn't good anymore.

At about 300 feet altitude and a half-mile out from touchdown, my aircraft took a barrage of ground fire that seemed to hit us all at once and made one helluva loud banging sound.

In that instant, we lost all our engine instruments, so we had no "real" engine performance indicators. In addition, we lost partial control of the aircraft, and we could not fly straight and level. Instead, the aircraft porpoised through the air. And to keep the aircraft from shuttering violently, we could only maintain 50–60 knots of airspeed. This was the result of a bullet shattering the sync elevator coupling that later fell off the rotor head control assembly during a rapid shutdown procedure.

After a quick cockpit evaluation, and checking with our crew chief, we learned that we also had a casualty who sustained a gunshot wound through the upper part of his leg. Luckily, one of the troops on board was the unit's medic. He took over, declaring the wounded soldier stable. This "positive" prognosis, along with the condition of the aircraft, contributed to my decision to make an emergency landing about a mile away from the fight.

Chapter 15

I handed command of the flight to one of my flight section leaders, and then broke out of the formation. Yellow flight continued into the landing zone, door guns blazing, and debarked another 42 troopers. There were now roughly 100 American "Screaming Eagles" on the ground, and as things went, they were slowly taking control of the situation. My co-pilot, 1st Lieutenant Dave Parsley, and I safely landed our aircraft and then worked with the ground guys to set up a defensive position utilizing the seven troopers we had on board, supplementing their weapons with our door-mounted machine guns.

Once the defensive perimeter was set up, the co-pilot and I inspected the aircraft and discovered 40+ entry/exit holes along with four spent rounds of undetermined caliber on the floor of the aircraft. One round hit the armor-plated seat directly under me, leaving a big pucker mark in the Kevlar, the material used in making the armor plate. Almost the million dollar wound I thought, but who wants to get shot in the fanny—and the way things work, it could have hit a much more important part of my anatomy!

Anyway, seeing how many rounds hit the aircraft, it was hard to believe that only one of our soldiers suffered an injury. It turns out that the remaining six aircraft in our flight sustained a total of only 11 hits throughout the entire day's operation, and they sustained zero on-board casualties. At the end of the day, my co-pilot and I looked at each other and simultaneously knew that the enemy keyed on our aircraft, intent on knocking down the flight lead, and I guess it could be said that they succeeded!

Looking back, fate was at work here. If the onboard medic had declared the wounded soldier as being critical, I probably would have attempted to fly back to our base where more immediate medical attention would have been available. But, as events unfolded, I soon discovered we would have shortly crashed with likely all aboard being lost. God was looking out for the whole bunch of us!

The 11 of us laid up against a rice paddy dike at the ready for the next hour and watched U.S. Air Force F-100 Super Sabers drop bombs onto enemy positions as directed by Air Force forward air controllers and infantry forward observers on the ground. For us, it was quite a show. We were positioned about three-quarters of a mile from the fight, and when the F-100s came in on a bomb run, they released their ordnance directly over our "defensive position."

Weapons release that distance from the target was necessary because of the speed at which the fighters were dropping their loads. We could see the release, could hear the bombs screeching through the air, and then heard and saw the thud, quickly followed by an ear-piercing explosion. These fighter bomber runs were followed by our own Tiger Sharks putting rocket, mini-gun, door gun, and

Chapter 15

40mm grenades onto the target area. At some point I asked the crew chief to get the camera that always seemed to be with the aircraft, saying some of these pictures could make it to *Life* magazine or perhaps the network news, or maybe even win a Pulitzer! If nothing else, maybe a little unit exposure. Well, so much for thinking about network news, magazines, and Pulitzers—the crew chief looked at me and said he left the camera in his tent and only realized it when we were taking off. You've gotta be kidding me, no camera—remember, long before cell phones!

About 45 minutes into our ordeal, the medic we had with us asked if a MEDEVAC could be brought into our area so that he could airlift out the soldier who had been shot. He still considered the soldier in stable condition but was concerned about the possibility of him going into shock at some point. I said we can arrange for that, climbed up into the cockpit of our grounded aircraft, lit up the radio, and requested a MEDEVAC bird through our Tiger Shark lead.

After getting the contact info for the MEDEVAC and his estimated time of arrival, 8–12 minutes, I went to see and talk to the wounded trooper. He was an Black-American kid who was in good spirits and suffering very little, if any, outright pain. His wound seemed very "clean" as the bullet had entered his leg from the underside, as he was sitting at the time he was struck, and exited

Vietnam, November 1, 1968: The Start of a Long Year!

through the top side of the leg. The round finally embedded itself in his flak jacket, becoming a souvenir. We made light of it, and he acknowledged that yes, it was quite a souvenir! There was no apparent bone damage and no major bleeding.

We made small talk, and I told him that he would probably be en route back to the States the next day. His greatest concern was what his mother would think, and he wanted to be assured that if anything "happened" to him he wanted his mother to know that he had been thinking about her. His concerns for his mother struck me—he was a Black-American kid and I was a White kid, but we had the exact same feelings! I never really thought otherwise, but it hit home at that moment in time, as I know I would have felt just as he did. How about that—he also bled red blood, just like all the rest of us! Again, never thought otherwise, but here it was in "real time."

I think about the term "diversity" and what's going on TODAY. Well, here's what our little group looked like then: of 11 soldiers, we had seven White kids, three Hispanic kids, and one Black-American kid. The White kids were of Irish, German, Swedish, and Polish descent. We were a pretty diverse group, and there was NO palpable animosity one to another. We were all concerned about each other, and that's how it was during my entire tour in Vietnam. And by the way, I never heard a call for assistance

Chapter 15

or MEDEVAC denied, prioritized, or even questioned on the grounds of race, gender, ethnicity, or nationality—NEVER—PERIOD!

MEDEVAC was now on short final, and within a minute "our guy" was on board and off to the medical evacuation point. His platoon members wished him well and assisted in getting him into the aircraft. We all thought that this soldier's war was likely over and that he would probably make a full recovery. We were happy for him!

Shortly after the MEDEVAC departed, our commanding officer, Major Paul Stringer, along with our unit maintenance officer, Major Bruce Nail, arrived on site to check us out and inspect the aircraft to see if it could be flown back to our base. Major Nail climbed all over the

1st Lieutenant Frank Fox in the cockpit of a Huey helicopter, Phan Thiet, Vietnam, 1969.

Vietnam, November 1, 1968: The Start of a Long Year!

downed bird and declared her RED X'd and unflyable due to combat damage. He went about arranging for a CH-47 Chinook to be brought in to "sling" the Huey back to our base. Both Major Stringer and Major Nail told us that we were damned lucky for not having flown that aircraft any further. Major Nail indicated that along with the sync elevator control being damaged, a push-pull rod coupling on what's called the swash plate was hit with a bullet of unknown caliber and had broken off in three pieces when he inspected it and while pushing it from side to side.

He went on to say continued flight would likely have caused a failure of that coupling, which could have resulted in the rotor head being "slung" completely off. Without saying, it would have been catastrophic. I was relieved on about three different levels after hearing that. I had briefly considered flying the aircraft to home base, but then thought otherwise. To fly any further would have resulted in 11 KIA. So, the timing of events, the world revolving around individual events, human impulses, good data/bad data, other fleeting inputs to the brain all collided and caused me to make a "gut" split-second decision, which in the end saved my life and the lives of 10 others. Yes, I was relieved, and the events of the day were SOBERING!

Our commanding officer offered us air crewmen a ride home as maintenance folks would handle the evacuation of the aircraft, so we all clamored into his bird, waved our

Chapter 15

goodbyes to our comrades on the ground, and took off for Phan Thiet. We made it back in time for lunch. What a weird war: shot down at 1030 hours, spent an hour or so in a rice paddy, counted bullet holes in my aircraft, watched the U.S. Air Force unload on the enemy, shared an emotionally raw "moment" with a wounded Black-American soldier, now having lunch, and hey, it might be early enough to get one of those warm showers everyone was after.

While we were "doing" lunch, our "grunts" continued to maneuver against the enemy, suffering five KIA and 12 wounded. They would stay in the field on high alert for the next 24 hours after consolidating their positions. I often thought about how the grunts had it—from the get go it was frightening, damned exhausting work, dirty and buggy with no thought of a "sun-warmed" shower or hot food at the end of the day, and one's reward for being a good "trooper" might be a horrible death.

I was commissioned an infantry officer and then later went to flight school, so I felt I had a bond with the "grunts." The only reason we were there was to support the infantryman. Everyone I knew and worked with in Vietnam thought that way and would drop everything to support the troopers in the field—and we did, day or night!

As the afternoon wore on, the aircraft that I had been piloting was airlifted by a CH-47 Chinook back to base and dropped, literally, in front of our maintenance facility tent hangar. The aircraft was dropped from a height of about eight feet and it spread the skids on impact. Imagine, we were able to get it to the ground after receiving a significant amount of gunfire with no further damage and then it got dropped by the Chinook. It probably had something to do with the giant dust cloud kicked up by the twin rotor Chinook, which likely caused what's called "brown out," and so the crew chief was guessing when he informed the pilots to "cut the load loose."

As it turned out, our aircraft was eventually sent back to the States for repair and refit. The "official" final count on the number of entry and exit holes in the fuselage and cabin area was upwards of 45. Instrument failure was caused by a round that came up through the floor and, when exiting through the roof, severed the one and a half inch diameter cable that ran from the generator to the cockpit instrument panel. Consensus from all the airframe and powerplant guys in the hangar was that we used up one of our nine lives as the damage to the rotor head, the shattered push-pull rod coupling, would have been fatal for all if flown much further!

In the early evening hours of that same day, I was hanging around our ops tent when a mission came in to fly an emergency resupply of ammo, rations, radio batteries, medical bandages, and water into the area where the battle

Chapter 15

had raged for most of the day. I volunteered to fly it because I wanted to be involved. The ops guys were more than happy to give it to me. We took off after dark and flew to the "downtown" Phan Thiet HQ of Military Assistance Command Vietnam (MACV) and landed in a courtyard within the compound that was just barely large enough to accommodate a Huey.

We shut down and waited for the aircraft to be loaded. Once loaded, we lifted straight up to a 20-foot hover, tipped the nose over, shuttered through translational lift, and low leveled up the river toward the mountains. I always liked flying in the early evening. The ground thermals associated with hot daytime weather and the winds that caused significant turbulent flying conditions normally abated after dusk; flying was smooth and the early nighttime breezes were cool. Although it was a combat environment and dangerous, it was also exhilarating.

About five miles out we climbed to 1,000 feet and contacted both the ground command and our own Tiger Sharks, who were on call providing gunship support for the ongoing ground operation. When I contacted the Tiger Shark lead, Captain Tom White, the gun platoon leader, recognized my voice and said something to the effect of, "Hey, weren't you the guy who 'lost' an aircraft earlier today?" I said yes, and Tom said, "Wow, think they should

Vietnam, November 1, 1968: The Start of a Long Year!

have given you the rest of the day off!" Come to think of it, it had been a long day.

The very next day, I flew a resupply mission out to the "contested" area of the day before and witnessed the aftermath of a nasty 18-hour firefight. The entire area smelled of gunpowder, fuel oil (?), filth, acrid smoke, and death. The fight started after a local Vietnamese militia-led, MACV-supported squad reconnaissance element detected movement of what turned out to be a battalion-sized mixed Viet Cong/North Vietnamese Army unit and initiated an ambush.

Once the fight started, it escalated very quickly and expanded into our committing troopers from the TF 3/506, 101st Airborne Division, the action that I took part in. The enemy suffered 166 killed, including the commander, 40 wounded and captured, 200+ individual weapons destroyed or confiscated, along with 12 crew served weapons, a mountain of ammunition, and an extensive amount of printed "intelligence" material in the form of ops maps, propaganda literature, currency, which included U.S. dollars, and unit communications gear. It was an awesome terrible sight! U.S. losses on the battlefield were six KIA and 16 wounded.

That afternoon, General Peers, 1st Field Force Commander, presented "impact" Distinguished Flying Crosses to our Tiger Shark gunship pilots. The very brave

Chapter 15

MEDEVAC pilot who airlifted the first casualties out of the hot landing zone was also decorated with the Silver Star. Well deserved all around—Hoooah!

After completing the re-supply mission and returning to Phan Thiet, I went over to the medical evacuation point to check on how the wounded Black-American soldier made out. To my shock, the emergency evac MDs told me that he had died en route to the hospital at Long Binh near Saigon. They were as shocked as I was because they thought he was going to be fine. He was alert and stable when he departed, and they, like the medic on my aircraft, thought the wound was clean and had missed hitting any bone.

Unfortunately, it seems the bullet nicked the femur or thigh bone in the upper leg causing the soldier to "throw" a blood clot, which caused him to go into cardiac arrest. The MDs at our location learned that the medical personnel aboard the evacuation helicopter could not revive him. I was sick at hearing of his death and over the years I have thought of him and his mother often. Two young men who met under unreal circumstances—a brief encounter for both of us that, for me, has lasted a lifetime and which I remember as if it occurred just last month.

Vietnam, November 1, 1968: The Start of a Long Year!

TR—Walk Softly but Carry a Big Stick!

February 1969 was a busy month. My unit flew daily combat assault missions mostly in support of TF 3/506, 101st Airborne Division. We also supported the 44th ARVN (South Vietnamese) Regiment, U.S. Army 75th Ranger Regiment, U.S. Navy SEALs, Military Assistance Command Vietnam (MACV), and elements of the 173rd Airborne Brigade. Our operations area ranged from our base along the coast at Phan Thiet to Vung Tau in the south; Bam Me Thuot and Da Lat (the French capital of Indo-China) in the west; and Phan Rang, Nha Trang, Cam Ranh Bay, and Dong Ba Thin to the north and east.

Occasionally, our unit would also be tasked to provide aviation assets well outside our normal operating area, and those type actions could take us to virtually anywhere in the country to support what would be called a tactical emergency (TAC E). I participated in one of these ops along the Vietnamese/Laotian border staging out of Bam Me Thuot at the end of February 1969. A TAC E was normally declared when a friendly unit developed a firefight into an evolving and ever-larger action that required "large-scale" troop reinforcements and/or resupply.

I made an interesting discovery while awaiting "mission orders" at Bam Me Thuot. The air crews on standby were to be fed near an old and longtime hunting club at one end of the airfield. That's right, a hunting club! In the French colonial days, this club hosted "prominent" people from all over the world to safari for Bengal tigers, elephants, monkeys, and water buffaloes, to name a few.

At the entrance to the club was a brass plaque commemorating President Teddy Roosevelt's visit to the club in 1905. I was astounded not because ole Teddy had been there but because in order to get there, one had to travel about 10,000 miles from the east coast of the United States, and in 1905 that was an "arduous" and long trip even when traveling in a presidential caravan. His visit to this region in Asia may have had diplomatic overtones, but the reason he was in Vietnam was to hunt big game. I don't figure that would go over so well in our present times. For me, I was never very wild about big game hunting—too beautiful to see in the wilderness; let them live!

Friendly Fire—"End of Fire Mission; Over"— Not Hardly!

Combat assault missions varied in type. One such mission I flew consisted of airlifting infantry and artillery troopers into a soon-to-be fire support artillery base about 40 miles southwest of Phan Thiet. There was a sequence as to how these types of operations unfolded, and it normally started with the preplanned selection of a piece of "high" ground on which to insert a battery of three to five field artillery pieces for the purpose of providing artillery support

Vietnam, November 1, 1968: The Start of a Long Year!

A Huey in flight... beautiful! Note the Tit Ti Mountain low in the background, the site of a terrible crash in March 1969.

in a 360-degree circle out to the max range of the guns. Once that was done, an artillery prep of the ground site selected was conducted to dislodge any enemy troops in the immediate area. This artillery prep also cleared a sufficient area of trees, which facilitated bringing troops in to secure the area, followed then by the artillery battery. This part of the mission was normally conducted by CH-47 Chinook helicopters.

Well on this particular mission, I was flight lead of five assault helicopters bringing in 30+ troopers to off load at the landing zone. We were in a holding pattern about five miles north of the landing zone watching the artillery prep work over the mountain top. Knowing the predetermined time for the artillery prep to stop, and having been briefed

Chapter 15

that the end of the prep would also be marked by white phosphorus (WP or Willie Pete) rounds, I turned the flight toward the landing zone at the first sign of the Willie Pete rounds hitting the target. We were two miles out and, thinking that the prep was over, we started letting down into a final approach. And then BAROOM! At about a half mile out and about 700 feet up on short final, five high explosive rounds hit the landing zone right in front of us.

With this, I aborted the approach, simultaneously breaking to the right out of the line of fire and beyond the gun target line. Our flight of five started a climb to a "safer" altitude and called the Charlie/Charlie ship, demanding to know WTF was going on and hey, didn't we have Willie Pete marking the end of the fire mission? Well, the answer was yes and yes, and the commander in the Charlie/Charlie ship, Lieutenant Colonel Alves, was one hot SOB who at that point was not about to mince his words. He realized, as we all did, that had the high explosive rounds hit 5–10 seconds later, my flight of five aircraft would have been on the ground in the target zone and we would have been shredded by our own artillery. The damage would have been catastrophic. We would likely have lost five aircraft and upwards of 50 soldiers. Lieutenant Colonel Alves relieved the fire support officer over the radio, in the clear, and on the spot while still airborne; we all heard it. Rumor afterwards was that the fire support officer was court martialed for "dereliction of duty."

I never heard any more about the alleged court martial and never heard of friendly fire knocking down friendly aircraft. And while I never heard of any friendly fire incidents, it could have happened to us on that day. I do know of an incident where enemy artillery fire downed a Chinook on short final to a landing zone.

I think I may have used up another one of my nine lives on this mission, bringing me down to seven, and at such an early age!

Turn on the Lights!

Sometimes, in a weird way, "funny" things happen in a combat zone. Every night, our unit would have a quick reaction team consisting of two gunship aircraft and one aircraft designated as the flare ship on stand by. These aircraft would be pre-flighted and loaded with ammo and flares at completion of the daytime mission schedule. Because everything had been pre-set, the pilots just had to jump in the cockpit, pull the ignitor trigger, and bring the engine and rotor up to full operating rpm. The flare ship was loaded with 80 1-million candle-power flares stacked from floor to ceiling, "programmed" to be dropped from 3,500 feet above ground level. These high-intensity flares illuminated a large area, aiding both our ground troops and

Chapter 15

the gunship pilots in acquiring targets (this was a full 20 years before reliable night vision targeting devices).

On this particular night, February 22, 1969, I was assigned to be the lead pilot on the flare ship. The aircraft was pre-flighted, loaded with 80 flares to the rear of the pilot's seats, and then repositioned to a revetment nearest our operations tent where it would sit until needed. Most nights were uneventful; however, on this particular night a portion of our compound known as LZ Betty was overrun by enemy troops.

When the firefight started, the gunships and the flare ship were alerted to "scramble" to provide illumination and fire support to assist in repelling the attack. As soon as the alert siren went off, I grabbed my flight gear and sidearm and ran out to the flare aircraft. At the time the runway area was receiving small arms fire and it was of the green tracer variety, which is what the Viet Cong/North Vietnamese Army used versus the red tracer used by U.S. and South Vietnamese forces.

After arriving at the aircraft, I got into the pilot seat and started the quick-start procedure, and after what seemed like 20 minutes but in reality was likely less than a minute, no one else had arrived on the launch pad. I couldn't fly the mission by myself, as there was no way to drop the flares from the cockpit. Thinking the other assigned crewmen might have been injured in the ongoing

Vietnam, November 1, 1968: The Start of a Long Year!

attack, I ran back to the pilots' tent area and got my roommate, 1st Lieutenant Chris Fecher, AKA "Step and Fech it," to accompany me back to the flight line. He didn't hesitate for a second and together we ran back to the flare ship.

The first "funny" thing that occurred was that in the dark, Chris didn't see a sign that was "planted" right behind our tent and, as a result, he ran right into it and all his "flight stuff" went flying. The sign read "Trash Collection Point #32." You had to be there—did "Step and Fech it" really wipe out on the "Trash Collection" sign? Well, yes he did, and together we nonchalantly gathered up his gear under strange conditions, tracers flying and all, and finally made it back to the flare ship.

By then, Captain Bill Bauer, the 1st flight platoon commander, had jumped into the aircraft thinking that all the assigned crew had been injured. The three of us were relieved that we could now get moving with two pilots, Captain Bauer and yours truly up front (always good to have two in the front seat), and 1st Lieutenant Fecher serving as the crewman/flare dispenser. We briefly waited for the enlisted crewmen to arrive, but they did not show. Not wanting to be further delayed, we took off.

As we climbed to altitude, the 4.2 mortar positions were compromised, sustaining multiple U.S. casualties, after which the adjacent ammo dump was blown up. The

Chapter 15

blast was huge and it sent shrapnel and debris in a wide diameter, causing damage to five of our aircraft on the ground and on the other side of the airfield away from the mortar positions. The damage ranged from small shrapnel holes peppering the fuselage to whole unexploded 4.2 mortar shells ripping gaping holes completely through an aircraft. The whole situation is not "funny," but here we are at 3,000 feet and climbing, witnessing our compound being ripped by explosions and now realizing it is time to deploy the flares.

Well, none of us had ever set the timing device on the flare canister as this was always done by the crew chief, but tonight we three pilots were "solo." The instructions were printed, in small print, on the side of the flare, but the lighting was so bad, Fech couldn't read it. We had a flashlight up in the cockpit, so we passed it to Fech, who couldn't hold the flashlight on the instruction panel with one hand and manipulate the "arming" wheel with the other hand. He did the best he could under the circumstances, and so he "set" the arming device and started deploying flares over the side of the aircraft.

Flares were igniting at about 500 feet instead of the recommended 2,500 feet, and so they were hitting the ground starting fires and in fact burned down an outbuilding on the edge of the compound. Captain Bauer asked that I climb over the pilot seat and work with Fech.

Vietnam, November 1, 1968: The Start of a Long Year!

So as we used to say, "No shit, 3,000 feet without a clue." I held the flashlight and Fech was then able to work the arming device with both hands. After two more "misfires," our altitude adjustment got better as we figured out how to set the ignition height properly, and we deployed the remaining flares over the next two hours without further incident. We dropped upwards of 65 flares on the first go and then put in for fuel and additional flares.

By the time we arrived at the "hot refuel" point, the enlisted crewmen caught up to us. One of them had been wounded by shrapnel in the lower leg, and his colleague got him to the aid tent for a quick pressure bandage to stop the bleeding. That caused them to miss the mission initially, but hats off to them for reporting back after being attended to.

During this refuel and reload break between missions, a cook's helper from the mess hall ran out to our aircraft with sack lunches and canned soda. He jumped up on the skid and handed them up through the cockpit window and said something like, "We folks in the mess hall just wanted to help out and thought you guys would need something to eat and drink. We're thinkin' 'bout you." He also brought lunches to the gunship guys who were at a separate refueling pad. We all thought that was neat—nobody asked for the midnight "lunches" but someone in their chain of command wanted them to play their parts in helping the

Chapter 15

best they could during an attack on OUR compound. The cooks and bakers weren't pulling a trigger, but hey, they were doing their best! They stayed at their duty stations, working to get the breakfast meal ready for those who would be coming off the "front line." This positive, can-do attitude was prevalent throughout all the units I came into contact with during my time in Vietnam while flying with the 192nd Assault Helicopter Company supporting TF 3/506th (Currahee), 101st Airborne Division.

Our mission that night lasted four and a half hours and only terminated when the sun started to break over the South China Sea. Our perimeter had been breached at the 4.2 mortar ammo dump, and we suffered nine KIA. In addition, we lost two 4.2 mortars in the explosion of the ammo dump. Throughout the compound we also suffered more than 30 wounded and had four helicopters sustain significant damage, requiring evacuation to the States for repair of the combat damage. It was a helluva night, but not the only one of its type during my year with the 192nd.

A Surprise In-Country Reunion

Wayman Hedrick, my former roomate from flight school, found out my location while in Vietnam, and he visited with me during a few off days that he had coming. He caught a random flight from Pleiku in the Central

Vietnam, November 1, 1968: The Start of a Long Year!

Me with 1st Lieutenant Wayman Hedrick (left), Phan Thiet, Vietnam, 1969.

Highlands and stumbled into my location in Phan Thiet on the coast about a hundred miles north of Saigon. We had a good Army time together—you had to be there!

On Wayman's first night with us, we were awakened by a mortar attack. Aside from the ready reaction crews that manned the flare ship and the ready gunships, we sleeping unit members scrambled into our bunkers for cover. It wasn't so bad—we had a couple of warm Carling Black Labels and waited out the attack. When the "all clear" siren sounded, we went back to our bunks, undaunted. The good news was our damage assessment team determined there were no soldier casualties, nor was anything of importance hit by the barrage of about 40 mortar rounds. It seems the Viet Cong gunners only hit the runway a few times with no damage. Most of the rounds hit the garrison garbage dump—that's right, the garbage dump. It happened a lot during my tour.

Chapter 15

The following afternoon, I was part of a helicopter combat assault mission that Wayman volunteered for just to compare how our unit versus his unit performed these similar types of missions. We conducted two separate assaults and airlifted about 60 troopers into an area in the high country about 30 miles north of our airfield toward Da Lat. To my recollection, we did not receive any fire and all aircraft returned safely to base. That night, while hoisting a few warmish PBRs—yeah, I know, look it up—our commanding officer made Wayman an honorary member of our unit, the 192nd Assault Helicopter Company!

Wayman tragically died in an airplane crash in 2002. He was piloting a Stearman aerobatic bi-plane and he crashed outside of Birmingham, Alabama. I was at Ft. Rucker, Alabama, attending a business meeting relative to aircraft survivability equipment the day he died, and in one of those unexplainable moments in life, I heard on a local news station that a bi-plane had crashed, killing the pilot. When I heard that on the news, my jaw dropped and I just knew—I don't know why, but I just knew it was Wayman.

When I got back to the Pentagon later in the week, I was able to determine, through a friend at the FAA, that Wayman was indeed the pilot. Although we didn't see a lot of each other over the years, we did talk occasionally on the phone. It was always good to talk to him, and I can

Vietnam, November 1, 1968: The Start of a Long Year!

never get over how easily we could slip into conversation—like it had just been a week since our last talk. There's something about having served in the military together, knowing that your life might depend on one another someday, and, while that notion is never talked about or even acknowledged, it seems to be a main ingredient for making easy friends for life. I miss Wayman, and I will always consider him a good friend!

That "Ridiculous" Thing Called Guard Duty

Some weeks later, the 192nd Assault Helicopter Company's perimeter defensive area was probed by an unknown-sized Viet Cong/North Vietnamese Army force. It was standard operating procedure for all units stationed at the Phan Thiet airfield to be responsible for a portion of the perimeter. The size and location of the perimeter to be guarded was likely based on unit size and perhaps expertise, as in combat "acuity."

The 192nd was assigned an area that was directly adjacent to our cantonment area and which sat on a cliff roughly 150 feet above the beach. We had two fortified towers directly above the cliffs oriented toward the ocean and three additional fortified bunkers that were oriented to the south along the beach and slightly more toward a flat plateau. I knew the area well, as one of my "extra" duties was that of perimeter defense officer, likely because I was

Chapter 15

commissioned infantry and, of course, because of that, as a 2nd lieutenant of infantry, I had it down—right!

Well, early on in my tour, one of my "trusted" 21-year-old sergeants and I surveyed the bunkers and developed defensive position "range cards." The cards were laminated and placed in the bunkers for reference. The information on the cards laid out grazing fire lanes, terrain dead space, areas to be covered by indirect fire, overlapping fire lines, and final defensive fire lines so that all positions could support and be supported one to another.

We also coordinated with our "organic" engineers for the emplacement of Claymore mines, and something called FUE gas, which was a mixture of aviation gas and a gelatin additive. This concoction was poured into a half-full

This perimeter tower was attacked with RPG and small arms fire in June 1969. There were two towers and three bunkers in our area. Our "guards" repulsed a determined VC attack for which all 15 men were awarded the Bronze Star for Valor. Ten of these men also received the Purple Heart Medal for having been wounded in action. Their actions that night likely saved many lives.

55-gallon drum that would be placed facing the enemy's approach "lane." When ignited with a block of C4 explosive, it created a large Napalm-type (read firebomb) explosion.

The Claymores and the FUE gas were ignited with an "electric" striker type device, which was initiated by those manning the bunkers. All this work putting this "defensive" plan together seemed benign as we went for five months with nothing at all happening. So, the guard duty became tedious and the maintenance required to keep things in tune and reliable was time consuming. Then all of a sudden one night—WHAM!

The center bunker was hit with a B-40 rocket-propelled grenade, wounding all three occupants. That brought all five bunkers on line in rapid succession and, within minutes, all the bunkers in our defensive area were under attack and receiving small arms fire and either 60mm mortar fire or grenade fire. In turn, our guys were returning fire with M-16 rifles and M-60 machine guns, and at some point at different times in the attack, they employed the Claymores and the FUE gas.

Our ops center scrambled the guns and the flare ship and in 15–20 minutes after the attack was initiated, they were on station and providing support. The 4.2 mortar platoon, which only three weeks earlier had suffered terrible losses during a similar attack, also provided indirect

Chapter 15

fire support with continuous fire along the approaches from the beach up to our barbed wire line.

This firefight lasted just under two hours and was chaotic. At one point, the bunkers requested an ammunition resupply and our officer of the day, who was in charge of the nightly posting of the guard, along with the sergeant of the guard, delivered ammo, water, dry rations, and "new" barrels for the machine guns while under constant fire moving along the bunker line. No other area in the perimeter was affected, and the best we could determine was that the enemy may have "thought" they could breach an area that was likely inadequately defended. Had they breached our area, they might have been able to destroy any number of aircraft and maybe ransack the pilots' living area, inflicting significant casualties. All of that would have been possible except for the "alertness" of the 15 soldiers on guard duty.

The determined defense of our bunker line guards, consisting of mechanics, prop and rotor techs, fuel analysis specialists, and a couple of cooks…yes cooks…saved the day! The nightly guard duty roster was made up of men from all the units' specialties and aviation units had a strange variety of what's called military operational specialties, or MOSs for short. Amongst our men, we suffered 10 wounded, none life threatening, and thankfully, none KIA. All of these soldiers were awarded the Bronze

Star with V device for Valor. Well deserved! Viet Cong casualties were 17 KIA and many blood trails leading away from the area, which seemed to indicate numerous wounded had been removed.

It was hard to tell, but a bunch of us living in that area who were sleeping at the time of the attack probably owe our lives to soldiers performing "moronic" guard duty the way it should be performed. Guard duty is something that is drilled into soldiers from the time you enter basic training. Most often, it is scoffed at as being "ridiculous"—here I am sitting in a tower overlooking the South China Sea at 0200 hours…nobody out here but me…think I'll go to sleep. BOOM!!!! While in Vietnam, I heard of Korean soldiers being executed at their post by their officer of the guard for falling asleep during guard duty, which jeopardized the entire command. Seems extremely harsh, doesn't it? But culturally, and in their Army, it wasn't even questioned.

Song Mao—Like My Father Used To Say, Nothing Good Happens After Midnight!

On a hot, humid, and stormy night in early August 1969 during the monsoon season, our unit's Ready Reaction Team of two UH-1C Tiger Shark gunships and two UH-1H Huey troopships was alerted to get ready for a quick departure to extract a U.S. Army Ranger

Chapter 15

detachment. This group of eight men from the 75th Ranger Regiment was in contact (a firefight) with the enemy, which had already resulted in two friendly KIA. I was assigned as a pilot in the lead gunship along with Chief Warrant Officer 2 Don Hancock, who would be the aircraft commander. The time was 0040 hours—really o'dark thirty!

This Ranger recon element had been inserted three days earlier into an area near Song Mao, roughly 12 miles southeast of Da Lat. Their mission was to recon and observe suspected infiltration routes that spun off the Ho Chi Minh trail, about 100 miles to the west. During these types of operations, our unit would be tasked to provide dedicated 24-hour emergency support so that if the mission had been compromised or the unit became engaged we could extract them.

Hueys from the 192nd Assault Helicopter Company, Song Mao, Vietnam, 1969.

Vietnam, November 1, 1968: The Start of a Long Year!

The established procedure for operations of this type was to have a "dedicated open" radio monitoring a single frequency in our air operations center (actually a general-purpose medium tent located at the north end of the Phan Thiet airfield). A single "listener" would be posted to the radio set 24 hours per day with the sole responsibility of monitoring any and all voice traffic coming over the designated frequency. In addition, air crews were on standby with aircraft pre-flighted and loaded, ready to be airborne in 10 minutes from notification to go.

So, this evening, our listener detected very low speech tones in English. What he was hearing was a call for immediate extraction, as the Ranger unit had been uncovered by an enemy patrol. A firefight broke out and the friendlies, our guys, had already sustained two KIA with several other team members suffering minor wounds. At the time of this call, they were "escaping and evading" to a prominent hilltop roughly 100 meters from the contact position, all the while carrying their dead through very rough terrain. With that info, our aircraft were dispatched to effect an extraction of the Ranger team. Our flight of four helicopters would join with and be accompanied and supported by one O1 fire support fixed-winged aircraft, whose operator and observer could provide artillery support if necessary, and an Air Force C-47 "Spooky" gunship with its dual rapid-fire mini-guns capable of delivering a large

Chapter 15

volume of suppressive fire on target. This type aircraft was a converted WWII cargo plane that was equipped with door-mounted 7.62mm mini-guns with an almost unlimited amount of ammunition and the capability of remaining on station for six to seven hours at a time.

Our 20-minute flight to the contact area was horrendous! The rain was so heavy it sounded as if we were being hit with hail, which gave you the feeling something was going to break—such as windscreens, the pitot tube (which tells how fast you are flying—important stuff), communications antennas, or, worse yet, rotor blades. Especially disconcerting was the potential for losing the tail rotor, which was possible under such conditions and which would have been catastrophic.

The visibility was down to zero, and although we were not on an "instrument flight plan," we were flying "instruments only" with no outside visual references for the better part of the flight. We had our top side rotating red lens beacons on in hopes that at least the other aircraft could see us and we them. The problem with that was it caused a phenomenon called "flicker vertigo," due to the spinning rotor blades and intermittent red light that was reflected into the cockpit, producing a whirling "disco ball" effect. This, coupled with the cockpit interior red and yellow lights on the dash, can cause one to lose visual perspective, become confused, and generally make one feel

Vietnam, November 1, 1968: The Start of a Long Year!

sideways with what's really happening with the aircraft. It can cause everything to go to hell very quickly and can be fatal while flying; think loss of control and inability to believe your instruments because your body, your sense of balance, is telling you differently.

Well, there we were, and we were fighting it and helping each other—calling out airspeed and altitude, turn and slip rate, wings level per the attitude indicator—while being ever mindful of the potential for one or both of us being victimized by "vertigo." And in addition to all this, we were monitoring three radio frequencies and attempting to establish contact with the Air Force Spooky, which, we hoped, would guide us into the general area. I had visions of six aircraft all flying to the same "spot," and because none of us could see the other, we all might literally just fly into each other. That thought, accompanied by a mental picture, kept rolling around in my head—who knows!

The good news was that my aircraft commander was Chief Warrant Officer 2 Don Hancock, a big burly "old salt" of a guy from Arkansas who I always looked forward to sharing flight duties with. Don was cool, with good piloting instincts and he knew the business. What more could I ask for? I was his co-pilot that night and would be working the mini-guns while Don was in charge of piloting the aircraft and firing the 28 17-pound rockets (meaning they had a 17-pound warhead). We also

Chapter 15

had two full up and ready door gunners manning M-60 door-mounted 7.62mm machine guns, and this wasn't their first rodeo.

So we were "dead reckoning" flying "time and distance" into an ongoing firefight with weather that was still bad when all of a sudden this very commanding voice breaks over our UHF radio: "Tiger Shark lead this is Spooky 12345, acknowledge." Don was flying so I answered with a snappy, "Spooky, this is Tiger Shark lead, acknowledged." "Tiger Shark, Spooky, I'm at flight level 7.5 'angels' and orbiting the target zone. I have a visual on six aircraft well below my flight level, and I can clearly see your rotating beacons. You are about 10 miles south of the target and you should be breaking out of the weather shortly."

Don and I briefly shot a glance at each other and said something like…was that the voice of GOD masquerading as a Spooky pilot? If it was, it couldn't have come at a better time for us. And then, almost on cue, we broke out of the foul weather into a crystal clear 15-mile wide "shaft" of clear air with thunder and lightning well to our west. We could see stars, and we even had a visual on Spooky. Still think God's not on our side? Well, Spooky sorted us all out and had us establish contact with the Rangers on the ground. We coordinated with them and affirmed their position when they deployed a "railroad" flare at center of mass. Once confirmed, we asked them where they were receiving fire from, telling them that we could suppress with mini-gun and rockets and that our wingman could lay down 40mm high explosive rounds along with door-mounted M-60 machine gun suppressive fire. In addition, the Spooky aircraft would provide continuous illumination with big flares and suppressive fire on locations away from the contact point.

When they returned the communication, we could hear the chaotic sounds of close contact—yelling in both English and some other indistinguishable language, the sound of crackling gunfire and muffled explosions, and the heavy breathing and tense, almost desperate tone in the ground guy's voice. On our first pass he wanted us to put mini-gun fire (me) 15 meters from the railroad flare on an azimuth (compass heading) of 60 degrees from the friendly location center of mass. That was really close to their location, 50–55 feet. Trying to shoot that close at night from a bouncing and "skidding" helicopter, flying at about 110 knots, in a shallow dive under the dim light of aerial flares, punctuated by outbound and inbound red and green tracers, was going to be a real "trick"!

We set up our gun run perpendicular to the ground guys' location, which was a smallish circle of men oriented north (on our right in the approach to target) toward the imminent threat. We needed to be perpendicular to their location so that when we fired the mini-gun, the "beaten

Chapter 15

path" or kill zone of our fire would not be coming in over their heads; ideally, it would be offset and slightly away from the friendlies and coming in on the enemies' heads. As we started our gun run, we alerted them to the fact that we would commence firing in xx seconds and when finished we would break right and away from their location. My heart was in my throat and my stomach was in a knot, not because we were flying in "harm's way," but because everything was so close that we could very well hit friendlies on the first burst.

We were followed by our wingman, who fired up an area adjacent to our target with 40mm. He would also cover us in our break from the contact zone, and we would do the same for him when he finished his run. The ground guy's response to our first gun run was ecstatic; he screamed into the radio handset and said we "hit 'em right in the freaking forehead." Thank you, God, I said to myself, and to say the least, I was relieved—and then the ground guy came back on the air and wanted us to DO IT AGAIN!

While we guns were working the target, a single ship Huey helicopter was approaching the contact area looking for an opening in the tree cover to drop a rope ladder down to the friendly forces. When the helicopter crew made visual contact, they hovered over the trees and received a heavy volume of fire opposite of where the gunships had prepped. The lift aircraft broke away and down the hill to

Vietnam, November 1, 1968: The Start of a Long Year!

assess for damage. Although they had been hit in the cockpit area, they determined that all critical components were operational and no flight personnel had been wounded. With that, they decided to attempt the extraction from a different direction. On this approach, they arrived over our troops and dropped the ladder through the tree top canopy. It never made it to the ground, and in fact had to be cut from the aircraft as it was severely tangled and ultimately could have caused the aircraft to crash.

Without a method for lifting the troops out, and with no area large enough to land, this aircraft had to redraw from the area. As the lift ship was departing the contact area, our gunship team shifted suppressive fire efforts to the reverse side of the hill to beat down the enemy fire that had hampered the first attempt at extraction. As the first airlift aircraft was departing, Don contacted the ground guy and relayed the situation to him, saying we had another lift aircraft inbound but we needed for the ground guys to move up the hill about 100 meters to a seemingly sparsely treed area. From our perspective, it appeared that the lift ship would be able to get a ladder down to the ground at that location with limited interference.

The ground guys understood and they started moving. We emphasized to them that we needed this evacuation to happen on the next pass, because after that the guns would need fuel and ammo, which meant we would have to depart

Chapter 15

the area. If that should happen, they would be somewhat uncovered, save for the Spooky aircraft, for a longer period of time than any of us wanted. That would not be good.

OK, so here we go. Lift ship was coming in, and we picked him up about two miles out and escorted to the contact zone, providing suppressive fire as we approached. We broke off the target and then our wingman picked up the fire support. The airlift ship got over the troops and again received ground fire, the green tracer type, which resulted in the pilot initiating a severe control over correction, which again caused the ladder to get hung up in the trees. This time, however, the airlift crew chief was able to free up the ladder and retract into the aircraft.

After this, we all "gathered" up on the radio and coordinated one more attempt at the evacuation. The airlift ship established another pattern into the area, and we guns established our gun support pattern. Right about when we were to commence the third attempt, my wingman called us and said he would have to depart the area for fuel. What that meant was we would have to cover the extraction with one gunship. Tactically, that was considered a no-no, because you can't provide adequate support as a team of one—there would be a big gap in coverage. You would also be very vulnerable to enemy fire. The enemy was smart to that, and when a one shipper would finish its pass, the enemy would concentrate its fire on the single departing gunship, without fear of being "caught" by the now-departed "covering" wingman.

Tactical no-no or not, Don and I thought our ship had enough fuel to complete one more attempt and still make it back to the nearest Special Forces base for fuel—or so we thought. We turned outbound and picked up the incoming lift ship again, and so as he was letting down into the area we provided suppressive fire parallel to his approach path. A thousand feet above us, our Spooky friend had dropped down to about 2,500 feet and was "hosing" down the opposite side of the incoming ship's approach path with a heavy volume of mini-gun fire. In essence, when the big C-47 Spooky gunship joined in providing suppressive fire, we became a very "unbalanced" two-ship gun team—maybe a first! I'm sure that was something to see and, as a result, our combined efforts gave the lift ship a clear path into the pick-up zone.

We loitered in the vicinity at about 150 feet with our door gunners responding to any sporadic enemy fire. These efforts effectively eliminated close-in fire, which gave the lift ship some breathing room. Out the door came the steel wire 100-foot ladder into the outstretched arms of the ground troops. Anchored by two soldiers on the ground, I could see another two soldiers scramble up the ladder into the aircraft followed by two more who "hooked" onto the ladder near the fuselage.

Chapter 15

Things were getting tense—four aboard with four to go, two of which were KIA. About this time, our 20-minute fuel warning light illuminated, meaning we had 20 minutes of fuel remaining—FUDGE! We were about 20 minutes to the nearest refueling point. What this meant was we needed to leave the area now, but we couldn't leave now and we sure as hell couldn't stay much longer! I punched the clock and started watching the time—we only had 20 minutes until out of fuel. Recognizing the severity of the situation, Don and I decided to reduce the engine power to a level just sufficient to maintain flight in the hope of saving some fuel and extending our time on station.

In what seemed like a long time, the two soldiers on the ground lashed the KIAs to the bottom of the ladder and then scrambled up and hooked themselves onto an upper portion of the ladder. The crew chief signaled the pilot that all were aboard, and the pilot slowly picked the aircraft up to a high hover. Making sure the ladder was well clear of all trees and while taking sporadic gunfire, the pilot nosed the aircraft over and off they went. I'll never forget—meaning I have an image burned in my brain, this Huey flying at 1,200 feet at maybe 40–50 knots with a ladder dangling from the fuselage with six very brave American soldiers hanging below and silhouetted against a pitch dark sky by the dying glow of "flares" dropped from our Spooky friend.

Vietnam, November 1, 1968: The Start of a Long Year!

Two lifeless forms and four very much alive and exhausted men just suspended in the dark over a strange land a long way from home. Seeing that Huey lift off and knowing we had "saved" six Americans with no further losses was a feeling I can't describe. It didn't always happen that way.

I never could find out who the Spooky pilot was, but the picture in my mind is that of an older, weather-beaten, likely lieutenant colonel, U.S. Air Force, who was probably a WWII vet. I suspect he had been flying C-47s for some time, and I imagine he had 20,000 hours of total flight time. He had a grandfather's radio voice with just the right touch to calm down 10 or so much younger Army pilots on a horrific night that produced great results!

Back in our cockpit, we are now 11 minutes into our 20-minute fuel warning light, which means theoretically we need to be on the ground in at least 9 minutes—but we're still 14–17 minutes out! Once the airstrip came into sight, Don maintained a 60-knot flight profile with approximately 750 feet of altitude, which would allow us, we thought at the time, the best chance of executing an autorotation to the ground in the event we lost our engine. At roughly a mile and a quarter out from the runway threshold, we started a fast "steep" descent through the "dead man's curve" to 100 feet while bringing our airspeed back to 40–50 knots with the intention of conducting a running landing.

Chapter 15

So, no shit, here we are, about to execute a 40–50 knot running landing to an unlighted airstrip, save a lone Special Forces Jeep shining its lights down the approach path. The runway was constructed of linked metal plates, which meant it would be like landing on an ice hockey rink. It got real quiet, very tense, and very heavy into concentration in the cockpit for the last two to four minutes. I was calling out airspeed, altitude, instrument readings, and "positive encouragement" while Don was flying. We crossed over the runway threshold and smacked that Huey down while doing 40 knots, sliding the length of the airstrip amid sparks, smoke, and a God-awful screeching sound. All the time, both of us were pulling pitch and easing the cyclic back to slow things down while also working the tail rotor control pedals to maintain heading as best we could. We finally ground to a halt, literally, when we hit the dirt off the end of the runway.

To our amazement, and delight, the engine was still running. We did not run out of fuel, and we flew 27 minutes into the 20-minute fuel warning light, or better put, we were 7 minutes over the limit and should have lost our engine due to fuel starvation. I'm sure glad the fuel low warning gauge, the BIG RED light, and the sensing unit were provided to the government by the lowest bidder—must have been somewhat defective or was it something else? Still believe God's not on our side?

Vietnam, November 1, 1968: The Start of a Long Year!

Shortly after we came to a stop, the Special Forces unit sergeant major came barreling down the runway in a Jeep pulling a trailer full of ice and cold beer. He was ecstatic; we were beyond that! I don't think I ever sweated so much; our flight suits were ringing wet with sweat, and we each probably lost a couple of pounds, which we replaced quickly with a couple of cold Ballantine's, brewed by P. Ballantine & Sons, Newark, New Jersey. How fitting and ironic for a Jersey boy! Oh, by the way, I burned off another one of my "allotted" nine lives; I think I was now down to six left.

While refueling and checking for damage, we discovered one bullet hole through the pilot side skid, one bullet hole through the rotor blades, and two bullet holes through the pilot side rocket pod. There was no apparent damage from our "fast" run on landing except for excessive wear on the "skid shoes"; guess we did it just right! All in all, we were very lucky considering all the multi-colored tracers that were flying around.

After our crew chief "repaired" the bullet hole in the rotor blades with "hundred mile an hour tape," we cranked up and headed back to Phan Thiet at sunrise, no worse for wear! It was a beautiful flight back to home base—Vietnam could be beautiful! The flight took about 35 minutes, and with the sun coming up over the South China Sea, the white ribbon of beach stretching as far as you could see, and the water-filled rice paddies shimmering in the first rays of

Chapter 15

sunlight, we each remarked that this place had the potential, at some point, for becoming a vacation spot. And after the war, it did just that! We landed at home base, wrote up the mission, checked the aircraft one more time, signed it off, and as a crew headed to the mess hall for a well-deserved breakfast!

It was an interesting place, this semi-permanent mess hall in a combat zone charged with dispensing probably 3,000 meals a day. It never shut down, was at work 24 hours a day, and because we had aircraft mechanics and guard personnel on duty throughout the night, the mess hall was knocking out pretty good food at all hours. What a difference two and a half hours makes! We went from really worrying about running out of fuel and maybe losing our lives to a hot breakfast served at four-person tables with tablecloths and flowers, fresh coffee served by dining room orderlies, and a day-old copy of the *Stars and Stripes* newspaper. The biggest decision of that morning for us would be deciding how we wanted our eggs and whether with pancakes or waffles! I took the scrambled eggs with pancakes. Talk about weird!

It really gets weird when you leave Vietnam for an R&R and end up in someplace like Singapore or Hong Kong—weird with a big dose of culture shock thrown in!

Fast-forward to around 1985. I was an Army aviation staff officer assigned to the Pentagon within the

Vietnam, November 1, 1968: The Start of a Long Year!

organization known as the G-3 (Operations). The motto of this organization is "War is hell, G-3 is a sonofabitch, and then you die" (dark military humor, except no one was laughing). It was no-fun duty, but it's what made the Army go. We were the people who developed the plans and funding requirements for what the future Army should look like and what equipment it would/should have to fight a future enemy.

Oh, and by the way, Army staff worked in concert with other Department of Defense organizations to determine who most likely would be the enemy. During my time there, Russia was enemy #1, followed by China and to a lesser degree Iran.

In the end, it was all about the budget and the Joint Staff (read the other services) and the Congress (read the purse strings). It was stressful and the joke to myself was that I had more time off in Vietnam than while in the Pentagon. Don't misunderstand, in Vietnam, we were "on duty 24/7" but there were slack times, crew rest because of excessive flight hours, bad weather days, aircraft down for maintenance, and so on. You could catch your breath, and I suppose one could say there was almost a normalcy to the organized chaos that was going on around us.

Here's maybe the difference: At one particular period during a budget cycle, the group I was assigned to was scheduled to brief Army Vice Chief of Staff General

Chapter 15

Maxwell Thurman, a single man who was "married" to the Army and who some doubted had a mother. The briefings were to be completed late on the Saturday before Mother's Day; however, things got real convoluted relative to the Army's "newly" conceived Comanche helicopter gunship program, and as a result we had almost a full day's worth of briefings to go. When we were dismissed early on Saturday evening, we were instructed to report back to the conference room at 0800 hours the next morning, Mother's Day. When General Thurman was reminded by his aide that reporting back for duty that early on Mother's Day would likely disrupt a fair amount of family plans, he agreed and told his aide to move up the report time to 1000 hours—get what I mean, pretty big of him, a whole "extra" two hours with the family.

And oh, in the mid 1980s we weren't in a shooting war with anyone! We briefed until 1800 hours that day and picked up again in the Pentagon at 0600 on Monday morning. General Thurman wasn't what I would call a real people person, but he was sharp as a tack and 125% dedicated to making "his" Army the Best it Could Be! Taxpayers couldn't have asked for more.

So that's the environment I was in through the 1980s. In another weird sort of way, it was exciting. We were contributing to something that would shape the future of Army aviation, and we needed to get it right. It was not an easy task in that we weren't working with absolutes, such as "if you do this, this will be the guaranteed outcome." There were no guarantees in this business. For the most part, however, we did get it right. This was the time when the AH-64 Apache attack helicopter (gunship and tank killer) was brought into the force along with an upgraded version of the OH-58 Kiowa, a light helicopter that mounted a target-designating "Mast Mounted LASER."

The OH-58 Kiowa worked in concert with the AH-64 Apache and its LASER designated (spotted) the target for the Apache's Hellfire guided missiles, which, during the Iraq War, decimated the early warning radar systems and tank columns arrayed across the desert in the opening hours of Operation Desert Storm. In addition, during this time the Army developed an "extended" life program for the CH-47 Heavy Lift Chinook helicopter. This aircraft is the "gold standard" for helicopters of this type and is still in operation today more than 50 years after first entering service with the Army. How's that for taxpayers getting their money's worth? Another success story in my world is the B-52—and while an Air Force "system," that aircraft in one configuration or another has been in service for almost 70 years and remains relevant today!

OK, so, one day in late 1985/early 1986, I was stuck in traffic on I-395 south out of the Pentagon with four other "car poolers," all Army pilots and Vietnam vets. As was the

Chapter 15

case, we start telling war stories and Lieutenant Colonel Ken McGinty, from some "gadawful" place in central Texas, mentions actions surrounding one horrendous night outside of a place called Song Mao. He goes on to describe how his team had suffered two KIA in an ambush on a very bad night and that his prospects were not looking good. Then "wah-lah," all of a sudden the "cavalry" arrived in the form of Huey gunships, a couple of lift ships, a U.S. Air Force Spooky gunship, and artillery spotting/observation aircraft, all on scene to support him and his beleaguered team.

Sounded reeeeeal familiar to me, and I looked across at Ken and asked if he was involved, as in, were you there? He said, was I there?! I was the 2nd lieutenant with the 75th Rangers on the ground, and I was there and in up to my neck! We locked eyes, and I told him that I was in the lead Tiger Shark gunship that provided fire support for him and in fact I may have talked to him over the FM radio that night 16 years earlier. We couldn't believe it! We kept telling the story over and over, "fleshing" it out and everything matched up, it was true, we were both there and in up to our necks!

McGinty attended flight school after returning from his ground tour in Vietnam, and he went on to serve a tour as an Army helicopter pilot in a second go-around in Vietnam. At the time we were together in the Pentagon, he

Vietnam, November 1, 1968: The Start of a Long Year!

was the program officer for the Army's "new" AH-64 attack helicopter, which is the premier attack helicopter in the world today. Sometimes the way things turn out is really hard to believe.

A New Aircraft Pick Up— What's That Got to Do With LBJ?

At some point in mid spring of 1969, I was asked by our then ops officer, 1st Lieutenant Brown, to accompany him on a trip up north to Da Nang to pick up a "new" rebuilt aircraft for our unit. This is something that occurred throughout the year I was in Vietnam. It was an "admin" type duty so to speak as we would, in essence, only be ferrying the aircraft back to our home base. We would be responsible, along with a technical inspector from depot maintenance in Da Nang, for ensuring all the aircraft equipment was on board and that a thorough pre-flight and short "test" flight was conducted prior to acceptance by 1st Lieutenant Brown as the senior flight officer in charge.

The trip to Da Nang included catching a ride on an Air Force aircraft out of Phan Thiet to Da Nang via two stops along the way. At one point, we had to "change" flights as the aircraft we had been on had a mission change and would now be going in the other direction. Not knowing our way around this particular airfield location, we sought the assistance of the first airman off the C-130, asking him

Chapter 15

for the whereabouts of "base ops." He told us to follow him up to the little shack that was air ops and, once there, he asked the flight scheduler to help us Army guys out. Upon doing so, we thanked him for his help and we all wished each other well.

It turns out that the Air Force sergeant who helped us was the C-130's loadmaster, whose name (on his uniform name tag) was Nugent. He had looked familiar to me and so I asked the air ops people about him, and they told me that he was Sergeant Pat Nugent, a son-in-law to President Lyndon B. Johnson. I had read somewhere that Nugent was in the Air Force, but I didn't know he was in Vietnam. I looked at 1st Lieutenant Brown and said, "I knew he looked familiar to me," followed by a "How 'bout that, LBJ's son-in-law!"

In a war as weird as the Vietnam War was, it was interesting to know that there were people who likely could have gotten out of serving but apparently chose not to. And Pat Nugent wasn't the only "first family" member serving. His brother-in-law, Major Charles "Chuck" Robb, married to LBJ's oldest daughter, was also serving in Vietnam with the Marine Corps. So, the Johnson family had "skin" in the game and they knew about the anguish families back home were enduring while dreading that knock on the front door by a uniformed service member!

Vietnam, November 1, 1968: The Start of a Long Year!

We arrived in Da Nang late afternoon and made overnight arrangements in the Air Force bachelor officer quarters. We stored our gear, took a "hot" shower, you know, Air Force, and went to the O Club for dinner. Well, to our surprise, a good surprise, it had happy hour every day followed by steaks to order at 6 cents an ounce—that's right, 6 cents an ounce or 96 cents a pound! We looked at each other in unison and said, "Incredible, we're in the wrong branch of service." As far as we could tell, the only thing this Air Force base was missing in a combat zone was a golf course with the appropriate clubhouse—I suspected the funding request was winding its way through channels seeking Congressional approval!

We hit the rack early and had an early wake up call to start our long day and flight back to Phan Thiet. The acceptance process went well with only a few minor hiccups and we were off the helipad at "Red Beach" in late morning. Our flight route back to home base would take us down the coast along the beach and slightly offshore, with planned stops for fuel at Chu Lai, LZ English, Tuy Hoa, and Dong Ba Thin near Cam Ranh Bay.

The beaches were beautiful and from 2,000 feet up it was hard to believe there was a war going on. We pointed out to each other the areas that would likely become "resorts" after hostilities ceased, and the future has seen resort hotels with accompanying golf courses

Chapter 15

spring up in more than a half dozen of those places. Just adds to the whole thing about trying to get your head around that war!

The Battleship USS New Jersey

In the March to April 1969 timeframe, the Battleship USS *New Jersey* moved from off the coast of Da Nang and points north to assume seaborne patrol duty and provide fire support missions to ground elements within our area of operations. The *New Jersey* had the largest ship-mounted guns in the world at the time: nine 16-inchers surrounded by about 20 five-inch gun batteries of two guns per. The main shell on the 16-inch guns was the "size of a Volkswagen," and it could fire these projectiles out to 25 miles with incredible accuracy.

When the USS *New Jersey* arrived off the coast of Phan Thiet, the "new" commander of the TF 3/506, Lieutenant Colonel Bauer, callsign "Rattlesnake," requested to fly out to the ship with his fire support group to meet with members of the ship's Naval Gun Fire Support Coordination Team. The request was granted and we, the 192nd Attack Helicopter Company, were tasked to provide an aircraft to transport a group of eight men from the TF 3/506 to the *New Jersey*. At the time, our commanding officer thought it would be neat if we could assemble an "all New Jersey" native flight crew to man the aircraft. We came up with three "native" New Jersey crewmen, and I was one of the pilots along with native Californian, Captain Bill Bauer, my flare ship partner from an earlier experience. To land on a ship, and this was one of the biggest in the world, was an experience we Army guys were really looking forward to.

And so, with no advanced training, and never having landed on a ship before, we flew about five miles off the coast and contacted the ship's operations control center for clearance to land. Pretty cool sequence of radio calls followed that went something like this:

"USS *New Jersey*, this is Polecat 3, request permission to land on your aft heliport."

The mighty USS *New Jersey* in all her glory off the coast of Phan Thiet, Vietnam, March 1969. We landed on the aft deck shortly after this picture was taken.

Chapter 15

"Polecat 3, permission granted to land on the aft fantail heliport. Contact heliport control on VHF frequency 118.5. Have a good day, sir!"

"USS *New Jersey* heliport control, this is Polecat 3 inbound to your location. Request landing instructions please."

"Roger that Polecat 3. Ever landed on a ship before?"

"No, sir!"

"Roger that, then listen up and strictly follow my instructions. Establish your downwind entry amidships at 1,000 feet indicated. For you ground guys, amidships is the center of that big beautiful 998-foot-long 'battleship' you are now pointing your Polecat nose at. It is also home to 3,600 proud American sailors. After you establish your downwind entry maneuver, initiate your crosswind turn to final as appropriate for an aircraft of your type.

Once on your final approach, align with the big white H at the center of the 'bullseye' on the fantail. For you Army guys, the 'fantail' is the big flat spot in front of the biggest shipboard guns in the world. Once aligned, establish a steeper than normal approach and be sure to stay clear of the crane at the very rear of the ship. It doesn't like Army helicopters, and it knows the difference between Army and Navy.

Also be mindful of the 8-foot seas the ship is currently cruising through. The wave action has a tendency to cause

Vietnam, November 1, 1968: The Start of a Long Year!

the ship to jump up and 'snatch' Army helicopters out of the air. Word of caution, if you damage your Polecat landing gear we have no replacement parts or a place to put 12 green guys up for the night. Have a good day, sir, and enjoy your stay on the mighty USS *New Jersey!*"

"Roger that heliport control. This is Polecat 3 turning crosswind to final at this time!"

There was not much we could say to that, and yes the big ship did come up and "snatch" us out of the air just like we were told it would. After touching down, a clean as a whistle Marine lieutenant came out, gathered up the air crew, and took us to lunch. The fire support guys went in another direction and off to work. We had a quickie lunch in what looked like the Marine section of a mess hall, and those who joined us thought it was novel to meet soldiers who had actually set foot on the ground in Vietnam. We thought they were novel too, and we liked their living quarters—air conditioned with two crew swimming pools on the quarterdecks (I have the pictures).

After lunch we were brought up to a deck level above the gun turrets and "watched" a fire support demonstration, which had all nine of the 16-inch guns fire together. When they were fired, this 70,000-ton ship moved sideways, noticeably, through the water, creating giant "whirlpools" at either end of the ship. The guns on that ship were an

Chapter 15

attention getter and the noise was deafening to the point of being disorienting.

Where is the mighty USS *New Jersey* today you ask? It is currently moored and on "display," open for tours in Camden, New Jersey, across the Delaware River and in plain sight of Philadelphia! It is one of America's most decorated "Hero Ships" and served in WWII, as Admiral Halsey's flagship, Korea, Vietnam, Lebanon, and the War on Terror in Iraq.

Navy SEALs and Army Helo Pilots— Working Together

In late spring of 1969, a Navy SEAL team deployed to our airfield with the mission of conducting "covert" operations. Our unit, the 192nd Attack Helicopter Company, was designated to provide tactical airlift and gunship support. The reputation of the SEALs preceded their arrival, and we Army aviation unit members thought it would be interesting duty to support them. It was interesting and very hush-hush, to the point that if you weren't involved directly, then you didn't have a need to know. I was the aviation ops officer at the time so I had a need to know.

I worked with the SEAL commander in setting up the aviation support he needed, such as how many lift ships, time and distance of flights, need for fuel, gunship

Vietnam, November 1, 1968: The Start of a Long Year!

coordination, disguising our movement, and routes in and out. The SEAL team group consisted of about 40 total people with only four Americans, the actual SEALs, and they were the commander, his XO, and two senior Navy enlisted men. They were very stand-offish and didn't mingle with us Army guys except to conduct operations. They were very professional and proficient in the conduct of their ops, and they never wore rank or any other type of ID. All four were very "weather beaten" from, I'm sure, many days in the heat of the jungle and blinding sunny days at sea.

The remaining members of the group were an odd collection of Montagnards, Chinese Nungs, and Malays, all mercenaries of sorts. The Montagnards had "skin" in the game and were indigenous to Vietnam from the highlands. They were distinctly different looking than "lowland" Vietnamese, and they spoke a variety of languages and dialects that made them all the more different. They reportedly didn't like the South Vietnamese government and they "hated" the North Vietnamese government. Our government, along with the South Vietnamese, "promised" them "things," such as money, medical support, some sort of autonomy, and land in return for them actively fighting against the north.

Well, when the North Vietnamese overturned the South Vietnamese government, we hung them out to dry.

Chapter 15

It seems we're good at that. The Nungs and the Malays were, for the most part, "soldiers of fortune," and were likely in it for whatever they could get—spoils of war. When the south fell, they were all long gone and likely out of harm's way. The Montagnards paid dearly at the hands of the North Vietnamese for supporting both us Americans and the South Vietnamese.

One particular mission in support of the Navy SEAL contingent comes to mind, not so much for working with the SEALs but because of the wants and desires of our unit commander, who we'll call Major "Dull." He took command of our unit from a really fine commander, Major Bob Elliot, who was summoned to duty in Saigon after only four months in command of our unit. Major Elliot was liked by all and sorely missed. Major Dull's first edict upon arriving at the 192nd was to declare, "There'll be no aircraft accidents on my watch" and "Such incidents will be severely dealt with," as if being in an aircraft accident wasn't severe enough!

Accidents happened under the best of circumstances and in the most conscientious of units. Unfortunately, it was the nature of the business—or is it the beast?—with things such as combat conditions, weather, maintenance, fatigue that starts looking like carelessness, vertigo that can be brought on by any number of reasons, and sometimes just plain bad luck! My unit lost more people to "accidents"

Vietnam, November 1, 1968: The Start of a Long Year!

that occurred while conducting combat operations than we did to actual gunfire.

In further dissecting the incidents, though, most were caused by uncontrollable circumstances directly associated with and related to conducting high-risk combat ops. An example would be poor visibility as a result of intermittent low-level clouds in mountainous terrain attempting to locate a recon team in contact. The aircraft wasn't shot down, but it was lost while conducting combat ops under very bad conditions in hopes of saving American lives on the ground. I don't think those things are accidents in the pure sense of the word. Another "uncontrollable" condition is "blaze," a nighttime condition that is caused by a flash explosion, the illumination of a flare, or the sheer amount of light from gunfire that can cause the pilot(s) to become disoriented while inducing vertigo.

Simply put, these risks came with the job and all of us accepted them. Why were we there if we didn't take these kinds of chances? On the flip side, we could have eliminated all the risk if we just flew under mostly ideal blue-sky conditions.

Major Dull was concerned because he thought it would hinder his chances at promotion if an aircraft accident occurred while he was in command. This likely happened sometimes, but it normally only negatively impacted one's career if it was determined that unit flight safety was an

Chapter 15

afterthought and that taking chances or "pushing the envelope" was over the top. In our unit's case, I don't think we were extreme. Rather, I think we were somewhere in the middle with a good group of conscientious guys who had been issued a fair amount of courage and a good dose of common sense at birth—and that's an element in all of this stuff that can't be taught or measured!

Major Dull was also a very nervous, chain-smoking sort who in general just seemed unsure of himself. I don't know how he ever got through flying airplanes and helicopters. He had been an Army fixed-wing pilot for maybe 10 years, and he had only transitioned to helicopters before coming to Vietnam. I'm not attempting to take anything away from the pilots, but Army fixed-wing ops were very low key in comparison to helicopter ops, save the OV-1 Mohawk reconnaissance aircraft and perhaps the O-2 artillery spotter aircraft.

Anyway, we had been assigned to develop a concept of ops to recon with the SEALs, then feign an op in one area but execute it in a completely different area. The objective was to rescue American and other prisoners of war (POWs) and to take a Viet Cong regional chief and any of his staff as prisoners. The information was supposed to be "top level" and the SEALs were confident it was for "real." The prevailing feeling was that it was going to be a dangerous mission as it was thought POWs would be

Vietnam, November 1, 1968: The Start of a Long Year!

heavily guarded, as American prisoners were prized by the North Vietnamese.

After developing and coordinating the mission with the SEALs, fire support, U.S. Air Force Spooky aircraft, and our own Tiger Sharks, we developed the air crew list. Our aircraft contingent would consist of two gunships, two lift ships, and our C&C ship, of which I would serve as pilot and air/ground mission coordinator along with Warrant Officer 1 Jim Lynch, who was the designated aircraft commander.

At some point, after seeing the air crew list for the mission, I was directed by Major Dull to select only unmarried crew members to man the aircraft. I immediately objected to this, as did every married pilot in the unit that I could tell. I objected strenuously on the grounds that this was an "unlawful" order, was discriminatory in nature, would wear on unit morale, and, above all, it was total BS!

I asked if I should regularly start assigning crews based on how dangerous a mission is determined to be. Initially, Major Dull dug his heels in, saying he wanted to "provide a level of protection for the married pilots." I said, "UNSAT. We all signed up for the same level of dangerous conditions, be they combat or weather or mountain flying. Flying is inherently dangerous! Should we just keep the married guys on the ground filling admin positions?" I think not, and I concluded by telling him that I would go to the 10th

Chapter 15

Me with Operations Specialist Roger Borrego after qualifying with M-16s, Phan Thiet, Vietnam, April 1969. Weapons "qual" was a quarterly event.

Aviation Battalion Commander, Lieutenant Colonel Stanley, who I thought would have the good sense to support me and the married pilots.

Major Dull acquiesced because I figure he thought being overruled on an issue like this by the battalion commander might also negatively impact his career. Afterward, my ops guys, Sergeant Joe Reese and Specialist 4 Roger Borrego, filled the flight crew slots with both married and single pilots, generally using experience and competency as their guide. We flew the mission to perfection. The only issue was that the POWs were not there, but the snatch of the Viet Cong regional chief along with some of his staff went as planned and the story goes they provided good intel for future ops.

There are some strange people out there with some strange ideas, and sometimes you have to challenge the BS. I met Major Dull some years later at Ft. Benning, and he was still unsure of himself, chain smoking, hand wringing, and all. The good news was that he hadn't yet been promoted to lieutenant colonel and he had "wrangled" himself a flying job supporting Army fixed-winged aircraft at Ft. Benning. Kind of out of sight, out of mind, and far from the maddening crowd!

Apollo 11—Americans on the Moon

On July 20, 1969, Americans landed on the moon! I remember a whole bunch of us looking up at the moon that night in awe, knowing that our guys up there were a long way from home. It was an interesting feeling of being proud of their collective accomplishment—maybe the greatest accomplishment of all time—but also being perplexed at the contradiction of our being in Vietnam and their being on the moon. The world is truly upside down!

We didn't spend too much time on analysis, just looked up again on a cloudless night at a bright and shiny near full moon. Good for those guys, and God Speed on their return home!

Go Mets!

The summer of 1969 saw a hot pennant race in the National League East, which centered on the Chicago Cubs and the New York Mets, an expansion club that was "born" in 1962, a mere seven years earlier. My brother and

Chapter 15

I were Mets fans from day one, and we "suffered" through some of the worst and losingest baseball one could imagine. In their first year they set a record for losses when they went 40 wins and 122 loses—and it was ugly!

The next five years were somewhat better, and the Mets built up a devoted fan base that likely consisted mostly of former Dodger and Giant fans, who were left without a team when those teams left New York for the west coast in the late 1950s. The 1969 "Miracle" Mets, as they were called, was a team of relatively "unheralded" position players supported by solid starting pitchers like Tom Seaver and Nolan Ryan, both future Hall of Famers, and Jerry Koosman.

As the baseball season progressed during the summer I was in Vietnam, there were about eight or 10 of us pilots who were Mets fans, and we would anxiously await the arrival of the *Stars and Stripes* newspaper so we could catch up on what was happening regarding wins and loses and the "standings" in general. At one point in the season, the Mets were nine and a half games behind the league-leading Chicago Cubs, managed by the indomitable Leo Durocher.

Well, the Mets caught the Cubbies during a near season-ending three-game set and then won the majority of their closing games. It was a "miracle," but it didn't ensure they were going to the World Series as the Major Leagues, because of growth and other things, had broken both the National and American leagues into two divisions each, an

Vietnam, November 1, 1968: The Start of a Long Year!

east and west division. What it meant was that the Mets would now have to take three of five games from the Atlanta Braves in order to move on to the World Series.

I think most thought that was an impossible task, as the Braves had a good ball club with a bona fide slugger in "Hammering" Hank Aaron and good pitching to boot! But, as things go in the land of "you gotta believe," the impossible happened and the Mets beat the Braves and moved on to the World Series of 1969. There they would face the Baltimore Orioles, another good baseball team with good pitching—think Jim Palmer (future Hall of Famer), Dave McNally, and Mike Cuellar; home run hitting, think Boog Powell, Frank Robinson (future Hall of Famer), and Don Buford; and good fielding, think Mark Belanger, Davey Johnson, and Brooks Robinson (another future Hall of Famer)—and he could hit too! All told, a real solid baseball team.

At this point in the season, Armed Forces Radio Vietnam (AFRV; think Pat Sajak, a one-time voice on AFRV) was broadcasting the games live from the States and we could listen in. The only problem was that the games, although played during the day in the States, were played in the middle of the night in Vietnam. That didn't deter the faithful however, and us faithful gathered up in Jim Lynch's "hootch" to listen to the broadcast, drink a few beers, eat some of Jim's famous Philadelphia pretzels (sent to him by his mom), and consume some of my Chef Boyardee meatballs and spaghetti or ravioli (sent to me by my mom)! My recollection is that the games would end right about the time the sun was coming up over the South China Sea and it was time to get to work. We were hoping that the day's events would be "easy."

By gosh, the Mets did win the World Series in five games. Clearly the underdog, they beat a very good baseball team in the Orioles with some very good pitching, stellar outfield play, a solid infield, and clutch hitting—and they lived up to their nickname of being the "Miracle Mets," or simply the "AMAZINS," in stellar fashion!

Military Affiliated Radio Station (MARS)

As the fifth and final game of the 1969 World Series was coming to an end, I placed a call to the MARS station on the compound. I asked them if they had a "connection" to the States, and they said they had one in New York. The reason that was good is because they could establish a VHF radio connection with the operator in New York and he could affect a radio/telephone "patch" and make a "collect call" (look it up) to my parents. The operator on my compound told me to stand by the phone as it would take about 20–30 minutes to make the connection all around, then once established, he would call me and we could go right into it.

Vietnam, November 1, 1968: The Start of a Long Year!

It worked like a charm, and I talked to my mom and dad for the allotted 10 minutes…OVER/OUT…about nothing but baseball and the Mets! It was a fun call, and to think, I was only two and a half weeks from finishing my tour and heading home. These types of calls were few and far between as atmospheric conditions weren't always right and so connections oftentimes could not be completed. I was very lucky that night, and it was a kick talking to my dad. My family, including my mom who became a fervent Mets fan, suffered together through all those losses over the first six years of the Mets existence as a National League expansion team. When they won the Series, it wiped all that "baseball misery" away!

Throughout my tour in Vietnam, I was able to make three MARS calls to my folks. Two of them were through the ground station on our airfield and one of them was from the very helicopter I was flying. On that particular day, I was a co-pilot with one of our more senior pilots and the aircraft we had been assigned was equipped with a VHF radio, which was a prerequisite for making a MARS call. So, we climbed up to 7,000 feet, cranked up the VHF radio, and started making calls in the blind across the frequency spectrum to see if we could raise anyone.

Step #1 was raising someone on the radio, and Step #2 was hoping that the atmospheric conditions were favorable and the "phenomenon" called skip would assist us. Under

Chapter 15

the right circumstances, radio signals could "skip" through the atmosphere, increasing the radio range "ad nauseam." On this day, after only four or five blind calls, we reached the airport tower controllers at, would you believe, San Francisco International. We couldn't believe that we actually raised someone, and they couldn't believe we were actually flying in a helicopter over Vietnam. The long and short of it was that they made the connections, because they knew how, and both my aircraft commander and I talked to our parents from high above Vietnam.

It was a weird feeling being in a combat zone talking to folks back in the "world," as it was referred to. On these occasions, our short talks were always "cheerful," but there was an underlying "fearful" tone in the voice at the other end of the line, especially when I briefly talked to my mom. It was understandable, as they watched the nightly news and the Vietnam War was on TV every night and the casualties were mounting. It was still good to hear everyone's voice and they were recognizable over the radio.

The MARS system in the States was a collection of HAM radio operators who volunteered to receive radio calls and then place the "collect call" to the final destination. They did good work and helped some GIs get over the rough spots—and I suspect hardly anyone knows about them. Hats off to the MARS system, the operators, and all the good they did!

Vietnam, November 1, 1968: The Start of a Long Year!

Could This Have Been a World Record?

One day, at the conclusion of flight missions, three of our aircraft were summoned to rendezvous at a makeshift landing zone about 15 miles from our base in Phan Thiet. All were told that the Vietnamese government troops were conducting a "relocation" operation and they needed our aircraft to transport civilians from the location in the field to the airfield at Phan Thiet. The initial reports indicated that we needed to transport about 50 total people and that we should be able to finish this in one or two lifts. OK, so when we arrived at the site, there's more like 200 people that needed to be airlifted out and there were more coming.

The whole operation took five or six lifts, and the last bird out was faced with leaving some folks behind or really loading things up. In an effort to lighten the aircraft and take on more passengers, the door gunner caught a ride in our C&C ship and then the crew chief unloaded excess ammo, C-rations, tools, water, and oil cans.

When completed, the crew chief skillfully loaded 52 people onto his UH-1 Huey helicopter—maybe a record! It really meant there were 55 total souls aboard including the pilot, co-pilot, and crew chief. It turned out that the pilot of that "last aircraft out" was Warrant Officer 1 Jim Lynch, who usually flew the C&C aircraft but on this occasion he was actually undergoing an "aircraft commander" check

Chapter 15

My friend Warrant Officer Jim Lynch, who might have set a world record when his Huey transported 55 "passengers" and crew near Phan Thiet, Vietnam, 1969.

ride. If anything had gone amiss, Jim surely would have flunked his check ride and all concerned would have looked real dopey loading up that many folks on an aircraft that was "officially" rated to carry nine fully loaded troops and four air crew members Oh well, everything went just fine!

Everyone was amazed when they touched down in Phan Thiet as the stream of people just kept coming off that helicopter. I know, 55 people, impossible you say—well, the Vietnamese were little people and this load was mostly women and children, so the mothers carried most of the children as others clung very close to mom. And because of their short and slight stature, they all stood up for the short flight of about 15 minutes.

The pilot and crew chief contended they could've put a few more folks on board as they were well inside the safety limits for weight, balance, and engine torque requirements.

Guinness Book of World Records—has the statute of limitations passed? Could this still make the record books?

Jungle Survival Training— Cubi Point Naval Station, the Philippines

In May 1969, my unit received an "allocation" to send one commissioned officer to the U.S. Navy's Jungle Survival School located at the Cubi Point Naval Station in the Philippines. It turned out that I was on orders as my unit's escape and evasion (E&E) officer, so my unit commander directed that I attend the course and then come back and "upgrade" our in-house E&E "program." I somewhat objected as I "only" had five months left in-country and I thought a "newly" arrived officer should go just because he would have about 10 months left on his tour in which to share the wealth. Well, the commander insisted that I attend because I was an infantry officer and, at the time, I was the unit flight operations officer, so he thought, and rightly so, that I was the guy to go.

Over the next couple of days, I packed my jungle fatigues and the one set of civilian clothes I had and made arrangements to get down to Tan Son Nhut airfield in Saigon. When I reported to the "passenger control point," I received a commercial airline ticket aboard Philippine Airlines to Clark Air Force Base, which also served as a commercial airfield.

Chapter 15

While milling around Tan Son Nhut, I ran into a lieutenant who had been my neighbor in the trailer park I had lived in while in Mineral Wells. We started talking and found out that both of us were headed to the Jungle Survival School hosted by the Navy. Good deal! So, we buddied up and shortly afterward boarded the Boeing 727 for the five-hour flight to the Philippines. It was an interesting environment insomuch as that while the flight was departing from a war zone, my new friend and I were the only military people on board. All the other passengers were Filipinos, Malayans, or Australians/New Zealanders who "worked" in Vietnam or Thailand and were essentially heading back home.

The flight was a nice respite from the daily grind of an aviation unit in Vietnam. We got a little sleep, were served a good meal (airplane-style meals were better then than nowadays—in fact, you rarely see meals on planes today), and had a couple of Filipino San Miguel beers! We arrived at Clark late afternoon on a Friday and were billeted in the transit quarters. After unpacking, we headed to the adjacent PX (a smallish department store) to purchase some additional sundry items and to see about getting some "new" civies. With this accomplished, we found our way to the Clark O Club where we figured we could catch dinner and chill.

Well, as it turned out, the O Club was fabulous! It was a beautiful building with a couple of neat bars serving

Vietnam, November 1, 1968: The Start of a Long Year!

up all the tropical/exotic drinks you could think of, staffed by very pleasant and charming people. Dinner in the main dining room was great and just about anything you wanted could be had off the menu at very reasonable prices. The entertainment for the evening was, we couldn't believe it, the Tommy Dorsey Orchestra! If you closed your eyes real hard, you might think you were in a stateside establishment.

So six to seven hours from the Vietnam War zone, and we ran right into "normalcy"—and people were even dressed like it was date night. I'm pretty sure we had steak and shrimp for dinner, couldn't turn it down, along with our share of the exotic libations being rustled up at the bar—you know, the drinks with the flowers floating in them that go right to your head!

Dinner being over, we thought we'd head back to our rooms to sleep and get ahead of an early wake-up to catch a flight down to Cubi Point. On the way out the door, however, we saw the sign pointing to the downstairs "Ratskeller"—that did it for us! We spent the next three hours carousing to "Beatles" hits being performed by a Filipino band, the type that played a lot of the Beatles songs as good if not better than the Beatles.

There was an interesting crowd in attendance. There were a lot of youngish American women (lovingly referred to as "round eyes"), who, we found out, were teachers in the

Chapter 15

American school system at the U.S. military bases, nurses with the military, federal workers, and contractors. We thought this was a pretty neat place to be assigned if you had to be overseas.

All good things come to an end, so we collapsed into our bunks well after 0100 hours and arose at 0500 to start our movement to the ops building to arrange for a flight to Cubi. After an hour or so we were called to the dispatch area and directed to an odd-looking, very low to the ground, wing over, twin-engine Navy seaplane that was heading back to Cubi. I'd never been on a seaplane before so it seemed like an adventure was about to happen. About 10–12 passengers boarded and once settled in we took off for the one-hour flight down to Navy country. This seaplane was WWII vintage and was used as a "ferry" plane between the various military installations in and around the Philippines.

When we started letting down, I was thinking we would be landing on a runway just like we took off from at Clark. Not so—we let down into the waters of the Cubi Point Harbor and taxied up the ramp in front of a seaplane/helicopter hangar. When the aircraft landed in the water, the sensation one had was that you were sinking, and once the plane "settled," the water was right up to under the windows. A very weird feeling!

My new friend and I debarked and headed to the training office to sign in. We were told we had the rest of

Vietnam, November 1, 1968: The Start of a Long Year!

the day off to explore. We were additionally informed that we would need to be in formation adjacent to the building we were standing in at 0700 hours tomorrow morning in our military jungle fatigues and combat boots. At that time, we would be issued web gear, canteens, first aid pouches, water purification tablets, a very limited amount of rice, and field mess kits. Additional food would be "harvested" from the land and streams.

So, free for the day, we walked down to the small Navy exchange to look through whatever it is they had. While there, my new friend runs into a Navy pilot who he went to college with (I want to say LSU), and they talked for what seemed like 15 – 20 minutes. The upshot was that the Navy pilot invited us Army guys to dinner aboard "his" ship, the aircraft carrier USS *Enterprise*, CV-65, which was in port for repair and replenishment. We accepted the invite, and he told us where to meet him at 1730 hours on the pier. He also requested we wear our Army uniforms, which for us meant "clean" jungle fatigues as that was all we had.

We met him near the ship, and he escorted us up the "gangway" through the ship and to his wardroom where his squadron took their meals. Not all squadron members were in attendance, as it was a Saturday night and a percentage of crew was permitted shore leave. The commanding officer was present, however, along with 40–50 pilots, and they made us feel right at home. They thought it was really neat

Chapter 15

that we were serving in Vietnam and had actually walked the ground, so to speak. We thought what they did was pretty neat! Their adventures over Vietnam were from 20,000 feet—there was a different feel to it. Navy folks ate real well. Anything you wanted off the menu was served by Navy stewards (mostly Filipino nationals who joined the U.S. Navy specifically for those jobs and to ultimately achieve U.S. citizenship). After the evening meal we were given a tour of the ship, hangar deck to flight deck to the island. Incredible—the ship was huge and sans its aircraft, which had been flown to the air station for maintenance. Empty of aircraft, the ship looked cavernous!

The USS *Enterprise* was scheduled to depart Cubi Point on Wednesday of that week for a four to six month deployment on "Yankee Station" off the coast of Vietnam to provide air combat support for ground ops. She carried upwards of 100 aircraft and a crew of almost 5,000.

What a cool weekend! Now it's on to the mountains with our newly assigned "negrito" native Filipino guide. Over the next four days, we plowed along jungle trails and streambeds, learning the dos and don'ts of survival in a jungle environment with little else than a small bag of rice for food. Our native guide instructed us in how to find edible "veggies" from the jungle floor, along with how to make a bamboo pressure cooker and how to float downstream and catch "crawfish" with a slender bamboo spear. The jungle

Vietnam, November 1, 1968: The Start of a Long Year!

was soothing, as it was quiet except for the rustle of the trees and cascading sounds of near waterfalls and rapids. We did a fair amount of "siesta" along with an equal amount of time "hunting and gathering" in prep for our evening meal. Although water was plentiful in this location, our guide "introduced" us to a rather benign looking tree that, when slashed with a machete, would leak sweet fresh water, which we collected into a large piece of cut open bamboo.

After four days of "surviving," our close-out "banquet" consisted of snake, which had been caught and skinned by our guide, along with rice, jungle "veggies," and crawfish cooked in the bamboo pressure cooker. All together, and when mixed with a local hot sauce that our "chaperone" smuggled into the training area, dinner was very good—not like the meal in the wardroom of the USS *Enterprise*, but very "survivable"!

After "graduation" my friend and I had to travel back to Clark Air Force Base to catch a chariot back to Vietnam. Instead of flying up from Cubi, we decided to take the 100+ mile bus ride, which traveled the same route as the "Bataan Death March." It was very interesting, particularly if you knew how tragic and massive this event was in the early history of WWII. Allied POWs, 30,000 of them, were force-marched the 125+ miles without food or water under sweltering hot conditions. Those who fell out of the column were summarily executed by the Japanese either by rifle fire, bayonetting, which the Japs thought to be sporting, or through decapitation! It wasn't hard to see why at the end of the war we had little sympathy for the island nation of Japan and the devastation that was brought upon them.

All along the "March" route, families of American, Australian, and Filipino soldiers, murdered by the Japanese, have erected small memorials to their loved ones. And while it's been a long time since those memorials have been placed there, they seem to be well maintained (kept clean, weeded, and even painted) by the local population along the entire route—hats off to them—something they will never forget! The meandering bus ride along the very rough and hilly terrain route is slow and sobering. The surroundings are likely little changed from how it looked during WWII, and I found it easy to envision the savage treatment those men endured. It will be a road traveled that I will never forget!

Custer's Last Stand—But Not Tonight!

Warrant Officer Terry Custer was a pilot in the flight platoon I was assigned to when I first reported into the 192nd Attack Helicopter Company. He was a likable cowboy type from Wyoming with an "aw shucks" kind of way about him just like you might see in a movie. He was three to four months senior to me in-country, and therefore

Vietnam, November 1, 1968: The Start of a Long Year!

I occasionally would be assigned to fly with him during my "break-in" period. I liked flying with Terry. He was savvy, likable, level headed, and one who wasn't easily rattled.

Anyway, Terry was selected/invited by the gun platoon leader, Captain Tom White, to become one of "them" and he readily accepted. Our flight platoon didn't want him to go, but such is life. Fortunately, he was not very far away as he only moved two tents down from our platoon's area, which meant we could still enjoy his company and work with him in a different capacity.

So, on a blustery, hot, humid, and very rainy monsoon night in the June/July 1969 timeframe, Terry was assigned as the aircraft commander on the lead gunship that was

Warrant Officer Terry Custer lived through a harrowing "blaze" experience while flying a gunship in support of Army Rangers. The aircraft crashed through the trees and was heavily damaged, "but flew pretty good at 40–50 knots."

Chapter 15

called out to support an infantry element in sporadic contact with an enemy unit. I don't know why these events always seemed to happen in the rain, at night, and in the mountains, but it never failed.

Upon reaching the target area, Terry initiated all the pre-mission checks with the grunts on the ground relative to the combat situation, including the friendly and the suspected enemy locations as part of the process to set up his first gun pass. The weather was intermittent with low clouds and fog, so Terry was flying in a limited-visibility environment with rain mixed in and flares being dropped through the cloud cover, causing a condition called "blaze."

This occurs when the high intensity light of a flare reflects off smoke, fog, rain, or clouds, and it can really play tricks with one's eyesight and perspective, which could lead to vertigo and complete disorientation. It was not a good condition when flying in close proximity to the ground at more than 100 knots. Well, into the gun run he goes from about 1,500 feet altitude starting at 80 knots in a shallow descent. Initially, everything seemed "normal" until his co-pilot called out "watch your altitude" at about the 300-foot level.

Terry remained in a shallow descent "fixated on the target," oblivious to his extreme low altitude until the co-pilot screamed "altitude" while he wrested the controls away, ultimately working in concert with Terry. In the split

Vietnam, November 1, 1968: The Start of a Long Year!

second after that, both pilot and co-pilot flared the helicopter into a nose-up attitude while pulling hard on the collective to gain altitude. With that, they descended below the tree level and pancaked off the ground, running through more trees while gaining altitude.

The aircraft regained flight but endured severe damage to the pilot side of the cockpit, which was crushed and devoid of the windscreen and chin bubble, and at that point was "garnished" with a good-sized tree branch with all the trimmings. This tree branch hit Terry in the face and head, and while still conscious, he was a bloody mess. The mini-guns were broken off the floor mounts and hanging by electric cables. The sync elevators, located to the rear of the fuselage, were half sheared off. The rotor blades were torn and ripped from the blade tips to the rotor hub. The aircraft, hard to believe, was flyable, but it was completely destroyed and rendered unserviceable upon returning to base.

After miraculously regaining control, the co-pilot radioed our unit ops and reported the incident, indicating that as battered as the aircraft was, they were flying and they intended to fly back to our base in Phan Thiet. He also reported Terry as being severely injured and losing a lot of blood. With that info, our ops notified the base medical team that we had an incoming casualty so that they could be prepared to provide aid. I went up to the MEDEVAC pad on our base to await Terry's arrival and couldn't believe

Chapter 15

what I was seeing when the helicopter came into view.

As described earlier, the aircraft was flyable but destroyed, with branches and leaves sticking out of all the doors, windows, skids, and in and around the rotor hub. Unbelievable! Terry had a big gash on his forehead and across his nose and was bleeding profusely. The co-pilot was also cut up, so in the 50-knot wind they generated while in flight, the blood was blown to the back of the aircraft, covering the two crewmen in a scene that resembled a mass murder.

I caught up with Terry in the medical eval room and was relieved to see that the crew would all survive and be no worse for wear with an incredible story to tell their grandchildren. I asked Terry, "Hey, how did that thing ever fly in that condition?" He essentially replied, "Aw shucks, it flew pretty good at 40 knots!" Thank goodness that evening did not turn out to be Warrant Officer Terry Custer's last stand!

The Oil Guys!

One afternoon, while I was the operations officer, four civilian engineer types arrived in our ops tent after stepping off an Air America (read CIA) flight from who knows where, looking for a flight to Cam Ranh Bay. While trying to determine if any flights were scheduled to depart for Cam Ranh, we started talking to these guys in their best

Vietnam, November 1, 1968: The Start of a Long Year!

"Abercrombie & Fitch" fly fishing outfits, and I asked them what the hell they were doing here in the middle of nowhere in the middle of a combat zone. The conversation that followed was revealing, to say the least. They told us they were petroleum engineers, and they had been conducting geological surveys off the coast of Vietnam in the South China Sea. The preliminary data indicated that there was likely more oil in this area than in all of Saudi Arabia and the Middle East. After hearing that, a few other GIs within earshot and I looked at each other and pretty much said in unison, well "think you know why we are here in Vietnam"—OIL!

Initially, I didn't want to believe it was all about oil, but through the years every now and again I would see a magazine article or newspaper piece, always in small print and on the back pages, about Royal Dutch Shell being awarded the rights to explore and drill for oil off the southern coast of Vietnam. Or Sun Oil being awarded the rights to "explore" the "Fish Hook" area of the outer Mekong Delta, and so on.

You gotta believe this wasn't occurring in isolation. Oil is the heartbeat of the world's industries, and I suspect that our upper echelon "leaders" within government and industry knew this was a significant contributing factor as to why our nation got involved in Vietnam. You know the CIA was aware, because it's their business to find out and know about stuff like this, and I have to believe any information this significant (more oil than in Saudi Arabia and the Middle East) was passed along to our commander in chief.

On the flip side, the Communist bloc (Russia, China, North Korea, and North Vietnam) wanted and needed oil to run their industries and fuel their worldwide ambitions! If it is the case that oil was a primary motivation for our being in Vietnam, I don't think many "normal" Americans were or are aware of it to this day. If, in fact, it was the reason for being there, then how do you think the Gold Star families of the 58,000 who died would feel about that? Were we there to deprive the Communist bloc of vast oil reserves? OK, but why couldn't we have been told that?

Rocket and Mortar Attacks

During the year I was stationed in Vietnam at the airfield in Phan Thiet (LZ Betty), our base was mortared and rocketed upwards of 75 times. These attacks were just mortar or rocket attacks and were not accompanied by a ground assault, except in the two instances I already described in which our perimeter was probed with the attack being repulsed and in another instance breached and partially overrun. We went one stretch where our base was mortared 38 nights in a row. All during that time the mortar attacks were ineffective and on some nights

Vietnam, November 1, 1968: The Start of a Long Year!

A CH-54 "flying crane" doing heavy lifting at LZ Betty, Phan Thiet, Vietnam, December 1968.

consisted of just a few incoming rounds. On other nights the "barrage" was more intense but still largely ineffective. Most attacks hit areas of the metal plate runways doing zero damage. Another favorite target, believe it or not, was the garbage dump, I'm sure unintentional and producing the same results…zero. In some cases, the rounds were "long," overshooting the cantonment area, and in fact hit the beach or landed in the ocean. None of these "attacks" resulted in U.S. casualties—someone was looking out for us!

Although not experiencing actual casualties, the net effect on our troops was that all unit members were deprived of sleep. And sleep is a most precious commodity. In our "line" of work, our flight and maintenance crews needed to be as "sharp" as possible and a good seven hours went a long way toward ensuring that result. So maybe, in fact, the Viet Cong were trying to achieve sleep deprivation, and while accomplishing that with haphazard mortar barrages, OK, and if by "accident" they hit something of significance, all the better.

One morning in early September 1969, just after sunrise, I was standing near the "water buffalo" adjacent to the pilots' sleeping quarters, taking a "spit" bath and shaving when BAROOM, BAROOM, and BAROOM happened 1,000 feet from my location. I was in the midst of a "daylight" rocket attack that occurred without warning and was over as quickly as it started. It was the only daylight attack against our compound that occurred during my time at Phan Thiet.

Two of the three rockets hit significant targets—an O-1 single engine spotter airplane, which was destroyed, and a wooden, tin-roofed barracks building, killing six members of our attached aviation maintenance unit who worked the night shift in the maintenance areas and who had just come off duty. It was a random, direct, and lucky hit that had devastating results. The third rocket hit in the middle of a small parade field surrounded by our ops building, the mess hall, and admin staff type buildings, causing no damage.

The irony of this attack is that all the enlisted men who lost their lives never participated in combat operations—they never fired a shot! They were "prop and rotor" people who kept our aircraft flying, and while not involved in the "shooting," they contributed significantly to the overall effort. Their loss hit our unit hard, and it was the highest single-day casualty count our unit suffered during its entire five plus years in Vietnam.

This Bud's for You—Or Would You Prefer a PBR?

Occasionally, we would be assigned a mission that seemed to have no beginning or end. One of those missions for us happened on very short notice—on the night before it was to happen at approximately 2200 hours with a pickup slated for near 0400 hours (OMG, now that's early). An 0400 hour pickup meant an 0200 hour wake-up call for the crews to receive mission briefings, pre-flight aircraft, and maybe catch a little breakfast (nothing like the 24-hour mess hall operation) before lifting off and forming up for the 30-minute flight into the ops area. We were tasked to provide four Hueys to fly up the coast about 50 miles and effect a pickup on the beach of 30+ GIs who hailed from an undisclosed unit at X marks the spot and conduct a combat air assault into a location that would be disclosed to us once airborne. That was "spooky," as normally we worked with units from the 3/506, 101st Airborne Division, and they knew how we operated and likewise.

Because the mission was a little "quirky" and we didn't know who these guys were, our crew chiefs thought we could have a little fun by placing empty beer cans in prominent places on the "pedestal"/center control panel of the aircraft. The idea was to get a "rise" out of our passengers by having them think we were "drinking and flying." Just to be upfront, we hadn't been "drinking and flying"—it never crossed our minds and never would, but the troops probably thought otherwise based on the supposed "reputation" of we "hell bent for leather" swashbuckling Army aviators!

Well, the "planted" beer cans along with pilot-initiated "wobbly" takeoff had the desired effect and just watching the wide-eyed grunts making hand motions and facial expressions to each other was fun—but only for us I suspect. The grunts/infantryman lived with constant risk of injury or death, and so I can just imagine what was going through their minds: "Jesus H. Christ—I lived through the ground phase of our op now I have to fly with a bunch of aviators under the influence?!" (After thinking about this for 50+ years, our little practical joke wasn't very funny under the circumstances.) We later assured them that the beer cans and the wobblies were all a prop, and as best we could under the circumstances we all laughed loudly under the drone of the turbine engine and whop, whop, whopping sound of the rotors.

Just a minute or so before touching down in the landing zone, the infantry platoon leader, who was riding with us in the lead aircraft, grabbed me by the arm and shouted into

Vietnam, November 1, 1968: The Start of a Long Year!

my headset something to this effect, "Loved the prank but can you make up for scaring the SH_T out of us with some 'live' beer as a gift on our way out the door?"

My crew chief heard the request over the radio and out of nowhere and in a second, thrust a case of Pabst Blue Ribbon (PBRs) into the 1st lieutenant's outstretched arms as he was jumping off the skid. In the instant that followed, me and the 1st lieutenant locked eyes and he gave us a big thumbs up! I never ran into that group again, but I bet the story of having conducted a combat air assault with a bunch of "drunken" Army aviators made its way around many Army gatherings and holiday dinner tables. Cool moment, and hey, what more can we do for our infantry brothers!

The Chuck Taylor Converse All-Stars

Long about March 1969, 1st Lieutenant Chuck Couey, a "left" coaster from Spokane, Washington, reported to the 192nd Attack Helicopter Company as a "new" replacement pilot. This happened throughout the course of one's yearlong tour as people were always rotating home, while "new" people were always rotating in as replacements. Chuck was assigned to the 1st Flight Platoon and was billeted in the tent next to mine.

As was the unofficial custom, when a "newby" was first assigned to the unit, the "old" hands would welcome him to the unit usually by sharing some heated long-range reconnaissance patrol field rations along with a couple of beers and always good conversation. While all this was going on, Chuck was unpacking his duffel bag and sorting through his unit-issued flight equipment while talking and filling us in on his hometown. At some point, out popped a pair of black, low-cut Chuck Taylor Converse All-Star basketball sneakers, the same type I used to wear in high school. They were top notch and expensive for sneaks then, and I believe they are still considered fashionable today, although not nearly as well made.

Anyway, when I saw them I said to Chuck, "Hey man, if anything happens to you I've got first dibs on the Chuck Taylor All Stars." He looked at me and said something like, "What's going to happen to me that would cause you to get my Chuck's?" I know what you're thinking—bad conversation, and you're right—but we were in a war zone and things did happen and so I said something like, "Ah, you know, we are in a war zone and…" He got it and said they'll be in the bottom of the locker for you!

Well, fortunately, I never got Chuck's "Chucks," and that was a good thing, but it has been something that we've shared a couple of laughs over throughout the years. We've kept in contact now for 52 years, and most recently, Chuck visited me in Park City, Utah, for a few days in the summer of 2022. We had a good time just talking, eating, and drinking. When I was arranging to pick him up at the Salt Lake Airport, I asked him what he would be wearing so I could ID him more easily. He replied, "Fox, I'll be wearing my Chuck Taylor All Stars." He did, and we both had a good belly laugh at that!

The Dog Pound

During my time in the 192nd Attack Helicopter Company, I was aware of four dogs that kept the officers and enlisted men "company" in various places throughout our unit. They were all mixed-breed mongrels with good dispositions. The dogs were named Mini Gun, Gear Head, S3/Brown's Dog, and Mama Son.

As you might guess, Mini Gun was the mascot of the Tiger Shark gunship platoon, and he was with them all the time. He looked forward to flying missions, and he couldn't wait to stand on the edge of the "gun" bay, sticking his snout out into the 90-knot "breeze," which caused his ears to flop all over his head. He seemed to love every minute of it. He looked like the dogs you see hanging out of the windows of cars and trucks throughout the country today. I'm just guessing, but it looks like it's in dog DNA—no matter what the vehicle, where the location, or what the breed, dogs seem to like hanging their heads out the window feeling the breeze.

Chapter 15

Mini Gun had great breezes but he had a tough "job"—as the noise from the guns was deafening, even with earplugs, and he would "shiver" and bark like the dickens when they fired. One of the crew chiefs fashioned a set of cotton swab-type earplugs, but he didn't like them and would always shake them off. Ever try to put a "hat" or a "bow" on your own dog's head? Same thing, right—they shake them off in 20 seconds. It's in the DNA! Mini Gun survived my tour in Vietnam, and I suspect he was with the 192nd until the end.

Gear Head was the best friend of the ground vehicle maintenance crews, more commonly referred to as the motor pool gang. His existence was less glamorous than Mini Gun, but he seemed to revel in the company with all the mechanics' attention. He was always riding in a truck with his head out the window, catching much more moderate breezes in the 25 mph range. Not much in the way of loud noises either. As I recall, the motor pool guys would get him on a flight mission about once a month so he could qualify for "flight pay"—just kidding, but he did fly occasionally.

S3, now there was a dog. S3 means "operations" in the Army and S3, our dog, was the epitome of operations. He was always in our ops tent; in fact, he lived there. He attended the morning briefs and the afternoon debriefs, and he seemingly barked in approval when the briefings were

Vietnam, November 1, 1968: The Start of a Long Year!

completed as if to say, "I liked it." He had his own monogrammed pillow in a shag carpeted remnant of a bed that was made by our ops sergeant.

His best friend was Lieutenant Brown, "Brownie," our one-time ops officer, and he rarely left his presence. And because of their relationship, he ended up with two names: S3 and Brown's Dog, and he would answer to either. S3/Brown's Dog was also a flier. Lieutenant Brown would take him flying whenever the ops aircraft was committed to liaison-type work and, yup, he too would stick his snout into the 90-knot breeze as soon as they were airborne. He ruled the roost and walked with a little bit of "fighter pilot" swag, different from "helicopter pilot" swag, and we attributed that to the likelihood he was probably the offspring of Japanese fighter pilot "dogs" who had occupied the same airfield just 24 years earlier. He did have curious eyes and a penchant for fish over rice. So who knows!

Mama Son was a permanent fixture in the aircraft maintenance section, and she was the only "she" amongst the dogs! She too answered to two names. Mama Son was her "formal" name, but her fun name was Rotor Head, you know, because of the helicopter blades. She flew with the maintenance officer on all our maintenance test flights and rumor had it that she barked a howling kind of bark in approval if all went well. Her bark meant she had

Chapter 15

Me with Captain Jerome DeSimone (center) and 1st Lieutenant George Dille (right), Phan Thiet, Vietnam, 1969. Captain "De" was our flight surgeon doubling as our veterinarian... he kept all of us dogs healthy!

"signed off" on the flight and the aircraft was therefore mission ready. Her biggest claim to fame, however, was that she had two liters of seven to nine pups during the time I was in Vietnam. Looks like the "boys in the pound" kept her busy!

And just so we all know, these dogs were all treated very well. The guys in the unit just flocked to them and as a result, they were all fed well and kept clean. In fact, I think some members of our unit had their mothers back home send "care packages" of doggie treats and canned food. They might have been eating better than we were. And whenever they appeared to be sick, they were taken immediately to Captain DeSimone's sick bay for an evaluation and maybe a shot of antihistamine. If, in fact, they were of Japanese descent, they quickly assimilated into becoming full-fledged "Americans" under our tutelage, and I think they probably thought they had died and gone to heaven.

Tit Ti Mountain— Warrant Officer 1 Theodore Thoman

Tit Ti Mountain was a twin mountain peak complex that jutted 800–1,000 feet up from the coastal plain about 12–15 miles northwest of our airfield. It was the location of a strategic communications radio relay site, and it was manned by a 40-man security platoon along with 12 or so communications specialists. There were no roads to the top, so they needed to be resupplied by helicopter for everything.

The peaks were connected by a narrow strip of ridgeline that was a couple of hundred yards long, featuring a walking path to either peak and a precarious helipad right in the center. When you landed on the pad, the aircraft nose would overhang and you would be looking through the "chin bubble" straight down the side of the mountain. Conversely, the tail boom and rotor would overhang to the rear. It was a tricky place to set a helicopter down, particularly because of the swirling winds encountered on the final approach and because of severe updrafts you would encounter the closer you got to touchdown. This occurred because when landing into the prevailing wind, they would burble up the opposite side of the landing area, catching

Chapter 15

approaching aircraft in the updraft right about the time the pilot would be anticipating touchdown. It could be severe, and it required a pilot's undivided attention and sometimes even that wasn't enough.

On March 30, 1969, Warrant Officer 1 Ted Thoman from California was the pilot in charge assigned to fly the local MACV support mission, which on this day would require a resupply mission to the top of Tit Ti Mountain. It was a crystal clear day with steady winds from the east off the ocean, which meant a pilot would be initiating an approach to the site from the west or the valley side. From all reports, everything appeared "normal" until the point of touchdown when the nose of the aircraft pitched up (likely caused by the updraft from the prevailing winds hitting up against the opposite side of the landing area). It all happened very fast. The nose pitched up and swung to the left as the tail boom and rotor pitched down to the right, contacting the ground causing catastrophic separation from the aircraft.

At that point, the aircraft rolled over and down the mountain roughly 100 feet, causing an explosion and fire. Four Americans were killed including the pilot, Ted Thoman, the aircraft door gunner from our unit, and two communication specialists who were to be dropped off on the mountain top. The co-pilot survived, as did the crew chief and four other passengers.

The entire event was tragic and terrible. Thoman had just a few days earlier turned 20 years old and our door gunner was 19 years old and a New Jersey native—very sad!

It was so traumatic for the co-pilot that he requested, and was granted, relief from flying duties, and he departed our unit within a week. I was the last one from our unit to see Thoman that day as I met the MEDEVAC aircraft at the medical pad. He was in very bad shape and was promptly prepared for medical evac to the Saigon area, where he died five days later of burns suffered over a large portion of his body. Thoman was a good guy, studious, and serious about his duties. I flew with him on numerous occasions and found him to have good piloting skills with a good dose of common sense. Rest in peace, Warrant Officer 1 Ted Thoman!

Captain Tom Campbell—"Okie"

At the end of one's tour in Vietnam, everyone was "offered" an opportunity to extend their tour in-country for six months. Those who chose to do so had the option of remaining in their current unit or requesting a transfer to another unit. I didn't know many pilots to do this, but the ones I did know normally elected to transfer to a different unit with a mission other than flying daily combat assaults into "Apache" country. All those who did take an extension were awarded a nominal monetary bonus, along with 30 days

Chapter 15

of "free" leave and an additional R&R to be taken during the six-month extension. It was attractive in an odd sort of way—continued flying assignments, a little more money, free leave, and an R&R, but I just couldn't do that to my parents as I'm sure it was hard enough "worrying" through a one-year tour let alone tacking on six more months.

Captain Tom Campbell, known to all in our unit as "Okie," being from Oklahoma and damn proud of it, chose to extend. Whenever he could get out of a flight suit or fatigues, Tom would wear "boot cut" Levi's with his lizard-skin cowboy boots topped off with a classic western shirt and a big silver belt buckle. We two, along with Chris Fecher, had come to Vietnam on the same day, which meant that we would be departing for home on the same day one year later.

As time wore on, toward the end of our tours, a few of us started talking about extending and about the pros and cons you know, possible command of a flight platoon, you'd be able to put more money into the Soldiers' Deposit program, and hey, you'd be eligible for an R&R to a place of your choice and 30-day "free" leave to start your six-month tour; all sounded good! Then again, you might die and for what? I don't think, by that time, any of us thought we were "fighting" to save our country; and hell, we all knew about the oil guys…sooooo! I dismissed the extension idea pretty quickly for the "parents" reason.

Vietnam, November 1, 1968: The Start of a Long Year!

Tom, on the other hand, signed up for the extension citing his desire to perhaps command the Tiger Shark Gunship Platoon at some point during his extension. He was also somewhat sure that he wanted to make the Army a career and that the added combat time would be helpful for promotion or advanced schooling opportunities. So, the morning my former flight school classmate, Chris Fecher, and I were packing out of the unit and heading down to the "transit" flight pad, we saw Tom, said our goodbyes, wished him well, and off we went to Cam Ranh Bay to catch the "freedom bird," as it was referred to, for home.

That night, while celebrating our imminent departure from Vietnam, we received word that our unit, the 192nd Attack Helicopter Company, had lost a gunship while supporting Army Rangers earlier that evening. Initially, we only knew of the aircraft loss, but about an hour later it was reported to us that Captain Tom "Okie" Campbell had been the aircraft commander and he was KIA.

Chris and I were incredulous and couldn't believe it. Tom should have been with us, looking forward to going home; instead, he was killed on the first night of his six-month extension! I couldn't help but think of my parents, his parents, how fickle fate is, the grim reaper and all that crap, and how tragic the loss of Tom Campbell, our "Okie from Muskogee," was. Rest in peace, Tom!

Chapter 16
"Freedom Bird" and Homeward Bound

Chapter 16

After only one night in the Cam Ranh Bay out-processing point, the very "savvy" and now-Captains Chris Fecher and Frank Fox were slated to board a military charter Flying Tiger airliner headed to Seattle/Tacoma International airport by way of a refuel stop in Osaka, Japan. On our way to the flight terminal, we literally walked into my old roommate in Phan Thiet, Dr. and Flight Surgeon Jerome DeSimone. He should have left for home months ago, but he explained that he extended to assist in surgery and to learn as much as he could about severe trauma of the type you would encounter in a war zone. We wished him luck and gave him a big handshake and a hug. I never saw or heard of Dr. De again, but I hope he enjoyed whatever life had in store for him.

What a feeling. It was hard to describe. To be 22 years old, alive, and unscathed after what we both had done and witnessed over the past year was staggering, and as I think I've said before, sobering! We had each accumulated more than 500 hours of combat flight time, endured numerous mortar and rocket attacks, got the crap scared out of us during the conduct of nighttime operations, and some broad daylight operations as well, kept our sense of humor, and labored through one incompetent commanding officer while working with two other very competent and well-liked commanders. Whew, what a year!

"Freedom Bird" and Homeward Bound

The mood on the Freedom Flight was somber and quiet in anticipation of actually taking off. Once the rear doors were secure, the captain welcomed us aboard, thanked us all for our service, and told us that we could expect to be airborne and on the first leg of our flight home in about 20 minutes. Stewardesses then flooded the cabin and passed out sandwiches and soft drinks with a promise of beer, wine, and spirits once aloft! OK, taxiing down the runway, slow roll at first followed then by full engine thrust, and after about 20 seconds we could feel the aircraft go nose up followed by the aircraft taking flight—we broke out in full throated and very loud cheering and clapping, all 220 of us, and it lasted a while. It was really happening, we were really on our way back to the States, the real world!

The refueling stop in Japan was uneventful on a very cold, wet, and just plain raw November day with a whipping wind. None of us had anything but short-sleeve uniform shirts to wear, so we froze, particularly after coming from 88-degree heat with high humidity. Ya think someone in the "chain of command" would have thought about issuing some cold weather gear just to get everyone through the flight, but no one did, and as a result, I'll bet virtually everyone on the flight came down with flu-like symptoms after arriving home. I did and it kept me down for five full days. Oh well, it was still veeerrry good to be on the way home.

Chapter 16

The flight from Japan to SEATAC in Seattle was about nine hours, and it was a good time to catch some sleep, as most aboard did. It felt like the night before Christmas when everyone is dreaming good thoughts and happy outcomes, and then you wake up to Christmas morning. In this case, those on board started to rustle around with about two hours to go before touchdown, and soon the whole airplane was abuzz.

And then it happened. Way out on the horizon on a very dark and moonless night there was a twinkling of lights and someone yelled out, "Hey, I think I'm looking at lights on the west coast," and sure enough they were the coastal lights of the United States of America. The aircraft captain heard all the hubbub and came over the intercom to assure us that in fact the lights we were seeing was the coast of Washington state. I still can't describe that feeling of seeing the lights on the horizon and knowing it was home. The remainder of the flight was nothing more than loud talk, "What's the first thing you're planning to do when you hit home," giddy laughter, handshakes, and believe it or not singing, as in "God Bless America," led by the senior flight attendant!

We were off the airplane, into a processing point, and had a briefing on the status of traveling in the States. The anti-Vietnam War movement had grown considerably in the year I was gone, and there was much hostility toward our government and the military. We were "baby killers" and all that. Accordingly, we were advised that returning soldiers, sailors, and airmen were experiencing some disrespectful crowds and individual hecklers and, as a result, it was recommended that we take off our uniforms—can you imagine, take off the uniform of our nation's armed services—and travel in civilian clothes across our own country. This, after a year's worth of seeing some people die wearing that uniform. It was hard to get your head around all of it.

Some claim they were spit at and had things thrown at them. I didn't experience any of that in person, but I did witness it on nightly news programs and for a time it was occurring regularly. Not that we were looking for it, but there were no "Welcome Home" banners or just "normal" citizens wishing us well—none of that. And as it turns out, we all just skulked back to where we were from just happy to be home. Sorting out the war and all the associated issues would have to be done by others. The entire atmosphere was ugly and, for me, it seemed to mark the start of much distrust of the government in particular and authority in general, and it has been somewhat downhill, in my view, ever since.

I landed at JFK International Airport mid-afternoon and was picked up by my parents and brother. It was a happy time. I went from there to home and spent the next five days in bed (remember the cold conditions in Japan?) with the crud or maybe the flu—long before COVID-19!

Chapter 17

*Vietnam—
The War and
Its Aftermath,
Still Hard to Figure*

Chapter 17

The Tonkin Resolution, which followed the somewhat murky engagement between a U.S. Navy vessel and North Vietnamese torpedo boats, became a blank check for the LBJ administration, and it led to the escalation of the war in Vietnam in 1965 and 1966, providing the legal basis for introducing large numbers of Army and Marine ground forces. Under Secretary of Defense Robert McNamara, the initial mission was ostensibly to provide airbase and local security for the sizable contingent of Air Force assets that had been conducting combat air operations in support of the South Vietnamese Army. As time passed, however, it legitimized the introduction of U.S. ground forces into the conflict. Their purpose was to conduct ground combat operations against North Vietnamese Communist forces infiltrating into and operating in South Vietnam. Congress never declared war against North Vietnam, even though the United States was in an open state of hostilities with the North Vietnamese for almost 10 years.

What kept it going was McNamara's fears, along with others within the administration, of what would happen to all of Southeast Asia if South Vietnam fell to the Communists. Their contention was that all the nations of that region would fall like dominoes (the so-called domino effect) if South Vietnam fell. Their concerns were seemingly legitimate at the time; however, 58,000 U.S. men and women lost their lives, and in the end, it appears as if we accomplished very little. And while South Vietnam did succumb to the Communists, the remaining dominoes (Cambodia, Laos, Thailand, etc.) did not fall.

We didn't really have clearly stated objectives or the power and authority of a declaration of war by Congress. It was all about politics; it seemed the men and women in Congress didn't want to commit to a formal declaration as this would have exposed their individual positions and their constituents would've known how their elected representatives really felt about the war. Might have caused a fair number of representatives to lose their elected positions. Sound familiar? And because of the growing anti-war movement at home, members of Congress were content to hide behind the Gulf of Tonkin Resolution, passing any and all criticism along to the president. Simply put, they were protecting their jobs by not really committing to the war effort in the face of heightened anti-war angst within our country. This high-level shell game almost brought our country down. It did bring the Johnson presidency down, as he refused to seek a second full term—who does that? He was worn out!

As a result, the war was fought with many restrictions being levied against U.S. armed forces, such as limited areas of operations, can't cross the border in pursuit, can't shoot back when fired upon until clearance is received (too late), no-fire zones even if you are fired upon or if enemy assets

Chapter 17

are marshaling, and no bombing supply ships in Haiphong Harbor (some of which were Canadian, loaded with fuel, food, and medical supplies—our ally trading with our enemy—what's that about?). The troops on the ground and in the air were fighting with their hands tied. You can't win a war and defeat the Communists like that. And on top of it all, we knew China and Russia were largely involved in supporting the North Vietnamese, and we resolved not to interfere with that.

Long after the war ended in 1973, McNamara stated that at some point he knew the war was futile and he had many regrets regarding decisions and policies he had championed in the execution of the war. Does that mean he knowingly lied about circumstances and events? Lots of people wish he had opened up about that during the conflict. Who knows? It might have led to a very different conclusion and likely would have saved thousands of lives on both sides!

Not knowing, at the time, all the intrigues and nuances surrounding Vietnam's history since WWII, and unaware of McNamara's misgivings, I thought we were there for good reason—to stop Communist aggression against a "fledgling" democracy in South Vietnam. Wasn't that our stated goal/policy toward Cuba in the late 1950s and early 1960s? Whatever the goal was, it turned out poorly for us and the Cuban people—maybe we should have learned then. So, it seemed that's what the U.S. policy goal was—to thwart Communist aggression. Well then, that said, it would have been nice if we had been informed as to what the end game was.

Was it to unify North and South and to support a "democracy" at the end of hostilities? Or was it to stop Communist aggression, thus maybe stabilizing the entire region, which included Laos, Cambodia, Thailand, maybe South Korea, Japan, and even New Zealand, Australia, and the Philippines! Not a bad goal in either case, but we needed a consensus strategy in place to achieve that, and we didn't have it. So, our involvement just floundered around aimlessly.

In my opinion, and from my perspective later as a participant, U.S. forces fought with distinction, and as well as any American forces in any conflict at any time in our history, under very trying circumstances and with no definitive goals. Our Soldiers, Sailors, Marines, Airmen, and Coast Guardsmen risked, and in 58,000+ cases lost, their lives, for a cause that after a time they knew we were not committed to winning as a nation.

After a while, for those of us who served in Vietnam, it didn't seem as though we were fighting for anything tangible. We were merely holding the line, maintaining the status quo. We fought to keep each other alive. We fought for hilltops with no names and isolated valleys that seemingly had no strategic value. We won these battles only to abandon the contested area over time.

When the North Vietnamese Army launched the Tet Offensive in January 1968, U.S. forces, along with the ARVN, fought tenaciously to defeat a very determined enemy in cities such as Saigon, Hue, and Quang Tri and in numerous other villages and hamlets across the country. Our enemy was defeated in detail on the battlefield, but we did NOT pursue a total victory. We made like Union General George Meade after the battle of Gettysburg and allowed the enemy to melt back into the interior or across the border into Laos and Cambodia to rearm, refit, and reconstitute.

This "policy" added years to the conflict and the loss of many more lives. There was a feeling that we Americans owned the day, while the Viet Cong operated underground and under the cover of darkness—all the while rebuilding. Our forces mounted many large offensive operations into places like the A Shau Valley, Michelin rubber plantation, Lam Son 719, Hamburger Hill, Dak To, and as I already mentioned, we defeated the North Vietnamese in the Tet Offensive, but we never pursued and pushed into the north. We never attempted to cut off the "head of the snake."

To underscore the fact that we soundly defeated the North Vietnamese in the Tet Offensive, North Vietnamese General Giap admitted, in a years' later interview, that his forces had been beaten badly. He further noted that it took the North Vietnamese five years in which to restore his forces to pre-Tet Offensive days.

So, by not pursuing the badly bloodied North Vietnamese forces following Tet, the United States, in essence, gave the north time to recover. As has been said a few times about the United States, most recently in Afghanistan, "the United States has the watches (like in wrist watches), but we (whoever you want to put in here) have the time." They wait us out. We think a year or two is a long time, whereas other cultures deal in decades, never giving up, when attempting to instill change! It was the North Vietnamese who fought a defensive war from Tet in 1968 until the United States pulled out in 1973. Two years after that, the North Vietnamese overran the country and took Saigon and the south.

The Vietnam War, at first glance, appeared to be a civil war—Vietnamese versus Vietnamese. It is just the type of conflict the United States should not, in my view, become involved in. That being said, however, if the conflict had been confined to just being a Vietnamese issue, that would be one thing—but it wasn't. And the dilemma for the United States then, and in the world we currently live in, is that looks are always deceiving and no issue on the grand scale is black or white—it's never that easy!

The South Vietnamese were ostensibly trying to maintain a democratic nation (don't confuse a Vietnamese "democratic" nation to be similar to what we know as democracy U.S. style—it's not, and this is an entirely different discussion). At least at the time, they, seemingly, were not interested in unifying south and north into a single Republic of Vietnam.

On the other hand, the North had been infiltrating the South, eyeing the creation of a left-leaning "single" People's Republic of Vietnam since shortly after the end of WWII. North and South Vietnam had been established somewhat arbitrarily and not necessarily along traditional, historic, and demographic boundaries, a sure recipe for discontent and internal strife. As the North's continued subversion of the South escalated during the 1950s and early 1960s, the Chinese and Russians supported the war effort through extensive training and equipping efforts to the point where Russian and Chinese pilots were flying combat missions against the South Vietnamese Air Force and later U.S. pilots, using very advanced aircraft for the times (MIG 19, MIG 21).

So as the situation deteriorated for the south in the face of a much more aggressive Communist North Vietnam, the United States increased aid to the south. U.S. assistance took the form of military training, arms, facilities, infrastructure, and so on. In the mid 1960s, and after the effects of the Gulf of Tonkin incident (USS *Maddox*, August 1964, attack by North Vietnamese gunboats), the

United States started introducing ground forces to bolster South Vietnamese forces and counter the North Vietnamese ground effort. Our involvement up to that point blunted the North's ambitions, and we successfully thwarted significant ground ops from being mounted against the South, that is until Tet in 1968.

Tet was a major offensive kicked off over the Vietnamese New Year that saw upwards of 100,000 North Vietnamese soldiers (regulars and guerrillas) conduct ground ops against many government and U.S. outposts throughout South Vietnam to include virtually every "major" city. Saigon was attacked, as was the U.S. Embassy, and if not for a determined effort by U.S. and South Vietnamese forces, the embassy and major portions of the city likely would have been overrun. The forces of the North were driven from the battlefields across South Vietnam, suffering "tremendous" casualties and equipment losses. They melted back into Laos and Cambodia and the vast underground network of compounds located throughout the south. They licked their wounds and started on a massive effort to rebuild, refit, and reconstitute.

When the war ended in the 1973–1975 timeframe, we thoroughly abandoned the South Vietnamese and let their country be overrun and now ruled by the North Vietnamese Communists. Many South Vietnamese, loyal to the war against Communism and to the United States,

Chapter 17

lost their lives as a result. Many of them departed their country to become "boat people." If they were lucky, they landed in the United States as refugees later to become U.S. citizens.

Unbeknownst to most in the United States at the time, the aftermath of the Vietnam War saw the unveiling and the emergence of a potentially "new" economic power along with a fledgling numerically huge and technically evolving military, which would have to be recognized across the world order—the Chinese, whose stated goal was to unseat the United States as the world leader. We, the United States, on the other hand, were ever so slowly sliding backward, selling ourselves out in order to achieve a foothold into the Chinese market, while cutting back on the size of our military knowing full well that we would not be able to handle a possible three-front war (Europe, the Middle East, and Asia).

You may ask…why should we be concerned about "fighting" a three-front war? Because the "free" world has looked to the United States to lead the way since WWII. It's interesting what's happening now in the Middle East (Israel, Iran, Hamas, and Hezbollah) while the Russians are at war in Ukraine, and we are supplying the material and money to the Ukrainians and the Chinese continue to "sabre" rattle in the South China Sea and against Taiwan. I'm hoping that we soon wake up and admit that our most significant threat is not diversity but rather the -isms.

Have We Not Learned a Thing?

As I sit here on a night in August 2021, we are doing the same damn thing in Afghanistan. Shame on us! We are withdrawing our forces as we speak and hanging the Afghans out to dry after 20 years of involvement in support of the U.S. "War on Terror." Many of those who had been loyal to the United States in the fight against terrorism and the Taliban will lose their lives. Those who aren't slaughtered will be "re-indoctrinated" and sent out to survive in the fourth-century society that existed prior to U.S. involvement.

Don't you think China will fill the vacuum left by the United States? So, we are contributing to China's expansionism and in effect helping them achieve world dominance. Look at the areas China now has a strong foothold—totally immersed in Panama (hell, they built the "second" Panama Canal, a prime military and economic strategic area right here in the Western Hemisphere about 1,200 miles from our nation's capital). In Africa, they built railroads, hydroelectric plants, and irrigation systems along with providing massive loans for development and infrastructure. These "initiatives" enabled them to have access to strategic, rare earth metals—think supersonic aircraft, nuclear weapons, battery technology, and renewable energy initiatives. A recent report indicated that the Chinese were seeking a "naval" base of operations in Equatorial Guinea on the Atlantic Ocean, which would allow them to operate off the east coast of the United States. That would be a first for them and an ominous signal to the west!

Oh, and should Taiwan be concerned? The Chinese want to take Taiwan back, as in invade and forcibly take control of an independent nation. Taiwan controls the world's computer chip industry (think the multi-national corporation TSMC). We cannot allow for that enterprise to come under the control of the Chinese Communists. All in all, things are not good! We, the United States, need to rethink our foreign policy efforts and determine how we can put a positive bent on how we work with third-world countries and provide them the ability to lift themselves up by their bootstraps.

Of late, in our own country, there is talk within certain circles about the "merits" of Communism over our Capitalist system. If the goal is to make everyone the same then Communism is for you. Capitalism surely has its faults however, it has created more wealth for more people in a shorter period of time than the world had ever experienced...it rewards hard work and creativity.

Communism, on the other hand, wherever it has been tried, has stifled creativity (no real incentive to be creative), punishes free speech if "threatened," and has not encouraged individual investment in broad-based economic growth, choosing instead for the state to control most aspects of business development. And, as an aside, millions under the Communist "yoke" have been murdered or banished to "work camps," never to be seen or heard from again. Look at the Soviet Union (Russia), China, Cuba, North Korea, Venezuela, and Vietnam! My thoughts, bleeding through the Vietnam experience—Amen!

Chapter 18

Life After Vietnam— And Then Some!

Chapter 18

How Things Unfolded

Remember me referencing how when we arrived in Vietnam, we all had an "opportunity" to nominate a person who was in-country to serve as an escort home in the event of one's death. Tom Jones and I each nominated one another, and so I was supposed to have escorted Tom's remains home to Maryland.

Well I was never "contacted" in Vietnam and only found out about Tom's death after reading the Pacific Edition of the *Stars and Stripes* newspaper about a week after his death. As a result, I didn't escort Tom home per his wishes. I found out after arriving home from my tour in Vietnam, the organization working those things could not locate me and so notified the grieving family. I was located about a week after the fact and Kathy Jones was informed.

But because of the delay that would have ensued, she declined me being sent back to the States believing it would be best to get on with the funeral. Tom was already home by the time I was notified and so the funeral went on, "per Kathy's" wishes, and I did not participate in any way. In an "ironic" side to things, a few days after being notified of Tom's death, Kathy notified my parents, who had met Kathy and Tom at our flight school graduation. Kathy told them that I would be escorting Tom home, and while the circumstances were terrible, she thought we would appreciate seeing each other regardless. After it was all

Life After Vietnam—And Then Some!

"unscrambled" and my parents knew I would not be coming home, they attended Tom's funeral anyway, and I was very happy to find out that they did that.

I have often thought over the years that if I had served as Tom's escort officer, and met the family under those traumatic circumstances, I might never have gone to visit Kathy and TJ with other flight school friends after returning from Vietnam. If I had escorted Tom home, and then returned to Vietnam, that would probably have amounted to "closure" for me and life would have moved on. But, as it turned out, eight months later upon my return, one of the wives suggested that a group of us who had been close to Kathy and Tom should consider visiting her and 16-month-old TJ at some point while on leave. The idea was to just share some time together and perhaps bring some closure to the family and to the rest of us. So, a trip was planned for a long weekend in November 1969, and I believe 10 of us showed up.

I had misgivings about going as one side of me thought a visit like that, not so long after the fact, might not bring closure at all, but in fact might be heartbreaking for Kathy, who had been grieving for eight months and now this! She was on a different timetable than the rest of us—we pilots and wives in attendance were happy to have survived Vietnam and we stood as a stark reminder and proof to Kathy that Tom would never return. I'm sure she suffered through Tom's loss again, but she was past it to a degree and we were just facing it from a totally different angle. In spite of what I thought, all went well and our visit was a good time of remembrance and maybe even provided some measure of healing for all concerned.

Another wife in attendance was Hattie Taylor. She was also a widow. Her husband, along with two other soldiers, had been executed by the Viet Cong after crash landing his helicopter and being captured. Her husband's name was Dean Taylor, and he graduated with my class, going to Vietnam as most of us did. Hattie was still very shaken and she lamented the fact that they did not have a child together. They had been teenage sweethearts, and she thought in retrospect that having a child would have insured Dean's legacy.

Many years after this get together with Kathy, friends, and family, I read in the *Vietnam Helicopter Pilots Association* magazine something about a woman who, along with her current husband, traveled to the location in Vietnam where a U.S. helicopter pilot had been executed. The story was about Hattie Taylor. She had been tormented for nearly 40 years and for her to go to that place completed the journey, providing her with a sense of closure and peace. She had remarried a former Air Force pilot who served in Vietnam, was very supportive of her, and helped set up their trip. I have often thought of her and

Life After Vietnam—And Then Some!

hope she found some degree of happiness and was able to move on.

After three days of visiting, the gathering broke up and we all said our goodbyes and parted ways. I asked Kathy to join me for dinner at a place in D.C. I'd heard about on the radio. It was Trader Vic's in the Washington Hilton Hotel, a very cool place with great tropical drinks and great not-so-ordinary "everyday dishes." My favorite drink was Navy Grog and Kathy's favorite turned out to be the Scorpion, which featured a floating gardenia—as you know, they go right to your head! I asked Kathy out to dinner so that we could have some alone time. I felt that prior to leaving for Vietnam, I was pretty good friends with the Jones' and I wanted to tell her how terrible Tom's loss was for me and how bad I felt for her and TJ. As I mentioned earlier, it took me a long time to get over his death and accept it for what it was. I understood that my loss wasn't as horrific as losing a spouse or child, but it was as deep a loss as I had ever experienced. The other such loss was my friend Nick Swidonovich, my map exam mentor!

Anyway, I just wanted to talk this kind of stuff out in person away from the maddening crowd. We had a nice time together, albeit emotional, and I think we both enjoyed each other's company. I didn't have designs on Kathy and I was sure she didn't have designs on me, but I think we found each other comfortable to be with, at least at that time. Kathy, for me, was easy to be with and, although she had been married to Tom and he was my best married friend, we knew each other reasonably well while in flight school so we didn't "stumble" through the "what to talk about" phase. I never had much trouble talking to Kathy, she was a good listener, had a good sense of humor, and we laughed a lot, and altogether that kept things moving. Throughout my time in flight school, I just kept "bumping" into Kathy and Tom Jones. They were good casual friends of mine. All told, we had "history" and talking about things seemed to come somewhat naturally.

Although talking to each other came easy, I wasn't sure what she "really" thought of me at that time. So, dinner together enabled us to find out a little more about each other. She had many questions about my time in Vietnam and "what was it really like for you" and was I familiar with the area that Tom was assigned to, which I wasn't. I learned how devastating Tom's loss was to Kathy and the turmoil it created within the extended family and a large swath of friends and acquaintances in the D.C. area. Tom had been an All-Metro football player in high school and he was reasonably well known.

I learned she was determined to be independent of her parents and former in-laws when it came to raising TJ and living her own life. In both instances she was under pressure to "move" closer to both parents and in-laws so they could all have a "hand" in helping Kathy raise TJ—not a good thing over time. She needed some distance and I understood, or at least I thought I understood, Kathy's plight, and I agreed with her plan for fully getting over her loss and getting on with life, which I assumed meant remarrying and having more children.

We laughed a little, and got a little emotional over the loss of Tom and life in general since departing for Vietnam. We talked of other friends lost, of time lost, and generally started to discover each other's likes and dislikes. When I look back on that first alone encounter, I was speaking from a different side of the planet. Only eight months had passed since Tom's death, and God only knows where Kathy's brain was. Time does heal, and the passing of time had eased the pain of Tom's passing for her and lowered the angst surrounding his loss. It made it easier for us to talk about Tom, the husband and friend, without getting overcome by emotion.

Over the next few months, our relationship just blossomed and the feeling of guilt associated with ultimately talking about ourselves and hey, what might the future hold for you/me, and TJ, as a family unit together just melted into the background. The feeling of guilt was an interesting emotion at a time like that. How can I be on the verge of falling in love with my best friend's wife? It was very uncomfortable, and it also evoked a feeling of why was

Chapter 18

Tom taken from us—a person who had so much to live for, a lovely wife and a son, and a loving extended family. And so why was I spared? I lost a fair number of classmates and friends in Vietnam; why them and not me? I'm certainly not the first to have these feelings or these questions, and I doubt I'll be the last. The whole thing does, however, give you pause to think about the bigger picture of why am I here and do I have a mission—and if so, what is it? I tried not to get overly hung up on those unanswerable questions. I just tried to do the best I could to handle it.

We started openly dating, burned up the telephone lines between Mineral Wells and D.C., and saw each other about twice a month for the next six or so months. We attended the 1969 Army/Navy football game in Philadelphia and spent the New Year's holiday at a flight school classmate's home in Mineral Wells. That New Year's Day, we attended the 1970 Cotton Bowl football game, which featured the University of Texas versus Notre Dame.

Wow, our first two real dates and both to sporting events. Things were looking good from the compatibility standpoint, she seemed to like what I liked. Although I do remember her saying something to the effect that watching golf and baseball was like watching grass grow. And as much as I like those sports, she might have been on to something!

In February 1970, while visiting with flight school friends in Atlanta, Kathy and I decided we were "compatible enough" to be engaged to be married. We both enjoyed each other's company, and I was totally accepting of TJ, something Kathy found out wasn't so easy for some. And hell, we had to get engaged and married, as our phone bills were breaking the bank! So, when you lay all this out in a timeline, it's just three and a half months after I returned from Vietnam, and one might think that was a little quick. It was quick, but there were extenuating circumstances. While I had only been back in the "world" for three months, Kathy lost Tom 11 months prior, and so she was "more ready" and probably sure in her mind to get on with "life." It really didn't feel like we were "rushing" into something, as we had known each other reasonably well from flight school days—so all things considered, we had that going for us.

I too wanted to get on with life, but initially I wasn't ready for marriage as I thought it important to complete a college education before making the marriage and family commitment. I thought having a college education would afford me more employment opportunities, which would enable me to be a "better" provider from a financial standpoint. I had no desire at the time to continue with flying helicopters in the civilian world, as the pay was minimal and the type of flying was dangerous—think flying

Chapter 18

out to offshore oil rigs and mountain rescues. I also, in my view, had to consider marrying right into a family situation, as Kathy had TJ, and so it would be we three from the get go. I had no misgivings about "taking on" a family, so to speak, but it meant that we wouldn't have any together time for "two" in which to slide into certain decisions like a career, or college while working, or for that matter more family members.

Although I was able to continue in the Army and make it a career, in early 1970, I wasn't sure what I wanted to pursue, and at the time there were no guarantees about staying in the Army. As the Vietnam War was drawing down, the size of the officer corps was being cut back. And in fact, a fair number of my friends and acquaintances would receive RIF (reduction in force/separation papers from the Army) notices throughout the course of the early 1970s. So it was hard to make career-type "employment" decisions and marriage plans all at the same time.

All those "things to consider" ended abruptly during one of our "discussions" while on a dinner date. I was hedging on "a short timeline" for marriage and stating the case for getting through college prior to getting married, which meant marriage would likely be another three or four years away. Kathy looked me straight in the eye and said, "Hey, I have babies to make, places to be, and people I want to see–and I can't wait three or more years, so it's up to you!" Well, I thought about that for about five "New York" seconds and said, "Gotcha," meaning I was in agreement with her and before the evening was over, we had a tentative June 1970 wedding date in the making.

So, did you see how FATE swept in and literally sealed my FATE all in one 30-second period—a real pushover was I, but it was the best decision I ever made and I never regretted it for a minute! So, that was that!

Chapter 19
16 Months an Instructor Pilot

Chapter 19

While our courtship, engagement, and wedding plans were happening, I was attending the Army's Rotary Wing Instructor Pilot School at Ft. Wolters. This was an eight-week course that brought me full cycle—student pilot in training, combat pilot, instructor pilot. I was happy in that course, and it was my intention to mentor my students the way my instructor pilots had mentored my colleagues and me. Vietnam was still an ongoing conflict and most of the student pilot officers and warrant officer candidates in residence at that time (1970) would likely end up flying helicopters in Vietnam. I passed my instructor pilot check ride a year to the day after I had been shot down while flying an air assault mission in Vietnam (February 12, 1969)—time flies when you're having fun!

I started teaching as an instructor pilot in mid February 1970 in Flight A-2 at the Dempsey Army Heliport in Palo Pinto, Texas. This was Phase II of primary helicopter training, which meant that all the students at this point could hover, fly straight and level, perform autorotations, and they had all proved themselves proficient in helicopter emergency procedures and overall airmanship. Phase II training would expand upon what they had already learned, giving them more opportunities to conduct solo flights in a mission-oriented environment, such as confined area landings and takeoffs, mountain top and pinnacle approaches and takeoffs, formation flying, and cross-country flights, to name a few of the "fun" things we did.

My first three students were warrant officer candidates who were resident student pilots living in WWII-type barracks on Ft. Wolters. Their ages ranged from 19 to 21 years old, and they all were very dedicated to their flight training and officer development. All three of them were good, solid pilots. The student in this group who stood out for me was a young 19-year-old named Barry Fivelson from Chicago. In essence, he was my "first" student, and he was a neat and very sharp guy. As his training progressed, he performed some things every bit as good as I did in terms of pilot technique and aviator situational awareness.

He was "gifted" to the point where I would have "contests" with him to see who could make the "best" landing to the ground while doing autorotations or who could initiate a high overhead approach from 1,500 feet of altitude to a stable hover nearest to the red "colored" tire that denoted the tightest confined landing areas. The "prize" would be a "glazed honey bun" and a Coke at the lesson debrief conducted in the snack area. Barry won more than a few "prizes," and it was fun having that kind of student/instructor relationship.

He graduated in the spring of 1970 from the primary phase and finished advanced flight training at Ft. Rucker, Alabama. I lost track of him after that until one afternoon

Chapter 19

in mid summer of 1972. At the time, I was stationed in Korea along the demilitarized zone and while scanning the *Stars and Stripes* Asia edition, I stumbled across Barry's obituary. He was KIA in Vietnam while aboard a CH-47 Chinook helicopter. I was shocked and deeply saddened.

Over the next 16 months of being an instructor pilot, I had 18 students and only had one eliminated from the program. He was a good guy and determined to be successful at what he was doing, but he always seemed a bit afraid of flying—that's not good. It was hard to explain, but he didn't seem confident and he was tentative in the cockpit. He was flight evaluated by my flight commander, who recommended he be evaluated by what was known as Flight Standards. Two separate instructor pilots from that organization flew with the student and he was eliminated. It was not a happy day as it marked the end of someone's dream, but it was overall likely the best outcome.

The last group of students I had before I was assigned to Ft. Benning consisted of two officer students. Captain Harry Thain, a West Point graduate, was one of them, and he had already served a tour in Vietnam as an artillery officer. He would technically be my last student as an instructor pilot (specifically due to the alphabet—T (Thain) was very near Z, and that's how we do it in the Army). Harry was another "gifted" student pilot and he, like my first student, Barry Fivelson, did some flying things better than I did. I also had "contests" with Harry, and he won more than a couple of beers with burgers from me. Again, it was fun having a relationship with a student like that, and we bonded in a way that I think only "fellow" pilots and Army officers can. In that group's last weekend before graduation, I had them over for a cookout. It was a nice way to close out their training.

Harry, like my first student Barry, moved on to Ft. Rucker for advanced training. Upon graduation and receiving his wings, he transitioned into the CH-47 Chinook helicopter. I lost track of Harry until one day in late 1972 or early 1973 when I saw his obituary in the *Stars and Stripes* Asia edition. He was piloting a UN/U.S. "peacekeeping" aircraft painted light blue when it was shot down on short final to a landing zone in the northern part of South Vietnam. Harry was one of the last American casualties of the war. I was sickened and pissed off knowing that the aircraft he was piloting was not a combatant and by agreement with the North Vietnamese was not to be engaged.

So, just to recap, in the space of three months, while I was stationed in Korea, and while I was just randomly thumbing through the *Stars and Stripes* newspaper, I stumbled upon the obituaries of my first and last student pilots. Did something draw me to the newspaper and then the obituaries on those particular days? I didn't have access

Chapter 19

to the *Stars and Stripes* on a daily basis, so a number of things had to happen for me to be reading them on those particular days. It's hard to know. All I can say is that while I wasn't looking for "closure," being aware of their deaths did provide closure and it kept them "alive" in my mind since. If you are often thought of, you're never "really" gone, at least in the mind of the beholder. I know, I know, you are really gone, but it did provide closure for me and I think of the people in my past as "friends" who live on.

In 1985, my oldest son expressed a desire to explore getting appointed for attendance at West Point. I worked with a couple of other military guys who each had a nephew attending West Point. So, after talking with them, they suggested that the nephews meet with my son so they could show him around the West Point campus and provide him with the real scoop.

We planned a trip up to West Point in the fall of 1985 and made a day of it, with my guy meeting up with the two cadets, and me, my dad, and our younger son taking in the sights. We later had a picnic lunch in an area near the West Point cemetery. While cleaning up, my dad took his grandson through the cemetery to view the tomb of Major General George Armstrong Custer, of "Custer's Last Stand" fame. I told him that I would catch up. About 10 minutes later, I cut across a small field to an opening into the cemetery. When I saw my dad and Andrew, I whistled to them and then stopped to adjust a camera I had strapped across my back. When I did that, by chance I glanced at the headstone that was directly in front of me, and I mean eight feet in front of me and centered, as if I was purposely there to pay respects.

It was Captain Harry Thain's grave—I was thunderstruck beyond words! How does this happen? What are the odds of me, or anybody, just walking up to a grave in the middle of a fairly large cemetery and have it be someone you are connected to? I didn't know Harry had been buried at West Point, and I wasn't looking for anything—so what brought me to that exact location? Coincidence? It was hard to believe. I have thought of Harry often in the years following, and I just feel that Harry is a "presence" and we have a connection—whatever that all means. I know, beyond a normal explanation and somewhere in the Twilight Zone, but my gravesite "visit" really happened!

Chapter 20
What a Day!

Chapter 20

One of the first things on the agenda after Kathy and I decided to get engaged was to inform my parents of our plans. I figured they wouldn't be prepared for that kind of announcement, but I didn't think they would be unhappy! I thought, however, they might consider our decision to tie the knot a bit quick. I also thought they would hope that we had seriously considered not only the marriage part but also the fact that we would be an instant family. The family part changes the focus a little bit. We would not be just normal "newlyweds."

It turned out they were very surprised but not unhappy. After it was all said and done, they "knew" Kathy from our flight school graduation party, and hell, we all appeared in the pictures together. They had attended Tom's funeral and spoke with Kathy afterwards. So Kathy was a known entity to them and they were fully aware of the circumstances, and I believed they "approved." As the weeks went by, I think they enjoyed the lead up to the big day!

The biggest issue they probably had was "explaining" the circumstances (widow, mother of a child, a little older than me, etc.) to the rest of the family like in my mom's sisters and brother. The "issues" weren't issues at all and it was just a matter of going with the flow. We, the betrothed, were happy and looking forward to the future and we hoped that all would feel the same way. If there was to be an "issue," Kathy quickly eliminated it by indicating that she would convert to Catholicism so we could be married on the altar in a Catholic Church. It wasn't important to me that she convert, however, it did simplify things. She thought that I was "stronger" in my Catholic faith than she was in hers; whatever that meant. She was Episcopalian with roots in the Lutheran church—her "converting" made it easier!

The next thing that had to be resolved was a little age difference, which of course can't be resolved! I was almost three years younger than Kathy, and I had told her a little "white lie" about my age a few months earlier because, at that time, I didn't think she would like the age difference. I was right, she didn't, but for the short term we "ignored" it and in all honesty, we weren't that much different in maturity and naivete.

Not sure what would have been the outcome if she did know about it earlier, but whatever the case it was resolved as there was nothing that could be done about it anyway—and we still liked each other! At this point in our lives, she is now in "vogue," you know, the classic "Cougar"! We "worked" through the age thing, but I have been reminded of it for the last 50+ years now. We get a good chuckle out of it all and hey, I think the little "white lie" was the smartest thing I may have ever done—and she is still a "Cougar"!

Chapter 20

Another little "issue" we worked through was the wedding dress. Kathy initially was inclined to buy something other than a white wedding dress because she had been married before, and I guess there was some type of voodoo associated with wearing white and having been down the aisle before. My view of the world was that Kathy had tragically lost her husband whom she had loved. I accepted all that and wanted her to be my bride, and I wanted her to wear white on our wedding day in spite of whatever voodoo was out there. She agreed and purchased a classic white wedding dress and topped it off with a blue head piece that had a shoulder length veil—stunning! She was the bride I wanted and she was happy with that!

We planned to get married in Annapolis, Maryland, and Kathy, with the help of a Catholic priest, Father Downs, from the University of Maryland, arranged for the ceremony to take place at St. Mary's Roman Catholic Church on Duke of Gloucester Street in Annapolis. We were married on June 27, 1970.

What a Day!

The beautiful bride! Kathleen L. Fox (nee Thwaites), St. Mary's Church, Annapolis, Maryland, June 27, 1970.

Wedding day! (Left to right) Lieutenant Colonel Dave Thwaites, USAF (Ret) and Mrs. Polly Thwaites, Mrs. Francis M. Fox (Kathleen) and Captain Francis M. Fox (US Army), Mrs. Francis M. Fox (Eileen) and Mr. Francis M. Fox.

Chapter 20

The bride and groom, Mr. and Mrs. Francis M. Fox, St. Mary's Church, Annapolis, Maryland, June 27, 1970.

Epilogue

Life comes at all of us from many different angles. Decisions we make, which seemed so benign in hindsight, may be the biggest decisions that had a lasting impact on the road we all traveled. Most of the time, we'll never know, but sometimes if we really take the time to think about life and its twists and turns, ups and downs, good times and bad, all of a sudden funny patterns emerge and one can almost connect the dots.

I believe such was the case in my life, and of all the things the pandemic gave me, one was the opportunity (meaning time) to ponder. I used to think about events I had been involved with all the time and how a certain set of actions/decisions on my part or on the part of other people caused one thing or another to happen. Some, maybe most, of these events are cumulative and essentially add up to one's life never having a very long thread and they just peter out; however, some affect a lifetime.

This book of reminiscences is my attempt to flesh out stories and determine how I and others were impacted after having had the benefit of 50 years to accumulate and live them out. For me, it has been a full, happy life and hopefully well lived!

Highlights

- Although at the time I didn't think so, I was blessed to have attended St. James High School, the small Catholic school that conferred "only" a business diploma. I brushed up against some great teachers who had interesting world experiences and whose experiences "rubbed off on me" and got me thinking. I also learned some "skills" that have lasted a lifetime.

- Oh the joy of working in a maximum overheated kitchen and being a pizza/sous chef while making "friends" with the "family." Pat Scaglione, whom I'll never forget, taught me how to make a great at-home pizza, and I still do that on my George Foreman grill!

- Chris Kergen and the 13 run pool, sticking with it even though lost in the numbers. I can still drive a stick shift, and in general, and right out of high school, working with all those WWII veterans was a great experience and an eye opener to the real world.

Epilogue

Our family—T.J. Fox (left), Kathy Fox, and Andrew Fox (right). The author was the photographer!

- Playing Russian roulette with the military draft system and thus taking this decision out of my hands likely had the biggest impact on my early life and sent me on the path to meeting the woman I would marry and spend the last 54 years with. Had I "intervened," it could have been a totally different story, which would have led to a whole different set of "actions" culminating in who knows what kind of ending. So, I followed my "gut" to spend a couple of extra weeks at the beach and it set the wheels in motion!

Epilogue

- Qualified to go to Army Officer Candidate School and accepted the offer in spite of some telling me I was nuts. I weighed out the pros and cons and took a chance, which could have had deadly consequences…one of the cons…but it didn't. It contained some of the stuff that life is all about and opened up some doors for me that likely wouldn't have been there.

- Qualified to go to Army Flight School having no formal "flight orientation" background. It was a dream that I harbored from the time I was a kid reading the stories of early flight pioneers and Eddie Rickenbacker and Lafayette Escadrille of WWI fame. Fate took over from here!

- Dream almost shattered but somehow fate intervened after a "malfunctioning" test was discovered, just in the nick of time. Reinstated, persevered, and made a friend on the "bus" who unknowingly changed my life. Tom Jones introduced me to a "slice" of life that I was unaware of up until that time—and the hand of fate or the Twilight Zone was guiding me through it!

- Kathy Jones has baby TJ and I get nominated by the officers' wives in attendance at our pool party to go to the hospital in Tom's absence to find out Kathy and baby's

Epilogue

status and report back to our group. I did and went to the hospital and introduced myself to the corpsman as Kathy Jones' (husband) and could I see Kathy and (my son). The corpsman was very obliging and got me up to Kathy's room. I didn't want to be there, but here I was and all was fine. I reported back to the pool party with the good news—but in retrospect, are you kidding me?!

- Flight school graduation, my parents end up in party pictures mixed in with Tom and Kathy. The morning prior, my father held/walked TJ, who was having a bout with colic, and settled him down. In retrospect, my dad would be the first of, essentially, three granddads to hold TJ—he was a future granddad, who knew—are you kidding me?!

- Prior to deploying to Vietnam, Tom invited me to his parents home in Maryland near D.C. to attend a party for himself, Kathy, and TJ. I attended and "served" as the bartender that evening. I also toured the Capitol Building after midnight with Kathy's friend Linda McGill. Great time and having been the bartender, I met and talked to the folks who would all play a very big part in my life—my future in-laws. Who da thunk—and again, are you kidding me?!

Epilogue

- I also attended a night out in New York City with Tom and Kathy the week before we left for Vietnam. I couldn't/ didn't want to get a date and attended as one. We went to see "Hello Dolly." It was a good time. The first Broadway show I ever attended! Kathy and I kept bumping into each other.

- I departed for Vietnam and met with Tom and other classmates in San Francisco. Interesting time—somewhat subdued as we all knew that this journey across the Pacific could have a tragic ending. Upon reaching Vietnam, Tom designated me to escort him home in the event of his death and I designated him to escort me home. Upon his death, I was never notified and as a result, it "set up" the reason for visiting with Kathy and TJ along with other flight classmates upon our return from Vietnam. The guiding hand of fate!

- After "meeting," talking out emotions, remembering Tom and others, recalling the events that seemed to push us together (just kept bumping into each other), and the adventure of Helicopter Flight School we had all experienced just a year earlier, we "bonded" for want of a better word and then watched our feelings for each other grow and blossom into a "love affair"!

Epilogue

Coincidence, fate, the Twilight Zone...who knows, but the end of this story is just the beginning of another story that had the sun, the moon, and the stars align for us, and they have remained that way for a good 54 years!

The End

Milton Keynes UK
Ingram Content Group UK Ltd.
UKHW022010091024
449514UK00019B/161/J